THE FIXES

ALSO BY OWEN MATTHEWS

How to Win at High School

THE FIXES

OWEN MATTHEWS

HARPER TEEN
An Imprint of HarperCollinsPublishers

HarperTeen is an imprint of HarperCollins Publishers.

The Fixes
Copyright © 2016 by Owen Laukkanen
All rights reserved. Printed in the United States of America. No part of this book may be used or reproduced in any manner whatsoever without written permission except in the case of brief quotations embodied in critical articles and reviews. For information address HarperCollins Children's Books, a division of HarperCollins Publishers, 195 Broadway, New York, NY 10007.
www.epicreads.com

ISBN 978-0-06-233689-7

Typography by Ellice M. Lee
16 17 18 19 20   CG/RRDH   10 9 8 7 6 5 4 3 2 1

First Edition

For Shan,
who took me to the wild side
and brought me back safe

I.

This is a story about a boy's first crush, ~~and how it blew up in his face.~~

~~And all of its explosive consequences.~~

(You know what? Forget it.)

2.

Let's start over.

Let me tell you why E set off that bomb.

3.

It's the first day of summer vacation. School's out. School's over. Everyone in Capilano is at the beach, on a boat, or up in the mountains on a lake somewhere. Everyone except Eric Connelly.

Eric Connelly is in a hurry. Eric doesn't notice that it's a beautiful day. Eric sure as hell doesn't have any plans to go to the beach. Eric is running late.

(Give him a minute.)

Eric's the kid parking his mom's Mercedes G-Wagen in the near-empty sprawl of the Cap High parking lot. He's the tall, blandly handsome kid climbing out onto the sun-scorched pavement, checking the time on that fancy Omega diving watch and swearing. Walking—*fast*—across the lot to the school, wondering how he's going to make it to his new internship on time.

Eric's the hero of this story. And Eric has places to be.

4.

On a normal day, Cap High is a microcosm of Capilano itself. The building is beautiful, all steel and glass and reclaimed timber. It looks right at home amid Capilano's towering mountains and endless beaches. And it's populated by the best of the best. The elite.

Film directors' kids. Hedge fund managers' offspring. The broods of rock stars, Fortune 500 CEOs, real-estate moguls, athletes, and white-collar criminals. They all call Capilano home.

On a normal day, you couldn't throw a stone around here without hitting, like, four or five Birkin bags. The school parking lot practically screams for a valet. The kids at Cap High are glamorous and gorgeous and they DGAF.

(They're better than you, and they know it.)

(And honestly, so do *you*.)

Today, though, the halls are empty. It's only Eric Connelly, hurrying toward the office. And if you're thinking our hero looks a little out of place amid these glamorous surroundings, you're not entirely wrong.

See, Eric never fit in at Cap. Four years in the place and even now, his senior year finished, he still feels like an alien walking these halls. Sure, he has the Mercedes and the flashy Swiss timepiece. He dresses like the crowd, and his parents have money. He's your typical Cap kid, a poster boy for the school—

(in fact, he's Student of the Year)

—but Eric's different. If you look close, you can see it. It's the sweat on his face as he *hurries* down the hall. It's the way he keeps checking that Omega. It's the way he looks *worried*, like the world *doesn't* revolve around him, like he's actually *late* and that actually *matters*.

People don't *hurry* in Capilano. They don't get *worried*. They pay people to worry for them, and if they're late, the world waits. It's not cool to be stressed, and Eric's stressed all the time.

Ergo, he's not really *of Capilano*.

You know?

FREQUENTLY ASKED QUESTIONS (FAQ)

Q: Why is Eric stressed?

A: Eric is stressed because he's late for the VERY PRESTIGIOUS internship he landed at his dad's old law office. He forgot to put gas in the G-Wagen this morning, and now he has to swing by Cap High to pick up his Student of the Year plaque—

(they spelled his name wrong the first time)

—but he got caught in beach traffic getting over here, and he has to be at his internship in, like, fifteen minutes, and it's all the way on the other side of Capilano.

Q: Why does a rich kid care about some stupid internship? It's the first day of summer.

A: Right. And for normal people, summer means vacation. Parties, beaches, regrettable hookups. Two glorious months of freedom before college starts. For Eric, summer = work. Eric's headed to law school. Gotta pad those extracurriculars to make sure he gets in.

Q: This guy sounds like a nerd.

A: That's not a question.

Q: Okay, why are you making me read about some dork who can't have any fun?

A: I promise you, Eric's going to have fun. He just doesn't know it yet.

Q: You just said he's rich. Can't he *buy* his way into law school?

A: Good question. If Eric were anyone else at Cap High, the answer would be yes. But Eric isn't anyone else. Eric's a Connelly, and Eric's dad believes Connelly men work for what they get. He's riding Eric hard to get into Stanford. Hence the internship. Hence Eric's nerd-like countenance.

Q: What happens at the end?
A: You really want to know? Eric kills the love of his life and goes to jail. His family disowns him. The end.

Q: Great. And what's Eric's hero's journey?
A: Uh, what? You're totally trying to crib for some essay or something, aren't you? Just read the book, dude. It's not even that long.

5.

Anyway.

The point is, Eric's stressed. Partially because he's late for the VERY PRESTIGIOUS internship, and partially because he's afraid his dad will find out he was late on his first day, and that would be VERY BAD for everyone.

But we're not going to talk about Eric's dad yet.

(You'll hear plenty about him soon enough.)

This book is fundamentally a love story, and love stories need two things:

1. A love interest.
2. A cheesy *meet cute*.

Lucky for us, we're about to get both.

6.

Eric's footsteps echo down the hall. He passes his old locker, the lunchroom, the computer lab. He makes it to the front of the school, the administration office. There are two people already inside the office when Eric walks in. One is Mrs. Adams, the secretary. The other is Jordan Grant.

Jordan Grant is Harrison Grant's only child. And that makes him **IMPORTANT**.

7.

Jordan Grant ~~was~~ *is* a senior at Cap High.

(We'll get to that.)

He's pretty well Eric's opposite in every respect. I mean, he looks like an Abercrombie model—tall, built, perpetually tanned—but it's not like Eric's ugly. It's more than that. It's more the way Jordan carries himself. It's the way Jordan looks like he's never had a care in the world.

Jordan's dad is Harrison Grant, one of the most IMPORTANT people in Capilano. He used to be a development executive at Lionsgate, but he quit recently to start his own company. He just sold a TV series about baby geniuses, and Cap High rumor is that he walked away from the deal with, like, low eight figures.

Whatever the truth is, Harrison Grant is obscenely rich. And Jordan Grant is his only kid.

Something else you should know: This last year was Jordan's first year in Capilano. He was living in L.A. with his mom before the school year started. He moved up here with his dad. Nobody at Cap High's really sure what the deal is. Eric heard a rumor Jordan punched out, like, Wiz Khalifa, and that's why he had to get out of town—but nobody's been able to corroborate.

Whatever, though. Jordan's up here now. And since his dad is rich and powerful and important, and Jordan looks like an Abercrombie model and even pops up now and then on TMZ and Defamer, well, he pretty much became king of the school the moment he walked through the front doors.

And Jordan lives like a king. His Instagram is like a magazine spread: Jordan on a speedboat with a couple of smoking-hot Cap High girls. Jordan at some movie premiere with Chris Pine. Jordan skydiving. Surfing. Jordan with his shirt off.

(Jordan has a six-pack, obvi.)

If Cap High is full of A-listers, Jordan Grant is A-double-plus. He does what he wants, when he wants, with *whoever* he wants—guy or girl—like he's some kind of god who doesn't give a shit about ordinary people's rules.

Jordan Grant is the Man.

(He's also going to be the Love Interest for the purposes of this narrative.)

8.

Does that scare you? The Jordan thing? Did you pick up this book thinking it was going to be all fast cars and hot chicks and explosions?

I'm sorry.

If it's any consolation, the Jordan thing scares Eric, too. Eric's still not sure he's entirely on board with this whole "liking boys" situation. It kind of crept up on him. It's not something he was planning.

Yeah. It scares Eric . . . a lot.

9.

Jordan Grant is sitting on a bench in the secretary's office while Mrs. Adams talks on the phone.

(Jordan's like a Lamborghini at a Taco Bell drive-thru right now, but here he is nonetheless.)

He looks up when Eric walks in, flashes a thousand-watt smile.

"Hey," he says. "What are *you* in for?"

10.

Eric kind of stammers. Looks at his feet.

(He's blushing already.)

"I mean," Eric says. "I'm just here to pick up my plaque."

II.

Mrs. Adams looks up from the phone, sees Eric. Covers the mouthpiece.

"Hi, Eric," she says. "Just give me a minute. I'll be right with you."

"What about *me*?" Jordan asks her.

Mrs. Adams gives Jordan a look. "I'll deal with you next, Mr. Grant. Just be patient."

She goes back to talking on the phone. Jordan lifts an eyebrow at Eric. "Guess she likes you better. What's your secret?"

Eric kind of shifts his weight again. "Pardon?"

"Never mind," Jordan says. "You're here for a plaque? Like, you won an award or something?"

Eric nods. "They spelled my name wrong when they engraved it, though. That's why I'm here."

There's an awkward pause. Eric can see Jordan doesn't get it.

"My last name's Connelly," he says. "Two *n*'s and two *l*'s. They dropped an *n*, so my dad made me give the plaque back so they could redo it."

"Aha," Jordan says. "So what was the award?"

Eric feels himself blushing more. Hates himself for it. "Student of the Year."

Jordan grins wider.

(Eric thinks: *#Nerd*.)

"Student of the Year," Jordan says. "Holy humblebrag. Congratulations."

"Why *are* you here?" Eric asks, to change the subject.

Jordan makes a face. "A math problem. Calculus class, to be exact. They won't let me graduate until I pass."

This is a strange story. It doesn't make sense. Teachers at Cap High don't just fail anybody, especially not anybodies who happen to be Jordan Grant. Rich kids don't fail. They pull C averages and move up the ladder, annoy their college professors for a while until their parents land them cushy jobs with seven-figure starting salaries.

(#CapilanoLife.)

Jordan sees the look on Eric's face. "Right? Fackrell failed me, though, and if I can't sort this out, I'm coming back to Cap next year."

"Isn't there any way out?" Eric asks.

(Translation: *Can't your dad, like, make it rain?*)

"I don't think so." Jordan gestures to Mrs. Adams. "I've been trying to work my charms on the administration, but so far, the best she can do is try to convince Fackrell to let me rewrite the exam."

Mrs. Adams overhears, and rolls her eyes.

Jordan sighs. "Fackrell says unless I pass the exam, he'll hold me back. I won't graduate. So I'm probably screwed. I barely made it out of math class junior year."

"I got a ninety-five in calculus," Eric says, before he even knows what he's saying. "I could, like, tutor you."

(Bingo. There's our cheesy *meet cute*.)

12.

It's about as cheesy as cheesy can get. Completely contrived.

(Because we all know Eric isn't going to spend more than a couple pages tutoring Jordan Grant.)

For one thing, tutoring is boring to read about. For another, Eric doesn't have time to be tutoring Jordan Grant. He should be kicking ass at his internship. Speaking of which—

"Shit," Eric says, checking his watch again. "I am really, really freaking late."

It's about this time that Mrs. Adams hangs up the phone. She smiles at Eric the way your grandmother smiles when you drop by for Christmas.

(The secretaries love Eric.)

(All adults love Eric.)

"Eric," she says. "You're here about your plaque." She starts shifting papers. "I know it's around here somewhere."

Eric tries not to look impatient. He's fifteen minutes late for his internship already.

(I don't know if I mentioned this, but it's a VERY PRES-TIGIOUS internship for which his dad pulled beaucoup strings.)

Then Jordan speaks up behind him. "You're serious? You could tutor me?"

Eric glances back at Mrs. Adams, still searching fruit-lessly. "I mean, sure," he tells Jordan.

"I don't know. I'm probably a lost cause." Jordan flashes

that movie-star smile again, and it kind of makes Eric's stomach do a flip. "But it's worth a shot to save the summer, right? You're good at calculus?"

"Pretty good."

"Then it's settled." Jordan holds out his hand. "I'll pay you for your time, of course. Double if I actually pass."

Eric starts to mumble something about how Jordan doesn't have to pay him. Then Mrs. Adams makes, like, a triumphant noise and lifts the plaque out from under a stack of report cards. "Aha!"

"Sweet." Eric takes the plaque from Mrs. Adams. Thanks her.

CAPILANO HIGH SCHOOL, the plaque reads. ERIC CONNELLY, STUDENT OF THE YEAR.

Jordan peeks over Eric's shoulder. "Student of the Year," he says. "Rad. Fackrell can *totally* suck it."

13.

Eric stuffs the plaque in his Herschel bag. He's twenty minutes late now—and counting.

"So when do you want to do this?" Jordan says.

Eric pauses at the office door. Half wishes he could stay here, hang out with Jordan Grant the rest of the afternoon.

But Eric keeps his poker face. He has places to be. "I dunno, tomorrow night?"

Jordan shakes his head. "Callum Fulchrest's party, remember?"

"Oh, yeah. Right. Of course."

(Eric remembers. Eric got the blast online, just like everyone else. But Eric doesn't really, you know, go to parties. It doesn't fit with his dad's Plan.)

(The Plan apparently includes sending his son through life with a serious case of FOMO.)

"I'll just message you," Jordan says. "We'll figure it out."

"Cool," Eric says.

"I have to go now," Eric says.

And he walks casually, exactly five paces away from the office door, before he breaks into a full-on sprint.

14.

Eric speeds the G-Wagen across town to Hockley, Hart, and Brent—

(his dad's old law firm).

On the way there, he berates himself for being so freaking lame. For wasting his time. *How are you going to tutor Jordan Grant when you don't even have time for your internship?*

It's a fact. Eric—

(and his dad)

—have the summer all figured out. Internship Monday through Friday, eight hours a day. On the evenings and weekends, there's college prep to be done. Picking courses. Finding a dorm room. Researching professors.

("And if you have any time left over," Eric's dad tells him, "you can get an early start on next semester's required reading.")

(Yawn.)

It's not the greatest summer in the world. But this is the kind of work you have to put in when you're building your future, right? This is how a Connelly Man lives his life.

15.

Eric has lived nearly eighteen years preparing for life as a Connelly Man. There are certain things a Connelly Man is expected to do:

1. A Connelly Man goes to law school. (Preferably Stanford.)
2. A Connelly Man practices law for a Reputable Number of Years, and then
3. A Connelly Man enters politics.

These are all Very Important Steps.
This is the code Eric lives by.
This is the Plan.

16.

There's one other fundamental tenet to fulfilling your destiny as a Connelly Man. It's arguably the Most Important Tenet. It must NEVER BE BROKEN.

(Are you ready?)

4. A Connelly Man must never, *ever*, under *any* *circumstances*, TARNISH THE CONNELLY NAME.

17.

Eric's grandfather went to Stanford. He came back to Capilano and built a career in litigation before running for mayor of the town, and winning.

(So he literally ran the town.)[1]

Eric's dad went to Stanford. He came back to Capilano and built a career in corporate law before running for the state senate, and winning.

(Eric's dad runs the state.)

Eric will go to Stanford. He will come back to Capilano. He will build a successful law career, and then he'll enter politics. Preferably federal politics.

("A Connelly in the White House," Eric's dad likes to say.)

So, you know. No pressure.

---

1. Not, like, *literally.*

18.

(One more aside on the whole "Connelly Man" thing:
Connelly Men are expected to get married.
Connelly Men are expected to have families.
Connelly Men *do not* hook up with guys.

Ever.)

19.

(No Connelly Man ever met Jordan Grant, though.)

20.

I mean, it's not like Eric's dad is, you know, overtly *homophobic* or anything. He doesn't explicitly hate the gays.

He just prefers to tolerate them from a distance. Stays out of their business, if they'll stay out of his. They don't jive with Eric's dad's worldview.

They sure as hell don't jive with his image of the Connelly Man.

And that's why this whole Jordan Grant thing is going to be problematic.

21.

That night, at the Home of the Connelly Men—

(and women, but there's no glorifying mythology about them)

—Eric and his parents are eating dinner.

"First day at the firm," Eric's dad says. "Did you make the family proud?"

Eric shrugs. "I mean, I think it went okay."

(In fact, it was kind of boring. Ann, Eric's dad's old assistant, pretty well locked him in the room with a bunch of old files and told him to enter the pertinent details into a computer. There are boxes and boxes of files to be entered. It's going to be a long, tedious summer.)

"Ann said you were late this morning. What happened?"

Eric mutters a silent curse. Pastes his best smile on his face. "I had to pick up my plaque from the school."

The plaque is resting on the china cabinet, waiting for his dad to notice. "See? Now the name's right and everything."

"That's great, honey," Eric's mom says. "We're both so proud of you."

But the attempted distraction doesn't work. Eric's dad looks the plaque over. Frowns and sets it aside.

"Late for your first day at a job?" he says. "It sends the wrong message. It's careless and unprofessional."

Eric looks down at his salmon. "I'll be on time tomorrow."

"Tomorrow's not your first day."

"I'm sorry," Eric tells him. "I'll be better. I promise."

"Your grandfather and I have worked hard to build the Connelly name, Eric. I know you'll do us proud."

Eric finishes the salmon as quickly as he can. Excuses himself, goes downstairs to his bedroom.

(Brings the plaque with him.)

(Debates throwing the plaque through a window.)

(But he doesn't, of course.)

Eric doesn't do anything but feel guilty.

(As usual.)

22.

I mean, Eric knows his dad's right.

Eric knows if he doesn't bust his ass, he won't LIVE UP TO HIS POTENTIAL.

He won't MEET EXPECTATIONS.

He'll fail.

"Not everyone's cut out to be a Connelly," his dad's always saying. "But the world needs ditch diggers, too."

Eric knows he has to show up on time. He knows he has to make a good impression. He's depending on a good letter of reference from Ann to impress the Stanford Law admissions committee, three or four years down the road.

Eric knows.

Eric takes it seriously.

Eric does NOT want to be a ditch digger.

It's just—

damn it,

sometimes being a Connelly Man is just
really
freaking

HARD.

23.

Whatever. Eric gets over it.

He forces himself to focus on the future, the long-term gain for this short-term pain. He shows up to the law firm on time. He inputs the pertinent details like a good worker bee. He smiles and makes conversation with Ann when she checks in on him. He meets expectations.

(It's not fun, but it's progress.)

Friday passes. Eric goes home, goes online, settles in to spend the evening choosing his courses for first semester at college. Picking out his electives. Working out a schedule.

Then his phone buzzes. A message on Kik—

(The user name says ThaINfamous, but Eric knows it's Jordan Grant.)

Callum Fulchrest's party tonight. U going?

Eric hesitates. *Nah.*

Why not? Friday night. Everyone will be there.

(*Not me*, Eric thinks.)

Stuff to do, Eric writes back. *Have to pick my courses for college. Make a schedule.*

College is in, like, September, Jordan writes.

There's a pause.

Then: *I really think you should come.*

24.

So Eric sneaks out.

(Duh.)

It's not the first time he's done it. Besides, it's the first week of summer, and his dad's out of town on some fact-finding mission somewhere. Eric has tons of time to make a schedule later.

He borrows his mom's G-Wagen and drives to Callum Fulchrest's house.

This is wrong, obviously. This is not the way a Connelly Man behaves. Connelly Men don't go to house parties. Too much illicit shit going on and too many smartphones. Eric knows his dad would be furious.

Still, Eric isn't sure if his heart is beating so hard because he's NOT LIVING UP TO HIS POTENTIAL, or because he's sneaking out to see Jordan.

25.

The party is off the chain.

It's like every party you've ever been to—except in a bigger house and the people are way better-looking.

Callum Fulchrest lives in a big estate on Marine Drive, the road that winds through the forest and hugs the shoreline west of Capilano. Callum's dad only runs, like, a mining company or something, so his house is on the north side of the street, away from the water. But it's still huge. There's a gate. There are trees. Someone has to buzz you in and then you have to drive up a long driveway just to get to the mansion.

Eric parks the G-Wagen between a couple of Range Rovers. Fixes his hair in the rearview mirror, checks his breath. Stalls a little bit, exhales. Then he climbs from the Benz and walks through Callum's front door.

There are kids everywhere, some Eric recognizes and some that he doesn't. They're dancing in the living room. Making out on the massive curving front staircase. Playing beer pong on Callum's family's antique French Revolution–era dining room table. Somewhere, someone's bumping A$AP Rocky at a high volume through artfully concealed wireless speakers.

(There's no sign of Jordan Grant anywhere.)

Someone thrusts a drink into Eric's hand. A red Solo cup. A clear liquid. "I'm good," Eric tells him. "I drove and all."

The kid takes the cup back. "Suit yourself," he says,

disappearing into the mix. "*Fag.*"

Eric flinches.

(#WordsHurt.)

"Fuck it, one drink," he starts to tell the kid, but he's talking to air.

26.

Everyone's drinking from a red Solo cup.

Maybe just one drink, Eric's thinking. *Maybe I'll just make it light*.

(You can probably guess how underage drinking fits into the Connelly Man, you know, *ethos*. Or doesn't fit, as the case may be.)

Eric asks the closest person where she got her drink. She stops dancing and looks at him. "The keg's in the garage," she says. "Hard liquor in the kitchen."

"What about the cups?" Eric says.

The girl looks at him like he's a monkey.

"I'll just go to the kitchen," Eric says.

He does.

He walks into the kitchen. It's jammed with Capilano kids in various states of inebriation. And smack in the middle, holding court like he really *is* the king, stands Jordan *motherfucking* Grant.

Jordan looks good. He's wearing jeans and a fitted linen shirt, the sleeves rolled up past his forearms. He's holding a red cup and a forty of Fireball. He's pouring shots for a group of Cap High *elite*.

There's Callum Fulchrest. There's Terry Miles. Lexi Tanner. Tristan West.

The A-list.

The beautiful people.

(Only Jordan's miles above them, and everybody knows it.)

They're all circled around Jordan, laughing and having fun, looking—every one of them—like they've never *stressed* about anything for a minute in their lives.

(And let's be honest, they haven't.)

Eric knows he's staring. Knows he probably looks creepy. Can't turn away, though. He's realizing, for the first time in a long time, just how much *fun* he's been missing. He's feeling just a little twinge of maybe, you know, *envy*.

Eric pushes the little twinge from his mind. *It's all worth the sacrifice,* he tells himself. *Someday you'll be a big, important politician and you won't regret missing out on this stuff at all.*

He's not sure if he believes it, though. Especially not when Jordan looks up from the row of shot glasses and catches Eric staring.

"Connelly with two *n*'s," he says, breaking into that movie-star grin again. *"Come do a shot."*

27.

Eric blanches. Eric feels the room looking at him.

(Eric hears the kid with the red Solo cup calling him *fag*.)

"Okay," he says, walking over to the group. "Just one, though, then I'm done."

28.

Except—
　　　Shots are like potato chips.
　　　　　　(Bet you can't drink just one.)

29.

"Don't fucking worry about it, Connelly. You can just crash on the couch."

Callum Fulchrest has his arm around Eric now. With his free hand, he's shoving another shot into Eric's hands. Eric's trying to argue, trying to tell Callum how he drove here, how his mom will be pissed if he doesn't bring the Benz back.

Callum isn't taking no for an answer. "Your mom will get over it," he's telling Eric. "Quit being such a baby."

Eric looks at the shot. Looks around at the group. Jordan's watching him. Jordan has crazy blue eyes. Jordan's smiling at him with those perfect white teeth like, *Come on, what are you waiting for?*

Shit.

"I'll just wake up early," Eric says. "I'll bring the car back tomorrow."

Callum slaps him hard on the back. "That's what I'm talking about," he says, thrusting the shot glass at Eric again. *"Down the hatch."*

30.

And from there, it's pretty much a gong show.

Two shots are enough to get Eric pretty drunk. He's thinking a third shot might actually kill him. Thankfully, the bottle's empty.

Then Lexi Tanner's in front of him. "You need a drink," she says. "You like gin?"

She hands Eric a red cup.

"I went a little overboard with the Hendrick's," Lexi giggles. "I hope you don't mind."

"Of course not," Eric tells her. "Not at all."

(He can nurse a gin and tonic, at least.)

(And he does.)

The group envelops Eric. The party surrounds him. Eric talks to Callum and Lexi and Terry Miles. They're making plans for the summer. Lexi's going to Spain. Callum's racing Ferraris with his uncles in Las Vegas. Terry Miles is staying in Capilano.

"I'm just going to party," he tells the group. "Get stoned at the beach and surf and get laid. Why complicate things?"

They all look at Eric. "What about you?"

Eric shrugs. "Why complicate things?"

31.

Someone passes a joint around. Eric hesitates.

"Come on, dude," Terry says. "Don't be *that* guy."

(#PeerPressure.)

Eric starts coughing, doubled over like a rookie. Lexi and Terry are laughing. Terry slaps Eric on the back, and when Eric looks up, gasping for air and embarrassed, he realizes Jordan isn't here anymore.

And Eric's just drunk enough to go looking for him.

"Excuse me," he tells Lexi and Terry, who start laughing again, and then launch into a conversation about the first time *they* smoked pot.

"I've smoked pot before," Eric says as he's leaving. Or rather, he thinks it. Doesn't say it out loud. The words never shake loose from his brain.

He puts down his cup. Sets off through the mob of kids in the kitchen. It's hot in the house, stifling hot, and Eric's sweaty and high and he's pretty drunk, too. If he's not careful, he's going to pass out or puke or otherwise make a scene—

(and he's pretty sure Connelly Men aren't supposed to get white-girl wasted).

Eric navigates the party carefully. Back through the vast living room, where couples are hooking up on the couches and some junior is at the piano, trying to play "Chopsticks" and failing miserably. And then Eric's standing in the front hall, dizzy as shit, wondering what to do and where to look, when he turns around and there's Jordan, right in front of him, like a magazine cover or something.

"Two *n*'s," he says. "How's it going?"

"Good." Eric blinks. "Better. I was looking for you."

Jordan laughs. "Oh yeah? Why's that?"

Because you're the reason I'm here, Eric wants to tell him. *Because I've been looking for you all night.*

Yep. Eric's just drunk enough to say it.

"You're the reason I came here," he tells Jordan. "I just wanted to see you again."

"You are going to see me again," Jordan says. "The tutoring thing, remember? I'll message you tomorrow. We'll set it up."

"No," Eric says. "I mean, yeah, that too, but, like—"

(*It's really hot in here.*)

(*This is a disaster.*)

"I was just kind of hoping we could maybe be alone," Eric finishes.

Jordan's eyes go wide. "Oh," he says. "*Oh.*"

"It's stupid," Eric says. "Just forget it. You're probably not even like that. Forget I said anything."

Jordan looks past Eric. Eric follows his gaze, sees a couple of not-so-popular Cap High girls in the open doorway, Paige Hammond and Haley Keefer—

(who are kind of weird people for Jordan to hang with)

—staring in like they're waiting for something.

Jordan holds up a finger, *One second.* Then he looks at Eric again. Studies him with those intoxicating blue eyes.

"You're sweet," he says. "And you're smoking hot, too. If I didn't have to bail, hell, I'd probably take you home."

This sounds decent to Eric. So Eric's thinking, *Why not?*

"But that's all it would be, just a one-night stand. And

then shit would get awkward, and I'd fail freaking calculus, and nobody would be happy."

Eric looks away. "It wouldn't have to be like that."

"Sure it would. You're a good kid. Fucking Student of the Year, man."

"Yeah, so?" Eric says. "What does that make you?"

"Me?" Jordan shrugs. Smiles that movie-star smile, but there's something else behind it, something darker. "I'm a bad influence. I'm a one-way ticket to nowhere."

Paige shows up at Jordan's arm. "We gotta go, Jordan."

"*Yeah,*" Jordan says. Eric blinks and Jordan's just Jordan again—that strangeness evaporating like some kind of hallucination. Eric wondering if it was real, or just the pot.

"I'll holler at you," he tells Eric. "We'll do that tutoring thing, okay?"

He's already following Paige to the door.

"*Wait,*" Eric says. "Where are you going?"

Jordan glances back. Winks. "Believe me, Eric, you don't want to know."

KIK -- CAPILANO HIGH PRIVATE MESSAGE GROUP
— 06/25/16 — 04:40 AM

USERNAME: SuIcIdEpAcK
MESSAGE: Something's burning, Capilano.
    Watch this space.

32.

"Dude, wake up."

Eric opens his eyes to bright daylight and Callum Fulchrest looming above him. Callum has a look on his face like he forgot to wear pants to the prom, and Eric sits up too fast and realizes two things immediately:

1. He's in Callum's palatial living room.
2. He's hungover as shit.

Ow.

The night comes back in snapshots. Shots of Fireball, shots of gin. Jordan—gone with Paige and Haley, the party raging on regardless. Girls, dancing, music, drugs.

And puking.

(Shit.)

Callum is pacing. Callum is running his hands through his hair. Callum looks like he's ready to cry.

"I can't fucking believe this," Callum is saying. "My dad's going to kill me."

Judging from the light coming through the living room windows, it's midmorning, or worse.

Eric's been here all night.

He still has his mom's G-Wagen.

(He thinks: *You think* your *dad's going to kill* you?)

Eric sits back, tries to shade his eyes from the light. Looks around for some water and sees only trashed Solo cups and empty bottles. Party detritus. A couple kids passed out on the opposite couch.

"You didn't see it, did you?" Callum asks Eric. "You didn't see if someone, like, took it?"

Eric shakes his head. "No, I didn't."

Then Eric frowns.

"Wait. What exactly are we talking about?"

Callum stops pacing, and now there really *are* tears in his eyes.

"My dad's *Basquiat*," he says. "Someone *stole* it."

33.

Eric doesn't know what a Basquiat is.

But according to Callum, it's worth a shitload of money.

"It's my dad's favorite painting," Callum says, leading Eric into his dad's den. "He paid, like, a million for it. And it's *gone*."

Callum gestures to a blank space on the wall. It looks like a good place to hang a painting. There's nothing there now but a forlorn picture hook.

"Yup," Eric says. "It's definitely gone."

34.

"What are you going to do?" Eric asks Callum.

They're in the kitchen now. Eric's drinking orange juice and fighting the urge to puke again. Callum is still pacing. Callum is openly crying.

"I don't *know*," Callum says. "My dad comes back in three days. Are you sure you didn't see anything?"

Eric thinks back. Still doesn't know what a Basquiat is supposed to look like, but he can't remember anyone walking around with a painting.

(You'd figure a painting would be kind of hard to hide.)

"I'm pretty sure," Eric tells Callum. "I got really drunk, though."

Callum moans. "He's going to freaking *kill* me. I'm as good as freaking dead."

Eric thinks about his own dad. About his mom, who is bound to be pissed that Eric still has her car.

Eric doesn't know anything about Callum's little problem.

Eric needs to save his own skin.

He's about to bail on Callum, when his phone starts to buzz. And then Callum stops pacing.

His phone's buzzing too.

35.

It's a message to the private Capilano High Kik group. But it's no user Eric has ever seen before.

"SuIcIdEpAcK."

(Eric sees they posted an earlier message, in the middle of the night. *Something's burning, Capilano. Watch this space.*)

There's no text in *this* message, though. Just a link.

Eric clicks the link, and it opens a Vine. He presses play. Across the room, Callum is doing the same.

THE VINE

FADE IN

INT. - CALLUM FULCHREST'S KITCHEN - NIGHT

A crazy HOUSE PARTY. Drunk TEENAGERS
everywhere. The camera is shaky, waist
level. Nobody seems to notice it's there.

In a corner of the kitchen, CALLUM
FULCHREST is talking to A PRETTY GIRL. They
are both holding RED SOLO CUPS.

As we watch, the girl turns away from
Callum to talk to A FRIEND. She puts her
cup on the counter.

Quickly, Callum removes A BAGGIE from his
pocket. He pours SOME KIND OF POWDER in the
girl's drink. Stirs it a little with his
finger. Nobody sees.

FREEZE on the Solo cup. HORROR MOVIE MUSIC.
(Think strings.)

Back to action. The girl turns around.
Reaches for her Solo cup, but before
she can take a drink, something happens

offscreen. She puts the cup down again.

CLOSE ON THE CUPS as someone walks past.
We only see gloved hands and dark clothing.
The hands switch the cups.

PAN BACK TO: Callum drinking from his cup.
Then CUT TO:

INT. - CALLUM FULCHREST'S LIVING ROOM
- NIGHT

One hour later. Callum slumps on a couch.
He's slurring his words. He's drooling.
(He's obviously been drugged.)

CUT TO:
EXT. - OUTDOORS - NIGHT

A bonfire. There's something burning in the
flames, something large. The camera zooms
in - it's CALLUM'S DAD'S BASQUIAT.

CUT TO:

A black background. A logo, a HANGMAN'S
NOOSE fashioned into a heart. Words:
SUICIDE PACK.

VOICE-OVER:
(disguised)

Be careful, Capilano. Next time we burn
more than the Basquiat.

FADE TO BLACK.

36.

Eric puts down his phone.

Callum has gone pale. He's staring at his phone with his mouth open like he wants to say something but there's nothing he can say.

Other people are talking, though. That message thread is blowing up.

#sleazeball.

smdh

Someone should kick that dude's ass.

Unbelievable. Always knew you were shady Callum.

LMFAO!

And there's Jordan Grant, ThaINfamous:

Holy shit!!!

(Plus a hundred laughing emojis.)

The hits keep coming.

Nobody's on Team Callum.

(#SocialSuicide.)

37.

Seeing Jordan's message reminds Eric of last night.

The awkwardness.

The drunkenness.

The point-blank rejection.

(*Shit*.)

Then Eric remembers how he was supposed to bring the G-Wagen back home and how he doesn't have time for Callum Fulchrest's little comeuppance, or the Suicide Pack—

(whoever they are).

He's in deep enough shit on his own.

He stands.

Callum looks up, his eyes hollow. "Dude," he says. "I didn't. That wasn't—"

But Eric's already heading for the door. "It doesn't matter, man," he tells Callum. "Whatever you did, I can't help you."

38.

Eric's mom is on the phone when he walks in the house. She hangs up quickly. "Eric, oh my god," she says, standing up from the table. "Where have you been? Are you okay?"

The fact that she's worried and not angry makes it even worse. "I'm fine," Eric tells her, letting her hug him. "I stayed out too late, is all."

"You're sure you're not injured? You weren't in an accident?"

"I'm not hurt; I'm fine," Eric says. "I'm sorry I messed up your phone call."

His mom blinks, shakes her head. "Oh, Monica was talking my ear off, anyway. You'd think the Summer's End Ball was tomorrow, the way she's carrying on."

She keeps talking. Eric feels the hangover returning. "I think I need a drink of water."

His mom takes a step back. "You were at a party."

"*Please* don't tell Dad," Eric begs her. "I know I should have called, and I should have brought the car home, but, like— he'll flip out if he hears this."

His mom doesn't say anything for a beat or two. She just studies Eric's face, like a judge mulling the death penalty. Eric holds her gaze and tries to look sorry.

Finally, his mom sighs. "I guess it's better that you didn't drive drunk," she says. "What your dad doesn't know won't hurt him."

Eric hugs his mom. "I swear, it won't happen again."

"It's normal to blow off steam," his mom says. "You worked so hard this year; I'm glad you're out with your friends. Just be careful you don't go overboard, okay?"

Eric pours himself a glass of water. Drinks it, and feels a million times better already.

"I won't go overboard," he tells his mom. "I learned my lesson, I swear."

39.

It's not exactly a lie.

    (Eric's hungover as hell.)

    (He thinks he's through with partying.)

    (He's thinks he's going to spend the summer BEING RESPONSIBLE and LIVING UP TO EXPECTATIONS.)

    (He thinks he's going to be the *perfect* Connelly Man.)

Holy shit, is he wrong.

40.

Nobody at Capilano knows anything about the Suicide Pack. There's, like, a whole cottage industry sprung up in the wake of Callum Fulchrest's personal fiasco, every kid in town trying to figure out who's behind that mysterious Vine.

But nobody claims credit. Nobody steps forward.

(There isn't even anything in the news about the Fulchrests' stolen Basquiat. And that doesn't seem right.)

(I mean, it sounds like a big deal, doesn't it? A million-dollar painting stolen. A whole school full of suspects—it's like the inciting incident in a shitty movie.)

But there's nothing in the news. No police come to take Eric's statement. Nobody's talking about the missing Basquiat—not in public, anyway. But everyone from Cap High is talking about the Suicide Pack on Kik.

But SuIcIdEpAcK stays silent.

And nobody else has any answers.

41.

Jordan doesn't message Eric. They never set up a tutoring session. Eric figures he was right; Jordan was just trying to make him feel better.

    Trying to let him down easy.

    It hurts, but, you know, it is what it is.

    (Anyway, Connelly Men don't have time for romance.)

    (Especially not with Harrison Grant's kid.)

    Eric feels like maybe, just maybe, he's been spared something. Like—maybe this is a good thing?

42.

Eric's dad comes home. He doesn't find out about the party.

Eric sweats out his hangover for the rest of the weekend. Picks his courses for first semester and downloads the textbooks. Eric shows his dad his schedule.

Intro to Political Systems.

International Relations.

Elements of Political Theory.

Statistics.

American Literature.

("I needed an arts elective," Eric tells his dad.)

Eric's dad purses his lips together and frowns. "Hmm," he says, in that way that tells Eric he should already be taking, I dunno, Advanced Corporate Litigation and, like, How to Be President When You're Only Seventeen.

"Hmm."

43.

Anyway.

Monday comes, and Eric goes back to the law firm. He goes back to the little room with the really old computer, and he spends the next eight hours inputting data from the stacks of paper files.

He does this on Tuesday.

He does this on Wednesday.

He does this on Thursday.

He does not pass Go. He does not collect $200. He does not have any fun.

He is the model of the perfect Connelly Man.

44.

And that's all that matters, right?

> You start young. You build your future instead of farting around—

> (or so Eric's dad is always saying).

> Short-term pain, long-term gain.

> Etc.

> Still, Eric drives past the beach every night on his way home. He looks at all the boats out on the sparkling water. He sees party pictures on Instagram and Snapchat, club nights and camping trips and bonfires, sees Jordan living it up with Paige Hammond and Haley Keefer, and it's hard not to feel just the tiniest little twinge of,

> > you know,

> > *FOMO.*

45.

Whatever, though. Eric figures he can party—

(or at least relax)

—when he's president.

For now, there's work to do.

(Monday.)

(Tuesday.)

(Wednesday.)

(Thursday.)

(Etc.)

And on and on, until Thursday night, Eric's online doing problem sets out of his first semester statistics textbook—

(This is what passes for a social life when you're Student of the Year.)

—and his phone buzzes with a new message:

ThaINfamous.

Jordan Grant.

(And Eric forgets about statistics.)

46.

JG: *You still up?*

　　EC: (After a long pause and a few lame false starts) *Ya. What's up?*

　　JG: *Cramming for calculus. The exam is tomorrow.*

　　EC: *How's it going?*

　　JG: *Bad.*

　　EC: *You need help?*

　　JG: *You still down?*

　　EC: *Sure, why not? I'm always down for whatever.*

　　Pause.

　　Long pause.

　　(During which Eric curses himself for his inability to have, like, just *one* interpersonal interaction that doesn't turn horribly awkward.)

　　JG: *Rad.*

47.

Jordan shows up at the back door a half hour later.

(Eric can hear his BMW from two blocks down.)

He's wearing a hoodie and board shorts, and his hair is artfully messed up and he's tanned, and he's grinning his cocky, mischievous grin. Just the sight of him gives Eric butterflies.

"So this is your place, huh?" Jordan says as Eric leads him into the kitchen. "This is where the Student of the Year magic happens."

Eric follows his gaze, sees everything the way Jordan must be seeing it, and feels instantly self-conscious. His parents have a nice house, but, you know, his dad's a *politician*, not a studio executive.

Jordan doesn't seem to care, though. He looks around, takes in the kitchen, the dining room, the hallway to the TV room. "Where do you want to do this?" he says.

(*How about the bedroom?* Eric thinks. Then he thinks about how messy and embarrassing his bedroom looks right now.)

"How about the dining room?" he says. "That table right there?"

48.

"What were you doing online?" Jordan says. "I hope you weren't, like, G-chatting with an underwear model or something."

(They've been working for an hour or so. It's going fine. Jordan is way behind and kind of lost, but he picks up concepts quickly. Eric can tell he's actually pretty smart, no matter what kind of laid-back slacker vibe he puts out to the world.)

"Not really important," Eric says. "Just doing some statistics problems."

Jordan looks up from his calculus textbook. "What, like, homework? Are you in summer school or something?"

"No, no," Eric says.

"I thought you were Student of the Year."

"I am." Eric searches for a way to say the next part without sounding like a supernerd.

(It's impossible.)

"It's for college," he says finally. "I looked up my courses online and downloaded all the textbooks already. I was doing some problem sets."

Jordan looks at Eric like he's from Mars. "It's. Summer."

Eric blushes. "I know, but, like, I want to get a head start, you know? This way, when college starts, I'll be sure I really know everything."

"You could be doing anything in the world right now.

Traveling to Europe. Racing cars. Learning to fly. And you're doing *problem sets*?"

Eric hesitates.

(It sounds really stupid when Jordan puts it that way.)

"I need to keep my grades up to get into Stanford Law," Eric tells him. "It's important. I can have fun later."

Jordan makes a face. Is obviously about to shoot holes in that theory when the floorboards unexpectedly creak in the next room, and Eric's dad appears in the doorway. "Eric?"

"*Dad.*" Eric feels a sudden rush of, like, *guilt*, like his dad just walked in on them smoking pot or hooking up or something. "This is, uh, Jordan. We're just doing some calculus."

"It's after midnight on a weeknight," Eric's dad says. "Surely your calculus can wait until a more reasonable hour."

Jordan's standing, hand outstretched, before Eric can reply. "You must be Mr. Connelly with two *n*'s," he tells Eric's dad. "I'm Jordan Grant. Eric was just helping me cram for when I retake the exam."

The creases on Eric's dad's forehead get deeper. "Helping you *cram*," he repeats. "That implies you haven't adequately studied already."

Jordan's smile doesn't waver. "Well, yeah. That's correct, sir. I've been busy with some, uh, other projects."

"The night before an exam is hardly the time to start studying," Eric's dad says. "And it's EXTREMELY IRRESPONSIBLE of you to conscript your friend into enabling this kind of behavior."

(*Mortifying*, Eric's thinking. *Dad, you're the worst.*)

"Yes, sir," Jordan says. "Extremely irresponsible, I agree."

"Our house is closed to visitors after eleven on weeknights," Eric's dad continues. "Even to those who are cramming."

"Of course," Jordan says. "I was just leaving."

"See that you do." Eric's dad turns to go. Stops and looks back. "Oh, and Mr. Grant?"

Jordan winks at Eric. "Yes, sir?"

Eric's dad gives it a beat. "It's *Senator* Connelly."

49.

"*It's* Senator *Connelly.*"

Jordan is whispering, a pretty good imitation of Eric's dad's voice. Eric is equal parts trying to shut him up and trying not to laugh.

"My dad will kill you if he hears you," he tells Jordan. "He'll kill both of us."

Jordan waves him off. "He's not going to kill anyone. He'd never get reelected." He shoulders his backpack. "Anyway, thanks for this. I'd better get out of here."

"I'm sorry about my dad," Eric says. "I'm sorry I couldn't help you more."

"Don't be sorry." Jordan opens the back door. "This was good. I learned a lot. I'm feeling optimistic."

He tosses a wave over his shoulder. Disappears into the backyard. Eric waits at the open door until he hears Jordan's BMW rev. Until he hears the tires chirp as Jordan peels out, until the block is dead quiet once again.

Then he closes the door, locks it. Stands in the empty kitchen.

(Statistics problems just seem like a letdown at this point.)

50.

"It's noble of you to want to help your friend out," Eric's dad says.

(It's the next morning, at the breakfast table. Eric waited all night for this.)

"But your friend is going to have to learn proper work habits if he wants to succeed in this world. Using you as a crutch isn't going to suffice."

"His dad's Harrison Grant," Eric says. "The studio head. His family's loaded. He doesn't need work habits."

Eric's dad lowers the newspaper. Stares at Eric across the table. "But *you* do. And staying up to all hours to help your rich slacker friends isn't going to help you one bit. You remember what we've said about time management."

Eric looks down into his cereal. Sighs. Then recites. "I need to be proactive in making the most of my time. I need to choose activities that will set me on the right course for the future. This is where I set the foundation for my life as a Connelly Man."

"Exactly," Eric's dad says. "And you're not building any foundations when you're wasting time with Jordan Grant."

Eric doesn't say anything. He knows his dad is right.

(But come on. It's summer freaking vacation.)

"Better finish up," Eric's dad says. "You're going to be late to your internship."

51.

It's back to the paperwork.
 Monday to Friday.
 Nine to five.
 File by file, stack by stack.
 (Half-hour break for lunch.)
 The little room is air-conditioned. There aren't any windows. It's freezing cold and sterile.
 Eric hardly sees the sun.
 (Short-term pain for long-term gain.)
 (Build a foundation.)
 (Meet EXPECTATIONS.)
 (Be a Connelly Man.)

52.

A few days go by. Interminable, unremarkable. Then Eric's on his lunch break at the little deli beside Hockley, Hart, and Brent, trying to decide between the egg salad and the tuna, when his phone vibrates—a text.

Jordan.

Just got my calc exam back.

Eric sets aside the tuna/egg salad question. *Oh yeah?*

Yup. 68%

Ah crap, Eric writes. *I'm sorry.*

Pause.

Ellipsis.

Are you kidding??? That's a solid C-.

Eric waits.

Means I passed, duh! Jordan continues. *That means I'm actually graduating. And it's all thanks to you.*

A paralegal clears her throat behind Eric. Eric pushes his tray forward. Pretends to study a cup of Jell-O.

Oh, he texts back. *Well no worries. My pleasure* ☺

Where are you?

Eric puts the Jell-O back. Considers the tuna/egg salad conundrum once more. *Working. My internship @ HH&B. Why?*

We're celebrating. I'm coming to get you. Be outside in ten minutes.

"No," Eric says aloud. The cashier turns to look at him.

The paralegal glares behind him. Eric mutters an apology, steps out of line.

I can't. My lunch break's almost over.

Tell them you're going home sick. No excuses. Be outside or I'll drag you out.

I can't, Eric writes. *Maybe after?*

Ten minutes, Jordan writes. *And counting.*

53.

Eric doesn't go back to work.

(Duh.)

What Eric *does* do is panic. Eric *stresses* for a good eight minutes. Eric thinks about hiding until Jordan gets bored and goes away.

But that's ridiculous.

(And Eric doesn't really want Jordan to go away.)

The files will still be there tomorrow.

(Stacks and stacks of them.)

Eric figures he's been working hard. He can take a half day, right?

(*Well, no.*)

(Not if he wants to meet EXPECTATIONS.)

(Not if he wants to BUILD a GOOD FOUNDATION.)

(Not if he wants to be a CONNELLY MAN.)

None of those things involve skipping out to hang with Jordan Grant. But Eric's skipping out anyway.

54.

"I'm not feeling so good," Eric tells Ann. He fakes a cough. "I think I'd better go home for the day."

Ann squints up at him from her workstation. She doesn't look like she believes him.

"I'll have to tell your dad," she says.

Eric feels his phone buzzing in his pocket.

"I'm sorry," he tells Ann. "I just really have to go."

55.

"We need to adjust your nomenclature if we're going to hang out."

Jordan's waiting outside the law firm beside his cherry-red BMW. He smiles wide behind his Wayfarers as Eric comes out the front door. Hits him with the *nomenclature* bit.

Eric glances back into the office. "Huh?"

"Your name," Jordan says. "What we call you. Eric Connelly is so, you know, *Student of the Year*. We need you to loosen up a little bit. Do you agree?"

"I mean," Eric says. "I mean, yeah. Okay."

"Agreed. Perfect." Jordan steps back. Holds his hands like a picture frame. "What we have here is . . ." Beat, then he smiles, satisfied. "*E*."

Eric blinks. "E?"

"E," Jordan says. "Simple. To the point. Badass. From now on you're E, got it?"

He's climbing into the BMW before Eric can answer.

56.

Jordan isn't alone. Paige Hammond and Haley Keefer are sitting in the backseat of the Bimmer.

"Ladies, say hello to E," Jordan tells them as Eric slides into the passenger seat. "E just saved my academic career. We owe him a good time."

Eric twists in his seat as Jordan pulls out of the lot. Waves an awkward hello to the girls. Haley just nods at Eric and goes back to playing with her phone, but Paige takes off her sunglasses. Meets Eric's eyes.

"Hey, Eric," she says. "Fancy meeting you here."

57.

(Here are some facts about Paige Hammond and Haley Keefer, for context:

Paige is tall and blond and beautiful—the female Jordan Grant, almost. Her parents are big-shot real-estate developers who got rich flipping mansions to foreign investors. Except her dad's in some legal trouble at the moment, some embezzlement scandal. It's all over the news, and Paige's stock at Cap High has taken a hit.

(She's, like, an A-minus right now. Or maybe a B-plus.)

You might recognize Paige from the photo spread she did in Italian *Vogue*, if you're into that kind of thing. But Paige is smart, too, Ivy League; she's going to Yale in the fall.

(So don't get too attached.)

Haley Keefer had her own little fall from grace a while back. She disappeared from school last fall, and rumor has it she was committed to some psychiatric hospital. *Eating disorder*, people said. *She almost died.*

Whatever happened, Haley's still alive. But the gossip was a big blow to her rep anyway. She's not exactly Jordan Grant material either.

Haley is kind of the opposite of Paige. She's shorter than Paige, in height and in hair. Where Paige is glamorama, Haley is punk rock. Pixie cut. Tattoos. Corsets and ripped fishnets.

Her dad was in a rock band back in the eighties. They

never really made it big in North America, but the residuals from his European sales are still paying for the waterfront mansion and the vintage Ferrari. You might have heard his stuff in, like, a Girl Talk mashup or some post-ironic DJ set.

Haley also has an older sister, Tinsley. Tinsley is tall and slim and pretty. Tinsley is an actress. Tinsley is her mother's favorite.

Talking about Tinsley is the easiest way to make Haley hate you. We won't talk about Tinsley.

Yet.)

58.

(Here is one more fact about Paige:

Paige and Eric used to hook up, back in the day. Back before Eric started to realize he was more into boys.

Eric never really told Paige about his change in, you know, sexual preference. They just kind of drifted apart.

(Well, Eric drifted. Right into a sea of textbooks and college applications.)

Needless to say, there's some unfinished business between our hero and the model in the backseat. There may even be some hurt feelings.

Awkward.)

59.

But Paige and Eric don't dredge up those hurt feelings yet. The weather's too nice to rehash ancient history. The sun's shining, the sky's blue, and there's a breeze off the water. This isn't the time to be *stressed*.

60.

So what do four rich Capilano kids do on a hot summer day?

    Easy.

    They take advantage.

    They make the most.

    They enjoy themselves.

    (And in this context, that means a boat day.)

61.

Jordan's dad owns the boat. He's never around, though, so it's pretty much Jordan's toy. It's a Sea Ray Sundancer, fast and low-slung and sexy, with a sundeck at the bow and a cockpit at the stern, and a little kitchenette and master bedroom down below. Jordan revs the throttle high and points them out into the bay, dodging sailboats and cargo ships all the way to the south shore, the university, out west toward Wreck Beach.

Paige and Haley are downstairs in the kitchenette mixing vodka sodas. Paige is telling Haley about how ███████████ ² tried to pick her up at the Cactus Club the other night. Haley's telling Paige how she's pretty sure ███████████ has a fiancée back home in L.A.

Eric isn't really paying attention to Haley and Paige, though. Eric doesn't care about ███████████. Eric isn't even really enjoying the weather. He's in the cockpit with Jordan, nursing a gin and tonic, telling Jordan how he can't actually be here right now because he should be at the law office.

"What were you doing at HH&B anyway?" Jordan asks him. "What could be so important that you would waste a day like this?"

---

2. He's a movie star, *very* A-list. The lawyers won't let me tell you his name, but you can probably figure it out. Think former teen idols and nautical disasters.

"I kind of work there," Eric tells him. Eric tells him about the internship. He tells Jordan how it'll look great on his law school application. How his dad had to call in favors with his old partners to get Eric in. "It's mostly just data entry, though," Eric says. "I'm not actually *doing* anything."

"So that's how you're spending your summer. Data entry. Problem sets." Jordan pilots the Sundancer around a slower, smaller speedboat. "Isn't law school in, like, four years?"

"It doesn't hurt to start early," Eric says. "My dad just wants me to work for what I get. He says everyone in this town is so rich they feel, like, *entitled*."

"So what would *Senator* Connelly say if he knew you were out on a yacht instead of working for a living?" Jordan grins. "I guess that's pretty obvious. Anyway, it doesn't matter."

He slaps Eric on the back.

"You're here now," he says. "Your dad doesn't know. And we're *not* turning around, so you're just going to have to enjoy it."

62.

Jordan motors the Sundancer around Point Grey and throttles down the engine, and they drift in toward Wreck Beach. This is hippie country, a bunch of leathery old nudists letting it all hang out in the breeze. Haley drops the anchor a couple hundred yards offshore; Jordan cranks up the radio until every hippie in the sand is glaring out at the Sundancer. Then he pours Eric another drink and flops down beside him.

"Don't you ever get bored in that cubicle?" He gestures in a wide arc: The boat. The beach. The girls. The drinks. The sun on the water and no clouds in the sky, the mountains looming high in the distance. "Look around, dude. Is this really worth passing up for *data entry*?"

"Not everyone's dad is Harrison Grant," Eric says. "Of course I want to be out here. But I have to think of the future."

"Fuck that noise. You really think your dad didn't have any fun? Shit, I bet he tore it up when he was our age."

"I doubt it," Eric says. "I don't think he ever had any fun. He was too focused on, like, *integrity*. And LIVING UP TO HIS POTENTIAL."

"Then he fucking missed out." Jordan flashes that movie-star smile. "I'm just saying, life's too short. Why be stressed? Live in the moment for once."

Jordan reaches down, produces a joint from somewhere. He stands and stretches, slips his shirt off and chucks it into the little cabin. Then he climbs up onto the sundeck. "Come on. We're ignoring the girls."

He's impossibly golden, standing out there in the sun. He's tanned and he's built and he's devil-may-care, and Eric could give two shits about being a Connelly Man, all of a sudden.

(Funny how that works.)

63.

Eric climbs up onto the sundeck and spreads out a towel and lies down in the sun between Jordan and Paige and lets the stress melt away, until he's not worried about his internship anymore, or what Ann will tell his father.

Until he's *Living in the Moment*, the way Jordan said.

And *the Moment* is good.

It's really good.

64.

They tan.

(Well, all except Haley. She doesn't really do sun. She doesn't really do *social*, either; after a while she retreats to the cockpit, pulls out a battered copy of *L'Étranger* and a package of Belmonts, and just sits in the shade and reads and smokes by herself, and Eric can't tell if she's happy, but she sure doesn't look *stressed*, anyway.)

They swim.

The water is cold but refreshing, and it's so clear you can see the anchor digging into the sandy bottom. And the boat bobs on the waves, and Eric floats on his back beside it, staring up at the blue sky and bobbing in the waves too, and the internship and his dad and all of Capilano may as well be a million miles away.

65.

"So Jordan says you saved his academic career," Paige says—

(They're back on the boat now, on the sundeck, on towels, letting the sun dry the water from their skin.)

"I'd love to hear *that* story."

Eric glances at Jordan, who's back in the stern with Haley. They're cuddled up close back there. *Real* close.

(Eric's kind of distracted.)

"I didn't really do much," he says. "Just helped him cram a little bit for the calc exam."

"Don't be so *modest*." Jordan climbs back up to the sundeck with a fresh round of drinks. "I would have failed that midterm without you. They would have held me back a year. Now I'm home free, and the summer is ours."

Paige takes her drink. Toasts. "The summer is ours."

She reaches over to touch glasses with Eric, but Eric's hardly paying attention. He's watching Jordan retreat back to the stern of the Sundancer. Watching Haley sit up when he gets there.

He's watching Jordan and Haley make out.

And he's thinking . . .

Son of a bitch.

66.

"So if you helped Jordan pass calculus somehow," Paige says, "you really *are* a hero."

Eric stops creeping on Jordan and Haley, lest Paige figure out what he's doing. He forces a laugh. "Come on."

"Maybe *I* should have failed calculus," Paige says. "Maybe you would have paid more attention to me."

Eric looks at Paige. Can't see her eyes behind her huge Dolce sunglasses. Paige stares at him, her expression inscrutable, and suddenly the boat seems very small.

"Shit," Eric says. "Yeah, about that. I'm sorry. I . . ."

He trails off, unsure of how to finish. Not sure how to tell Paige about how scared he was, toward the end of their little fling, when he realized he wasn't feeling the whole hetero angle. When he figured out he kind of, sort of, was more into guys.

(Scared? Fucking terrified. Fucking *ashamed*.)

But Eric still can't explain it. And Paige is watching him through her sunglasses, waiting for an explanation. The seconds drag on. It's awkward.

Then Jordan speaks from below deck. "Who *cares*?" he says. "He's here now, isn't he? E's back, baby. Better than ever."

Paige's still watching Eric.

"Yeah," she says. "I guess we'll see, won't we?"

67.

Jordan's phone buzzes. He trails a lazy hand over the pile of towels to get it, smiles when he reads the screen.

"Someone on Kik just sent a blast from the airport," he tells the others. "Apparently Callum Fulchrest was just seen boarding a nonstop flight to *Barcelona* two hours ago. The bastard is fleeing the country."

Nobody replies. Eric lifts his head from the towel, looks around the boat just in time to see Haley and Paige exchange glances. But neither of them says anything.

"Do you think it's true?" he asks. "Did he really do what they said?"

"Of *course* it's true," Haley says. "Didn't you watch the Vine? It's all there."

"Well, yeah, but—"

"But nothing. That guy was shady as fuck. He tried to slip a roofie in my drink at prom, like I wouldn't freaking notice." Haley picks up her book again. "He got his, though, didn't he?"

"They always do," Jordan says.

Eric replays the Vine in his head. The hidden-camera trick was pretty rad, pretty sneaky. Whoever pulled it off had balls and skill. He's been racking his brain, trying to remember the party, searching his mind for any memory of the person behind the video.

But he can't remember much.

(Eric was really drunk.)

"I don't know how they got that painting out of there, though," he says. "Wouldn't somebody have noticed a million-dollar painting leaving a party?"

Another round of meaningful looks.

"Not necessarily," Paige says. "And it's a six-million-dollar painting, actually."

Jordan scoffs. "If it was real."

"Which it totally wasn't," Haley says. "Callum Fulchrest's dad can't even afford waterfront property. You think he can pay for a Basquiat?"

"Why do you think there hasn't been any news about it?" Paige says. "Callum's dad is too freaking embarrassed to report it."

"And anyway, his son's a wannabe date-rapist," Haley says. "He knows if he calls the police, it's his own ass that gets nailed."

"So how do you guys know all this stuff?" Eric asks them. "I mean, you all left the party early, right? Did you, like, see who took the painting or something?"

Jordan looks at Haley. Something passes between them. Then Jordan turns back to Eric. Smiles.

"We saw something," he says. "Yeah, I guess you could say that."

68.

(Let's cut to the chase. I'm just going to tell you now:

Jordan and Haley and Paige stole that painting.

But you already knew that, right?)

69.

It's almost full dark by the time they're back in Capilano. Jordan brings the boat into the marina, and they tie it to the dock and walk up to the parking lot to Jordan's BMW. Eric gets there first, and when he looks back, he sees Paige and Jordan and Haley huddled together. They're talking about something. Haley's shaking her head. It looks like Jordan's trying to convince her.

Finally, Haley just holds up her hands like she's disgusted. Turns and walks away from the others. She doesn't look at Eric as she approaches the BMW.

"Do you mind giving me a ride back to the law office?" Eric asks Jordan when he and Paige are within earshot. "I left my mom's ride when I bailed on my internship."

Jordan unlocks the Bimmer. "Heading home, huh?" he says. "Big day tomorrow?"

"Those files aren't going to enter themselves."

"Right," Jordan says. "It takes a man with integrity."

"Or something."

It all suddenly sounds *so* boring. It all sounds so *unfair*.

Paige and Haley climb into the BMW's backseat. Jordan circles around to the driver's side. Studies Eric over the roof of the car.

"I can take you back to your mom's Benz if you really want," Jordan says. There's a wicked glint in his eye. "Or we could all have some *real* fun."

The way he says it gives Eric a shiver. He flashes back to the boat, Jordan's tanned skin, his six-pack.

Real fun.

(Yes, please.)

But Eric forces himself to hold his poker face. "What do you have in mind?"

Jordan's grin gets wider. He gestures to his car.

"Get in," he tells Eric. "It's easier if we show you."

70.

"Where are we going, exactly?"

They've been driving for ten minutes now into an industrial park on the outskirts of Capilano. The streets are quiet; all business is done for the day, and this is a sleepy town after dark anyway, even on a Friday. Most of the real action is in the clubs across the bridge, in the city itself.

Nobody is speaking. Nobody's on the roads. Even the radio is turned off. It's like driving through a post-apocalyptic dead zone with the volume on mute. Eric plays along until he can't take it anymore.

"Um, guys?"

His voice seems intrusively loud in the silence. Nobody replies. Jordan keeps driving. He reaches an intersection and turns right, down a long road lined with warehouses and empty office buildings and almost zero streetlights.

Eric tries again. "Hello?"

Jordan slows the BMW. Peers out the window like he's checking for an address.

"Go easy on Eric," Paige says. "It's his first Fix."

"It's *my* Fix," Haley says. "I'm not wasting it just because of the new guy." She shakes her head. Mutters: "He shouldn't even be here, if you want my opinion."

"*Fix?* What are you guys even talking about?" Eric says.

Paige just shrugs. Jordan says nothing. Haley scowls out

the window. They're creeping down the road. A pickup truck passes in the other direction, and then they're alone again.

(Eric's starting to feel a little, you know, *nervous*.)

Then Haley's voice breaks the silence. "There it is," she says, pointing. "There's the spot. Get your game faces on, ladies."

"Where the hell are we?" Eric says, squinting into the darkness. "Are you guys going to tell me, or what?"

Jordan pulls to the side of the road. Stops the car and kills the headlights. "You'll figure it out," he says. "You're a smart kid. You'll get it eventually."

71.

"It's your first Fix," Jordan tells Eric, "so we'll bring you in easy. Just hang out with me here until the girls do their thing, cool?"

Paige flashes Eric a crooked smile. "We won't be gone too long," she says. "Assuming Haley knows her shit."

Haley gives her the finger. "Just watch me, *betch*. You assholes stand guard."

Paige and Haley walk up the road toward a long, low-lying warehouse. Eric watches them go. Beside him, Jordan's lighting a joint.

"It's amazing what you can learn on YouTube these days," he says. He blows out a smoke ring. "Like, there's everything. How to shave. How to give a good blow job. How to build a bomb. . . ."

It's the blow-job line that throws Eric, but it's just for a moment. "Why are you telling me this?"

Jordan inhales. Tilts his head back and blows smoke. "This world is filled with hypocrites, Eric. Would you agree?"

"Uh, I guess so."

"Capilano, especially. Your dad's kind of an asshole, but he's right about this place, I'll give him that. I knew it the moment I got here; this town has no soul. It's all rich motherfuckers who think they can do what they want because they have money."

Jordan passes the joint to Eric. Eric tries to wave him off.

"Take Callum Fulchrest, for instance," Jordan is saying. "The guy has a buttload of money, and he's still a slimy fucker.

And the worst part of it is, he gets away with it too, because his family's tight with the freaking police chief. Awful, right?"

"I mean, yeah," Eric says. "It's pretty messed up."

(*What the hell are we doing here?*)

(*Where's Haley and Paige?*)

"This town's full of shit like that, though." Jordan leans back on the hood of his car. Blows a cloud of smoke up toward the stars. "Racist teachers. Corrupt cops. Spoiled little rich kids who can get away with murder."

"That's what my dad says," Eric tells him.

Jordan nods. "Your dad and I are on the same page."

(Somewhere in the darkness, a door hinge whines open.)

(Electronic beeps follow, like punching in a keypad.)

"We just have different ways of dealing with it."

Eric squints toward the warehouse. "I still don't get it. What are they doing?"

"It's just something Haley's been working on," Jordan says. "A YouTube tutorial she's trying to master."

Suddenly, the front door of the warehouse lights up, bright fluorescent white. The lights flash twice, and Eric can see Haley waving from inside. Then the lights go dark again. Jordan smiles. "Looks like she nailed it," he tells Eric. "Let's go."

72.

Eric stares. Can't put the pieces together.

"I don't get it," he says. "What is this place? Did they just, like, break in or something?"

"This place," Jordan says, walking up toward the front doors, leaving Eric no choice but to follow. "This place is the West Coast headquarters for *Beauty Queen* magazine; you've heard of it? Kind of a low-rent *Seventeen*, trashy celebrity gossip and beauty tips for, like, fifteen-year-olds?" He looks back. "And yeah, they broke in. Paige picked the lock. Haley successfully overrode the master alarm."

Eric stops following Jordan. He's struck dumb. His heart's racing too fast to let him concentrate, and all he can think is how being here is *really* not cool for a Connelly Man.

"But . . . why?" he manages.

"We fix things," Jordan says. "That's what we're doing. That's what this town needs."

He gestures to the front door. Paige and Haley are waiting in the shadows.

"It's Haley's turn to choose the target. Maybe you heard she had a bit of a situation last fall. She left school for a while."

"I heard," Eric says.

Haley makes a face that Eric can just barely make out. It's not a happy one. "I don't want to talk about it," she says. "The point is, these fuckers in there contribute to exactly the kind of mentality that screwed me up last September."

"Haley has a bit of a body-image thing," Jordan says.

"Yeah, like I think it's all *bullshit*. This *Beauty Queen* stuff is dangerous shit, man. It really messes with you."

"And Capilano's all about that," Paige says. "This town is so superficial."

"One-hundred-percent superficial."

"So, what?" Eric says. "Breaking into this building is going to fix everything?"

Haley scowls. "Of course not. But it's sending a message." She looks at Eric, hard, through the dim light. "We're not just breaking in, dude. We're *trashing* the joint."

73.

Haley pulls the front door open. Disappears inside. Paige is right behind her. Jordan has his phone out. He's filming the whole thing.

And that's when Eric catches up with the rest of the class.

"Holy shit," he says. "*You guys!* You are the ones who stole Callum's painting."

(Well, duh.)

"You're the Suicide Pack!"

Jordan holds up his hands. "Guilty as charged. You've discovered our secret identity, E. Congratulations."

"But . . . why? Why are you doing this? Why did you bring *me* here?"

"Because we need you," Jordan tells him. "*I* need you."

(Shiver.)

(*Shit, what?*)

"I was wrong about you at the party," Jordan says. "You're not just a nerd. I can see that now. You *know* this town's broken, and you're ready to actually do something worthwhile, instead of fucking *data entry*. Am I right?"

Inside the building, Haley has another light on. She's in, like, an outer office. She's kneeling down with Paige, working on another locked door.

"You *know* I'm right," Jordan tells Eric. "That internship

you're working isn't doing shit for the world. I'm asking you to help us. I'm asking you to make a difference."

Haley has some kind of tool in her hand. Eric watches her fiddle with the door, can't think for the sound of his heart pounding in his head.

(Connelly Men don't break into office buildings.)

Haley stands up, triumphant. Tries the door. It swings open, revealing a long line of desks and computers, posters of magazine covers with, like, airbrushed Emma Stone. Airbrushed Emma Roberts. Oh, and look over there. Airbrushed Haley's sister.

Paige pokes her head out the front door. "You guys coming, or what?" she says. "Don't be ashamed to be feminists, boys."

"Go," Jordan tells her. "We're right behind you."

Paige disappears. Through the window, Eric can see Haley walking farther into the office. She stops at a desk piled high with papers. Cocks her hip to the side, looks back over her shoulder at Eric and Jordan, an innocent expression on her face as, ever so slowly, she topples the papers to the floor.

(*Who, me?*)

Jordan tilts his head at Eric. Smiles that movie-star smile. "So, what do you think? Are you with us?"

74.

Well, shit.

(*Yes!* Eric's mind is screaming. *Yes, of course I'm with you. Wherever you want me to go, I'm going.*)

But he's also thinking: *Gaahhhhh.*

(Connelly Men don't trash office buildings.)

(Connelly Men don't do vigilante justice, or whatever it is that Jordan and Haley and Paige—excuse me, the *Suicide Pack*—think they're doing.)

(Connelly Men don't get wound up in insane schemes that will land them in jail. They just don't.)

Jordan watches Eric, supremely calm. "Tick-tock. A security guard's bound to show up eventually. And we need to run the Fix before he gets here."

He shrugs. "But it's totally up to you. You can go back to your mindless data entry and your bullshit problem sets and your Student of the Year plaque if that's what you want."

(*No. No, it's not what I want.*)

"Or you can trust me, trust *us*, and have the most amazing, most meaningful summer of your life. Which do you want more?"

Paige and Haley are gone now. The whole night seems to be holding its breath, waiting on Eric's next move.

"What if I say no?" Eric asks.

"If you say no?" Jordan shrugs. "We get in my car, and I

drop you off at your mom's Mercedes and you never have to speak to any of us again. The end."

Eric says nothing. Can't calm his thoughts long enough to form a coherent answer.

"It's your choice, dude," Jordan says. "But you'd better choose something quick, or I'm going inside and you can fend for yourself." He winks at Eric. "I have a good lawyer. Do you?"

(*Gah.*)

Eric's thinking he wants to go with Jordan. He's thinking he'd follow Jordan off a freaking bridge, probably.

But it's not just Jordan. Shit, this town is messed up. It's *wrong* that the rich people get to ignore the laws. And it's not like Eric's going to be in any position to change anything for, like, another ten years.

This is worthwhile, even if it's crazy.

(*But.*)

"You can live a long life like a hypocrite, or die young with integrity," Jordan replies. "Which is it going to be, E?"

Eric hesitates.

(A little longer, just to build the tension.)

Then he sighs.

"I can't do this with you guys," he says. "I'm sorry."

75.

The ride down the mountain is silent. Eric keeps glancing across the car at Jordan, keeps wanting to tell Jordan he's sorry, wanting to explain himself. But he knows Jordan doesn't want an explanation. And he sure as hell doesn't want an apology, either.

Jordan wants someone who's brave enough to take risks. Break rules. And Eric isn't really a rule breaker.

Jordan pulls into the parking lot outside Hockley, Hart & Brent. Stops the BMW beside Eric's mom's G-Wagen, the only car left in the lot. Eric sits there a moment, but there's nothing to say.

He reaches for the door handle.

"So I guess that's it, then," he says, stepping out of the car. "I'm sorry I, like, let you down."

Jordan's face is expressionless. "Hey, you gotta do you, right?" He leans across the car and pulls the passenger door closed. Finishes the conversation through the open window.

"I'm just saying, though, you seem to think pretty highly of your dad's concept of integrity," he tells Eric. "But everybody has secrets, E. Nobody's *that* pure."

He shifts the car into gear.

"Anyway, I gotta get back to the girls. The Pack sticks together; you understand."

And before Eric can answer, Jordan's peeling out of the lot, the BMW's engine roaring as it disappears into the night.

KIK -- CAPILANO HIGH PRIVATE MESSAGE GROUP
— 07/07/16 — 08:15 AM

USERNAME: SuIcIdEpAcK
MESSAGE: Magazines are soooo 20th century.

76.

CAPILANO POLICE STYMIED IN BEAUTY QUEEN BREAK-IN.

Two paragraphs on page A6 the next morning. Everything vague; no details. Police called to the outskirts of town to investigate a break-in at the *Beauty Queen* offices, arrived too late to identify the perpetrators.

A detective named Dawson is quoted. "It seems like a case of simple vandalism; the building was trashed, but according to the employees we talked to, nothing appears to have been stolen."

Still, the detective says, the PD's actively investigating. He encourages Cap citizens to keep their eyes open.

77.

"Feeling better, Mr. Connelly?"

Ann doesn't bother to hide the sarcasm in her voice. She watches Eric walk through the office toward her desk, her features pinched and mean.

Eric ignores her. Keeps his head down all the way to the doorway to his little room. To the piles of paperwork waiting to be manually entered into the shitty old desktop inside.

"One more absence like that and I'll have to tell your father," Ann calls after him. "We don't tolerate slackers here, and he knows it."

Eric shuts the door. Surveys his little cell. Sighs and sits down and gets back to work.

Integrity is a real bitch sometimes.

78.

Truth is, Eric *isn't* feeling better. He lay awake half the night thinking about Jordan. About Haley and Paige.

About the events of the evening.

Yeah, it was scary when Haley broke into that building. It was freaking *terrifying*. Eric knows he was gambling with his entire future just by being there, and he's mostly not sorry he bailed.

But still, the fact remains that it was the most exciting thing he's done in, like, years.

It doesn't help when Eric watches the video. SuIcIdE-pAcK has the Vine on Kik by lunchtime, a close-up on a stack of *Beauty Queen* covers, then the footage Jordan shot of the Pack's destructive efforts.

And the destruction is total: we're talking wrecked computers, shredded files, furniture ruined. Even those artfully airbrushed cover posters are torn off the walls and kicked through their frames. (One with a bit more gusto than the rest, truth be told.) The place looks like a tornado hit. And then there's the Suicide Pack logo and some crazy girl laughing.

(It sounds a little like Haley, but, like, if she was on helium.)

Reaction from the members of the Capilano High message group on Kik is overwhelmingly positive.

Eff that magazine. It's trash anyway.

Kind of liked the mag but this is hilarious TBH.

[A long string of LOLs and one hundred emojis.]
Got off lucky compared to Callum. LOL.
SMH. SMDH.

The message board is anonymous. Everybody's an avatar, a username, and that's it, and anyway, nobody from outside Cap High can access the group. It's easy to stay hidden.

Still, Jordan isn't taking any chances, Eric sees. *Loving it,* ThaINfamous writes. *So fkn dope.*

Eric closes the app. Tries to pretend like he doesn't care. Like he doesn't miss Jordan and the others already.

79.

Jordan doesn't text Eric. Jordan doesn't Kik. Jordan leaves Eric alone to think about the *Beauty Queen* fiasco, about the Suicide Pack.

To hear Jordan's parting words resonate in his mind.

Everybody has secrets.

Think about it.

80.

Eric thinks about it. Then Eric does more than think. He locks himself in his bedroom one night after dinner, runs a Bing—

(just kidding)

—Google search on his laptop for Senator Donovan Connelly. Gets, like, twenty million hits in 0.19 seconds.

It's all bullshit. There are news releases from his dad's campaign office. There's a profile on Huffington Post, a bunch of glowing reports about Eric's dad's pet causes—

(the environment and, like, immigration reform).

Eric even pops up in one or two articles, evidence of his dad's devotion to family—

(yeah, right)

—but there's nothing big and secret and awful, no crazy revelations, and Eric wonders if Jordan actually knows anything, if he has dirt on Eric's dad or if he was just being a troll.

So Eric refines his search. Delves deeper into the weirder corners of the internet, the conspiracy theories and the crazy fanatics. He's still on his laptop when he should be doing statistics problem sets to get ready for freshman year, stays up past his bedtime.

And then, as Eric's eyelids are drooping and his iPhone's

reading five hours until he has to wake up for work, Eric finds what he's pretty sure Jordan was talking about. And it wakes Eric up like he's mainlining Red Bull.

81.

Somehow, Eric has landed on a right-wing political blog written by some far-out fanatic.

(Not the most reputable source of information, but still.)

Whoever the author is, he seems to have a big hate-on for Senator Connelly. There's plenty of dirt.

There are posts about how Eric's dad financed his reelection by taking secret donations from Big Oil, even when he campaigned on the environmental vote.

There are posts about how Eric's dad supposedly had an affair with his campaign office manager, a pretty woman in her twenties named Maggie Swenson.

And then there's the big one.

HATE CRIME COVER-UP!

This is the story that rocks Eric's world.

HATE CRIME COVER-UP!

What is it about rich liberals that makes them believe money—and connections—can wash away all of their sins? Maybe the fact that it's true?

First Ted Kennedy, now Donovan Connelly. The lefty state senator has campaigned hard for the environment and immigration reform, even as his political career is propped up by Big Oil. [See attached link.]

What we've stumbled across now, though, blows any hint of Connelly's other hypocrisies right out of the water. The Daily American has learned that Donovan Connelly, while a junior at Stanford University, was arrested with two fraternity brothers for his role in the beating of a homosexual man in San Francisco's Mission District. The fraternity brothers went to jail; Connelly was bailed out by his rich liberal father, pled out by his rich liberal lawyer, and saw his sentence suspended and his record expunged. Any record of Connelly's arrest was later ordered sealed by the governor himself.

The Daily American was contacted by one of those frat brothers, who declined to give his name.

"Connelly's lawyer showed up to the courthouse with a couple big checks," the source told TDA. "Made us sign confidentiality agreements if we wanted to keep the money. Said they'd sue for every nickel we had if word ever got out. So we kept our mouths shut, went to jail, did six months or so each. Had a big pile of hush money waiting when we got out."

The victim of Connelly's hate crime, whom our source described as "flamboyant but harmless," has long since disappeared, though our source was certain he'd been paid off, to boot.

"I heard his street name was 'Roger Dodger,'" our source tells us. "He got that big check and took off for the better life. I never saw or heard of him again."

82.

JG: *Did you ask him about it?*

Eric texts Jordan the next day. Ships him the link to the HATE CRIME article. Asks him if this was what he was talking about.

Asks him how he knew.

I didn't know, Jordan writes back. *But I suspected. Every politician is shady. And your dad didn't exactly strike me as a choirboy.*

So how do I get the truth? Eric asks Jordan. *Everything's sealed and, like, locked away. And this is the only site with the story.*

A convicted felon against a state senator, Jordan writes back. *A RICH state senator, too. I can see why the mainstream news wouldn't touch it.*

EC: *Either that or it's phony.*

JG: *Did you ask him about it?*

EC: *Not yet.*

There's a long pause. Eric drums his hands on the desk in his little office. Watches the ellipsis as Jordan types.

JG: *You should ask him.*

JG: *Tell me what he says.*

83.

Eric doesn't get a chance to ask his dad, not right away. Not before the fund-raiser, anyway.

84.

Eric's dad is guest of honor at some big environmentalists' gala downtown. Tickets cost a thousand dollars a plate, all to hear Senator Donovan Connelly talk about hybrid cars and solar panels and, like, protecting the wetlands. Eric's mom has a suit laid out on Eric's bed when he comes home from his internship.

"Aw, no," Eric groans. "Don't tell me we have to go too."

"Your father wants us beside him," Eric's mom replies. "It's important that we show our support."

"You mean he wants props. He wants people to see his nice, well-adjusted family."

Eric's mom clucks her tongue. "He's proud of you, Eric," she says. "He thinks it'll be good for you to see what *you* can do, if you keep following your path."

85.

So Eric goes to the gala. He gets dressed up in his suit and rides downtown in the backseat of the Chrysler 300 his dad hardly uses—
(he has a GMC Yukon, with a driver).

Eric sits in the crowd with his mother and eats over-cooked pasta and listens to an army of environmentalists talk about how wonderful his dad is.

Midway through the dessert course, Eric feels his phone buzzing. He checks his pocket. It's Jordan.

You ask him yet?

Eric's mom taps his shoulder. Motions to the front of the stage. It's Eric's dad's turn to speak.

AN ABRIDGED TEXT OF SENATOR DONOVAN CONNELLY'S SPEECH TO THE SIERRA CLUB

By Eric Connelly

[Applause]

Donovan Connelly: Thanks very much. Thank you so much. Please—no, thank you. Thank you very much. I—you're too much, really.

[Insert unfunny warm-up joke here; the crowd roars with laughter.]

DC: You know, I've always felt a kinship with the environment. Blah blah blah, blah blah, blah blah my father, who blah blah blah blah blah, blah blah stewardship. That's why blah blah, I am proud to blah blah blah . . .

[This continues for several minutes; Eric tunes out. He's thinking about that blog he found. About Big Oil. Maggie Swenson. About Roger Dodger.]

DC: . . . blah blah blah, blah blah. But I won't ramble on too much longer—

[Thank god.]

DC: But before I leave you to your dessert and this delicious wine, I want to recognize my beautiful wife, Marla Connelly, and my son, Eric, who is already setting the course to follow in my footsteps and who I know will serve his country, when the time comes, with integrity, discipline, and honor.

[All eyes in the room turn to Eric. It's a sea of adoring faces.]

[Eric blushes and looks down at his plate.]

DC: . . . blah blah blah, good night!

[Standing ovation for, like, twenty minutes.]

86.

Eric's dad clasps Eric's hand when he returns to their table. Pulls Eric to his feet, wraps his arm around Eric's shoulder. Presents him to the crowd.

(The standing ovation is still rolling. It shows no sign of stopping.)

"This is why we do it," Eric's dad is saying into Eric's ear. "This is why we work so hard. One day, they'll be cheering for you."

Eric smiles out at the audience. Lets his dad hug him. Pretends like he's happy to be here.

This is why you work so hard.

One day, this will be you.

This is where you're going.

The idea should thrill Eric.

(It doesn't.)

87.

"Dad."

Eric's dad looks up from the kitchen counter later that night. He's making himself a sandwich while Eric rummages in the fridge.

"*Eric.*" Eric's dad is all smiles. "What can I do for you?"

Eric hesitates. Wonders if he really wants to do this. Knows he'll always wonder if he doesn't.

Okay.

"The last election," Eric says. "Did you ever, like, get any donations from any oil companies?"

The smile disappears. "What? Of course not. Eric, I'm an environmentalist. How would it look if I took money from those people?"

"I know," Eric says. "I just heard something somewhere."

"Did one of your friends tell you that?" Eric's dad shakes his head. "Because my campaign finances are public record. Anyone can look them up. You of all people should know that."

Eric closes the fridge. He's shaking a little bit. "Yeah. I just heard maybe they were *secret* donations or something."

Now Eric's dad is frowning, his brow furrowed into deep creases. "Eric, that's illegal. Who's telling you this?"

"Nobody," Eric says. "Never mind. It's nothing."

"Well, I hope you'll tell them they're full of shit, if you'll pardon the expression," Eric's dad says. "And then maybe you'll think about who you're choosing as your friends."

Stonewalled.

A straight denial. Nothing proved.

(But then, a hypocrite *would* deny everything.)

"What about Maggie Swenson?" Eric asks his dad. "Did anything ever happen with her?"

Eric's dad turns around fully. Forgets about the sandwich and looks at Eric, his expression bemused. "Son," he chuckles, "*who* has been feeding you this stuff?"

"I just read it somewhere," Eric tells him. "I read that maybe you cheated on Mom with someone on your campaign. Someone named Maggie Swenson."

Eric's dad opens his mouth. Closes it. Exhales.

"Listen, whatever you're reading or hearing from *whomever* are lies, Eric," he says. "People are going to try to bring you down in your life, especially if they don't like what you stand for. They'll use whatever means they have at their disposal, no matter how slimy."

He sighs. "I'm sorry you had to learn about this so early."

"Yeah," Eric says.

"Now get to bed. You want to be at the office early tomorrow—make a good impression."

Eric turns.

Should he? Yeah, he should.

"What about Roger Dodger?"

His dad's brow furrows. His mouth gets real thin, and mean-looking. "What did you just say?"

Eric has never quite seen *this* expression before. It's . . . scary.

He blinks. Gives a "Hey, no big" chuckle.

"Roger, you know. Like ten-four? Over and out?" He

gives a little salute. "Good night and good luck?"

His father eyes him warily, then turns his back.

The interrogation is over.

88.

JG: GUILTY!! *What did I tell you?*

EC: *I mean, I don't know if it's true or not, but you should have seen his expression . . .*

JG: *Of course he's guilty. He's probably guilty of more, too. You just never know with these guys.*

Eric doesn't know what he's feeling right now. He's feeling like his dad *did* look guilty, just for an instant, when he heard Roger Dodger's name.

And that causes a little piece of Eric's secretly gay heart to crumble into dust.

JG: *Still want to be a Connelly Man?*

Eric stares at his phone. He's thinking he still has no credible evidence that his dad's anything other than who he's always claimed to be. He's thinking he's grasping, if he believes some fanatic's blog.

But that look.

Is that the same expression Roger Dodger saw just before Eric's dad and his buddies kicked the shit out of him?

Fuck it.

Maybe not, Eric tells Jordan. *When's your next Fix?*

KIK -- CAPILANO HIGH PRIVATE MESSAGE GROUP
— 07/10/16 — 02:56 PM

USERNAME: SuIcIdEpAcK
MESSAGE: Spikes are for Louboutins, not
    homeless people.

89.

"It's a competition," Paige tells them. "We all go in at the same time. Whoever comes out with the most stuff—without getting arrested—is the winner."

"What do we win?" Jordan asks.

Paige shrugs. "Pride, I guess." Then she grins. "And a lot of free stuff."

They're sitting in the food court at Pacific Center, the high-end mall downtown, listening as Paige lays out her Fix.

Haley raises her hand. "I'm confused. When you say 'the most stuff,' do you mean by volume or value?"

"Value," Paige says. "Sticker price. So save your tags."

She looks around.

"Any other questions?"

Eric kind of coughs. The others look at him. "I mean, it sounds fun and all. But what's the, you know, *point*?"

"Oh god." Haley rolls her eyes. "Is he going to wuss out again?"

Jordan holds up his hand. "No, it's a good question. Paige, what exactly are we fixing by being here?"

"I'm glad you asked, E." Paige finishes her soda. "Maybe you guys heard, but last week the store owners decided they were sick of seeing homeless people camped outside their doors. But instead of *doing something* about the problem, they had little spikes put down on every flat surface near the doors, so nobody could lie there."

She shakes her head. "It's total bullshit. They sell three-thousand-dollar coats and that's how they treat people."

"Sounds like a good enough reason for a Fix," Jordan says. He claps his hands and stands. "Yup. Let's teach these dickheads a lesson."

90.

The Fix:

Swarm The Room—

(the luxury department store at the north end of the mall)

—*en masse*. Steal as much as possible without getting caught.
(No points for dye packs or damaged merchandise.)
In and out. Lightning fast. Blitzkrieg. Rendezvous at the cruise ship pier, three blocks away. Lose security in the crowds.

Don't. Get. Caught.

91.

The Room is three floors of fun.

Women's wear on the top floor. Sunglasses, jewelry, and cosmetics in the middle. Menswear on the bottom. An open atrium in the center, two spindly escalators. It's a Sunday, so the store is jam-packed, mostly with rich kids spending their parents' money. The Suicide Pack will fit right in.

(Except they're not *spending* shit.)

Eric and Haley and Jordan and Paige stand at the third-floor entrance from the mall. They're all wearing baseball hats to hide their faces from the security cameras. Paige's long blond hair is tied up, out of sight. They're wearing shoes for a track meet. They're ready to run.

(They're wearing GoPros, too, to record the insanity.)

(Hey, gotta satisfy the fans.)

Eric can hear his heart beating, *feel* it pounding in his chest, like he's standing at the top of a high cliff, and he's about

to jump

o

f

f

(Splat.)

92.

There's a security guard by The Room's entrance. He's a big guy, old, half asleep. He looks slow. He looks complacent.

He looks like he has no idea what's about to transpire.

Paige raises her hand. Tenses up like Usain Bolt in the gold-medal race.

"Mark," she says.

"Set."

"*Go!*"

93.

And they're off.

Paige and Jordan take off running. Haley's right behind them. Eric hesitates a split second, watches Jordan body some preppy city douchebag to the ground. Watches the security guard perk up and take notice. Then Eric's running too.

Jordan peels left, to the Chanel mini store. Paige is at a rack of bras, snatching and grabbing. People are gasping. People are pointing. Staff are converging from every direction.

Eric and Haley dodge past them. Let Paige and Jordan play decoy. They take the first escalator down to the second level. Jewelry. Cosmetics. Haley darts across to the watches. The sunglasses. Eric lets her have them. He's going to the bottom.

Another escalator. Shouts from above. Eric's whole body is electric with adrenaline and terror. Opposite, on the up escalator, it's chaos. An army of The Room staff running topside. The bottom floor is strangely serene when Eric touches down. All the crazy shit's happening above.

Eric looks around. Clock is ticking. There's a wall of Gucci motorcycle jackets over there, a couple thousand dollars a pop. Eric hurries over. Tries to act inconspicuous. Pulls the first jacket he finds and turns to GTFO.

(ERROR)

The jacket won't go. It's tethered to the wall. Security measure. Eric drops it to the floor as a snooty-looking salesman comes over.

("Can I help you?")

Eric ignores him. Starts for the denim. Rag & Bone. J Brand. Nudie. Acne. True Religion. Eric grabs whatever's closest, no accounting for style. Size. Taste. Just speed. The salesman's still behind him. The salesman's yelling now—

(*"Excuse me!"*)

Eric doesn't slow down. Eric doesn't look back. People are staring, now. People are putting this together. Eric looks around for the exit. It's ahead, to his right. Two hundred feet, maybe. Maybe a little less.

Eric runs, arms full of designer denim. His feet struggle for traction on the polished floor, but he's closing the distance anyway. A hundred and fifty feet. One hundred. The security guard's by the escalators, out of position. He must have been heading upstairs to check out the commotion.

Eric's in the clear.

Eric's freaking *made it.*

Eric's just about ready to believe he'll get out of this alive.

Then the salesman blindsides him.

(*Oof!*)

An insane body check.

And Eric and his armload of jeans go sprawling

d

o

w

n

to the polished floor.

94.

The salesman falls too. The jeans go flying everywhere. The salesman claws and scrabbles at Eric's ankles, trying to hold him back.

("No. You. *Don't*.")

He's red-faced and angry. This is a personal affront.
Nobody comes into *his* store and pulls a stunt like this; no way,
buddy boy. Not on his watch.

Eric kicks himself loose. Scrambles away. The jeans are
scattered all over. There's no time to retrieve them.

Eric stands up. Starts running. Looks back and the salesman's tripping over his feet trying to continue the chase. As Eric
watches, the salesman falls again, lands hard on the marble.

Eric locks eyes with the salesman. The salesman pants
for breath. Eric pants for breath too. Eric looks around, grabs the
closest thing he can find—

(a Burberry trench).

The salesman looks at Eric like—

(*Don't you do it. Don't you dare.*)

Eric stuffs the trench under his arm.

Then he runs.

95.

Chaos. Terror. Hysteria.

Eric bursts out onto the sidewalk with the coat under his arm. There's no sign of the others anywhere. No matter.

It's time to go.

Granville Street is a zoo. Tourists off the cruise ships and Sunday shoppers, street kids and panhandlers and suburban staycationers. Eric turns north and bobs and weaves through the crowd, watching for police and slow walkers and more mall security.

He's gasping.

His lungs burn.

This is serious freaking exercise.

Three blocks to the cruise ship pier.

Don't look back.

96.

Eric makes it to the pier.

Two cruise ships are in today, both of them massive. The pier is crawling with old people walking slow and snapping pictures. The rallying point is the souvenir stand by the west entrance. Paige is already there, half hidden behind an extended Asian family buying goofy hats. Paige is holding a souvenir bag of her own.

Eric hurries over. Paige gives a weak smile when she sees him. She's panting for breath too. She's perspiring.

"The others?" she asks Eric.

Eric shrugs, looks around. "I saw Haley in jewelry. Then I bolted. Jordan was upstairs with you."

"Guess we're waiting." Paige nudges Eric's arm up. Examines the jacket. "Burberry. Nice. You went classic, I see."

"I was trying for jeans, but some salesman freaking tackled me," Eric tells her. "What'd you get?"

Paige opens her souvenir bag. A tangle of lace and a postcard at the bottom. "Just some underwear," Paige says. "La Perla and Frederick's. Probably isn't even my size." She gestures to the souvenir stand. "I just bought the postcard so they'd give me the bag."

"Did you have any trouble getting out?"

"Nah. After Jordan body-checked that dude in the entrance the whole store was focused on him. I just got as far away as possible. Nobody even saw me."

"They were hard on Jordan, huh?" Eric frowns. "I hope he got out."

"He got out," Paige says. "They both did. We just have to wait."

97.

They wait. Minutes pass. Long, agonizing minutes.

     Eric wonders what would happen if Jordan and Haley were caught. He wonders if Jordan's big talk about having a good lawyer is actually true.

     He wonders—

          (selfishly)

               —if the police could trace Jordan and Haley to him.

He wonders if this will fuck up his law school application.

98.

Just when Eric's deciding that yes, having two friends booked for Grand Theft Luxury will probably affect his future—

(and just when Eric's starting to *stress*)

—Paige nudges his arm. Points through the crowd.

"Bam," she says. "What did I tell you?"

Eric follows her gaze. Sure enough, there's Jordan and Haley, limping and staggering onward like they just fought a war.

Jordan's still grinning, though.

(That cocky smile.)

And they're both holding armloads of stolen merchandise.

"Had to get a little creative," Jordan says when they're all standing together. He nudges Haley. "Had to bail this one out of a little fiasco."

"Security had me cornered," Haley says. "I forgot there's no mall exit on the second level. Dumb."

"Anyway, we all made it," Jordan says. "So let's see who won."

99.

They drive back to Jordan's ~~house~~ big freaking mansion. Eric's buzzing like a live wire, amped up on adrenaline. He can hardly sit still in the passenger seat, keeps squirming around as they drive back across the bridge, checking behind them for police lights.

Haley catches him looking, rolls her eyes, like he's the lamest human being in all of Capilano—

(which he might be)

—but Paige smiles at him, just a little, before she turns to look out her own window again. They're all wound up, caught in the adrenaline afterglow. Personally, he feels so terrified he could puke, but it's kind of all right, too. They're in this together. It's been a while since he's had, like, actual *friends*.

(Probably since he and Paige broke up.)

Jordan's house is on Marine Drive, way west of Capilano, even farther than Callum Fulchrest's place—

(and Jordan's is waterfront).

It's surrounded by forest: big, tall spruce and cedar trees, hedged in from the road and the neighbors so when the driveway gate closes, you might as well be on another planet.

Jordan parks the BMW. Eric climbs out, takes a breath of fresh air.

They're free. Mission accomplished.

Fix complete.

Survival achieved.

100.

"Paige. What's your haul?"

Paige unloads her souvenir bag onto Jordan's couch. "Underwear," she tells the others. "Lots and lots of underwear."

Jordan sifts through, examining price tags. "Estimated value: about six hundred dollars. Agree?"

Paige checks his numbers. "Give or take." Then she holds up a lacy bra. "Shit. None of this stuff is my size."

"Let me see." Haley grabs for the bra. Checks the tag and smiles wide. "Bingo."

Paige chucks the rest at her. "Merry Christmas, bitch."

"Six hundred dollars," Jordan says. "Who's next?"

101.

"I blew my wad," Jordan says. "I was aiming for Chanel." He shows the others his haul: a black evening gown. "Instead I wound up with Badgley Mischka."

"Shoot for the moon," Haley says. "At least if you miss, you'll land among the stars."

"That's, like, *so* deep." Jordan holds up the price tag. "Eight hundred dollars."

Paige snatches the dress. "Give me that." She holds it against her body. Haley and Eric applaud. Jordan whistles.

"I guess I could fit into a size two." Paige smiles. "I mean, it would be a shame to waste this."

Haley shakes her head. "Size two. Sometimes I really hate you."

102.

"Is that a Burberry trench, Eric?" Haley says. "Damn, I can't beat that. You win."

Eric holds up the trench. Tries it on. It fits okay, but not great. It's too broad in the shoulders.

(It would look perfect on Jordan, though.)

"Wait a second," Haley says as Eric takes off the coat. "Let me see that."

Eric hands it over. Haley examines the collar. Makes a victory noise.

"*Ha*," she says. "Burberry *Brit*, retail nine seventy-five. E, I always knew you were a basic bitch."

Eric takes the coat back. Sure enough.

(*Phooey.*)

"So what did you get?" he asks Haley as he chucks the trench to Jordan. "With your big attitude."

103.

Haley stands at the front of the room. Makes sure everyone's looking at her. Enjoys the moment. She smiles out at them like an actress on Broadway.

"I went for watches, first thing," she tells the audience. "I thought I could bag me a nice Chanel J12. Really knock you clowns out of the water."

She's holding a shoebox. She's hiding the brand. It doesn't look like she stole a watch.

"Anyway, those display cases are damn hard to smash," she continues. "And you need a key to get them open. I thought I was screwed!"

"But you obviously weren't," Jordan says, rolling his eyes. "So end the suspense already."

Haley glares out at him. "You people have no concept of a good story," she says. "But fine. Here you go." She opens the shoebox. "Gaze upon my works, ye mighty, and despair."

Eric and Paige and Jordan crowd around like it's the Holy Grail. It's actually a pair of shoes. Sneakers. Red leather. A band of stars across the strap.

"Givenchy high-tops," Haley says. "Star Tysons. I snatched them right out of some dude's hands as he was trying them on." She laughs. "You guys should have seen the look on his face."

They're a hot pair of shoes, Eric has to admit—

(though he was kind of feeling good about winning his first Fix).

"How much?" he asks Haley.

"Retails for nine hundred and ninety-five dollars," Haley tells him. "On sale at The Room for just nine hundred and ninety-five dollars."

She grins at them again.

"Beat you by twenty bucks, E," she says. "Eat it."

104.

Haley wins the Fix.

    (Consolation prize: Those Givenchy high-tops are a size ten.

        Eric's a size ten.

            "Congratulations," Haley says, handing him the box.

                "Looks like you kinda won anyway, huh?")

105.

They admire their misbegotten goods for a while. Then they go outside, array themselves around Jordan's pool.

The afternoon wanes into evening, and Jordan turns the pool lights on, and the water glows multicolored. They change into swimsuits and jump in—

(and the water's, like, *perfect*)

(and the lights are psychedelic)

(and Jordan's six-pack looks amazing)

(even if he is still making out with Haley).

They towel off again, refreshed. Lie down on the deck chairs and watch the sunset. They don't say anything, just watch the sun dip down behind the islands to the far west, and they lie there and enjoy the Moment.

Eric gets wasted and thinks about his dad and shit. Thinks about how he should be home. Doing problem sets. Planning. Living up to EXPECTATIONS.

He thinks about how this is better.

How much he'd rather be here.

(He looks at the others, and he can tell they're thinking similarly. He watches the sunset reflect in their eyes.)

Jordan catches him looking. Jordan sidles up beside him, puts his arm around Eric's shoulders. "I knew you were my kind of guy, E," he says. "Welcome to the Suicide Pack."

106.

Eric wakes up disoriented. It's only when he sits up and sees the others that he remembers where he is.

Jordan's mansion. In the theater room. A bunch of couches and comfortable chairs facing a huge projection screen.

They celebrated last night, Palm Bays and pizza and a half-ounce of weed. Crashed on the couches and had a movie marathon.

Now it's Monday morning, and someone's phone is buzzing. The title menu for the *Bling Ring* Blu-ray is playing on repeat on the screen. Beside Eric, Paige groans and rolls over. Eric has a vague recollection of them sharing the couch, while Jordan was fooling around on the other couch with Haley.

(Eric tried to ignore it. Tried not to feel, like, *jealous.* Tried to hold on to the way Jordan looked at him at Callum's party—

(You're sweet, and you're smoking hot, too.)

Eric's still holding out hope, like a

loser.)

Haley mutters something and slaps at her phone. The buzzing continues. Eric looks around for the source. It's under his couch. It's his phone. It's Ann.

Shit.

The call goes to voice mail. Three new messages. Three missed calls. It's eleven forty-five, and Eric should be at work.

Eric stands up too fast. "*Shit,*" he says. "*Shit, shit, shit.*"

A sleepy-eyed Jordan pokes his head up from the other couch. "Something wrong?"

"I'm supposed to be at the office," Eric tells him. "They said if I missed one more day I'm freaking fired."

Jordan checks his watch—

(a gold Jaeger-LeCoultre).

"I'd say you're fucked, E," he says. "It's almost noon."

"Tell me something I don't know," Eric says, quickly fixing his hair. "Am I calling a cab or can you give me a ride?"

Jordan yawns. "How about neither?"

Eric stares at him. "What?"

"How about you accept that you're probably fired and forget about it," Jordan says. "Sit back down, smoke a bowl, and put on another movie. I'll order some food and we'll spend the day by the pool."

Eric looks around for his shoes.

"Just relax, E," Jordan says. "You and I both know you would rather be here."

107.

Well, of course he would.

(But that's not the point.)

"My dad's going to kill me," Eric says. "He called in so many favors to get me that job."

"Your dad will get over it," Paige says. "It's not like your life's over just because you got canned from a shitty internship."

"I need that reference letter, though," Eric tells her.

"Your dad is fucking *Donovan Connelly*," Haley says. "Any law school on the West Coast is going to lose its shit when it finds out his son's applying to *their* precious program. You're going to be fine, dude."

"Anyway, what do you care?" Jordan says. "It's not like you're a freaking juvenile delinquent. We got more accomplished in The Room yesterday than you'll get done pushing paper all summer. And it's not like your dad can be pissed at you anyway, not anymore."

Eric thinks about it.

Roger Dodger.

(They make a good point.)

His phone starts buzzing again.

108.

This time, Eric answers.

"*Eric*." Ann sounds exasperated. "Young man, what did I tell you the last time? You'd better have a good reason you're not at your desk."

"Not really," Eric tells her. "I kind of slept in. Late night last night."

Ann sputters. Now she sounds mad. "You *slept in*? And you think that's a valid excuse?"

"It's not an excuse. It's the truth."

"Your attitude is *completely* unacceptable," Ann says. "You've been a bad egg since day one, young man. Don't bother coming in to work again."

Eric yawns. "I wasn't going to, but thanks anyway."

Ann sputters something else.

"Have a good day," Eric tells her.

He ends the call. Looks around the room.

"So, *that* happened," he says. "Which way is the pool?"

On their respective couches, Haley and Paige and Jordan break into spontaneous applause.

109.

They go cliff-jumping instead.

You have to drive up the coast a little bit to get there. Then you park at a train crossing and walk down the tracks for half a mile or so, past a big No Trespassing sign and into the forest.

The tracks cut through the mountain, high, steep rock walls on either side. There isn't much clearance.

If a train comes, Eric thinks, *we're all screwed.*

But no trains come. The tracks curve toward the water, and they can see the sun shimmering on the ocean through the trees. They reach a little trail into the woods, and climb up and over some boulders, and then they're at the cliffs, forty feet high and nothing but blue water beyond.

Eric's only been here once. He didn't jump off the high cliff. He was nervous. Cautious. It didn't seem safe.

(What if there's a log below the surface?)

(What if you land on a rock?)

Eric made the smart play.

He regretted it all the way home.

110.

Look, you're smart. You can see the metaphor I'm going for here, with the cliffs and the jumping and the making of the smart choices. I'm not going to belabor the point.

Suffice it to say, Eric jumps off the high cliff today. He hems and haws at the top for a long time, in typical Eric fashion, but then, ultimately, he takes the leap.

And whether it's his own little act of rebellion against his dad, or the need to prove something to the others—

(or even just the way Jordan's looking at him)

—I'll let you decide.

Whatever suits your concept of the narrative so far.

The point is, Eric jumps.

But that's not entirely the reason I brought you here.

III.

They all jump. They scream as they're falling and they hit the water hard, and the water is shockingly cold and exhilarating, and they come up to the surface laughing and hollering, and then they swim over to the rocks and climb back up to the top of the cliffs and they do it again, all afternoon.

(And Jordan is the craziest of them all; he does backflips and gainers and long, graceful swan dives, climbs up to the *high* high cliff, the seventy-footer, and yells out like Tarzan as he leaps off the edge.)

They drink Palm Bays at the top of the cliffs, watching the sun shimmer on the water, and when they're all good and high and just, like, *mellow*, Eric asks the question he's been wanting to ask since the start.

"So, like, *why?*" he asks the others. "Why are you guys so determined to do this stuff, anyway?"

112.

Why?

I mean, what could possibly incite a bunch of beautiful rich kids to this kind of rebellion?

Why would they risk it?

Capilano's pretty much their personal playground, right?

113.

"I told you, E," Jordan says. "We're sick of the hypocrisy and the bullshit in this place."

"This town's a bunch of assholes," Haley says.

"As soon as my dad's face showed up in the paper it was like I didn't exist at Cap High anymore." Paige pauses. "I suddenly had *zero* friends. And none of my so-called 'BFFs' will even text me back."

It's more than that, though. It has to be, doesn't it?

"This place is rotten, E," Jordan says. "It's as bad as L.A., maybe worse. As soon as I got here, I figured it out: everyone here, all our parents, the teachers, even the other kids, every last one of them is *full. Of. Shit.*

"This town needs fixing," Jordan tells Eric. "And we're the only people who can see it."

114.

CITY POLICE SEARCHING FOR THE ROOM SNATCH-AND-GRAB GANG

City police don't have any suspects yet in the brazen snatch-and-grab robbery that shocked staff and shoppers alike at the city's most exclusive department store. The four gang members, who appeared to be teens or young adults, struck Sunday afternoon in a coordinated assault on The Room at Pacific Center mall.

The attack lasted only minutes, but a store spokesman confirmed the thieves were able to escape with nearly four thousand dollars' worth of merchandise. All of the gang members evaded capture.

A police sketch artist who spoke to witnesses produced these pictures of the suspects:

[Pictures follow. They're laughably bad. E's makes him look vaguely Mediterranean. Jordan might have Down syndrome, and Paige looks like a man. Haley looks kind of like Haley, but not enough to be worried. Nobody's tracing *those* pictures to the Pack.]

KIK -- CAPILANO HIGH PRIVATE MESSAGE GROUP
— 07/12/16 — 10:24 PM

USERNAME: ThaINfamous
MESSAGE: Wooo that new Suicide Pack Vine is
     SICK. Anyone know who they are? My dad
     wants to preempt the movie rights.

115.

"I don't get it," Eric says, reading Jordan's Kik post on his phone. "Why do you want people to try and figure out who we are?"

"I'm just trying to build us some buzz, E," Jordan replies.

"Okay, but why do we really *need* buzz? Isn't the point just to fix things?"

"Well, sure," Jordan says. Then he grins. Wraps his arm around Eric's shoulders and pulls him close—

(*real* close)

(like, more-than-friends close)

—"but we have to keep the fans happy too," Jordan says.

(And he smiles even wider.)

116.

He's right. Within the Capilano social sphere, the Suicide Pack are superstars.

Jordan posts the department store Vine to the Cap High Kik group the day after the Fix. The Vine blows up *huge*.

It's a sexy little clip. The GoPros picked up crazy footage, the whole store in chaos, like a totally bonkers shopping spree the morning of Black Friday.

There's footage of the spikes outside The Room's front doors, too. A title card overlaid:

SELFISH CAPITALISTS—FIX YOURSELVES OR WE'LL DO IT FOR YOU.

Then the Suicide Pack logo.

The laughing girl.

Fin.

117.

Cap High goes wild.
    Balls out!!
    Amazing.

    So fkn rad.
    Can't wait to see what they do next.
    Who are these guys?
    Anyone know who did this?
    Who the eff is the Suicide Pack?
    And how do I get in on all this cool shit?

118.

"Ann called me this afternoon," Eric's dad says. "I was in a meeting, but I took the call, because my professional relationship with Ann is important. And do you know what she told me?"

(Eric and his dad are standing—

(off)

—in the kitchen.)

Eric shrugs. "I guess she told you I slept in the other day. And then she probably told you she fired me."

"She told me you were rude," Eric's dad says. "She told me you were flippant and disrespectful and completely out of line."

"I mean," Eric says, "I think that's a slight exaggeration."

"I pulled a lot of favors to get you that posting." Eric's dad's brow is creased into canyons. "And you *pissed* all over it, and the Connelly name in the process."

"I think the Connelly name will be fine," Eric tells him.

(*It survived you committing a hate crime*, Eric thinks.)

(But he keeps his mouth shut.)

"It's not *just, like, a summer job*. It's another STEPPING STONE on the PATH to YOUR FUTURE."

(*Ah yes. Right.*)

"Ann's word could have opened a lot of doors for you. Now you're starting from scratch again." Eric's dad glares at him. "And if you think you're spending your summer lazing about, you have another think coming, Eric. If you want to live under my roof, you're going to start taking YOUR FUTURE seriously."

Eric sighs. "Look, I'll get a new internship, okay? I'm sorry I messed things up with Ann, but I just wasn't feeling that job. I want to do something, you know, *meaningful.*"

"Well, you're going to have to do something," Eric's dad says. "And don't think I didn't notice that you snuck out last night." Eric's dad doesn't move from the stairs. Doesn't let Eric by. "Wherever you spent the night, it won't happen again. You're grounded until I say otherwise."

"*Grounded?*" Eric nearly laughs in his face. "I'm *almost eighteen.* And how am I supposed to find an internship if I can't even leave the house?"

"You'd better find a way, Eric. We don't give free rides in this household."

Yeah, right, Eric thinks. *From what I've heard, free rides are a Connelly tradition.*

But he doesn't say this part, either.

Not yet.

119.

Grounded, Eric tells Jordan. *And I'm supposed to find a new job. Except I can't leave the house, so . . .*

    Grounded? Jordan texts back. LOL. UR 18.

    That's what I said. It didn't help. Anyway, it's the middle of July. Everybody's internships are all mostly filled up.

    What are you going to do? Jordan asks.

    I have no idea. Eric sighs. *But I need to get out of here. I'm going insane in this house.*

120.

Eric languishes for a couple of days. Makes a lot of cold calls to, like, Legal Aid and such. Emails his résumé around—

(avoids mentioning Ann in his cover letter).

It's slow going. It's soul-crushing. He'd rather be at the beach. Jordan's pool. Out on Jordan's boat.

(Hell, he'd rather be anywhere, but no dice. His mom and dad have him on lockdown.)

Then Jordan calls one day, early evening. "What are you doing?" he asks Eric. "I have a hookup for you. An internship opportunity."

Eric's locked in his room in the basement, wondering whether to send a résumé to the Capilano Police Department—

(wondering if that would be totally crazy).

"Great," he says, reaching for a pen and some scrap paper. "Where? What's the deal?"

"I'll be there in five minutes," Jordan says. "Be ready to go."

121.

Luckily, Eric's dad is at his office.

"I'm just going to check out a volunteering thing," Eric tells his mom as he ties his shoes. "I know I'm supposed to be grounded, but I have a good feeling about this one."

"You *are* grounded," his mom replies. Then she sighs. "But I told your dad I don't see how you're supposed to find a job if he won't let you out of the house."

Eric stands. "That's what I'm saying."

"Come straight home," Eric's mom says. Then she kisses him. "And good luck, sweetie."

(Shit. Eric almost feels guilty.)

(Then he walks out the door and sees Jordan's BMW parked at the curb, and the guilt more or less disappears.)

Jordan leans over and pushes the passenger door open as Eric walks up. "Your dad give you any trouble?"

Eric shakes his head. "Working. I told my mom I had a lead on a job."

"Perfect." Jordan shifts into gear. "So let's get the hell out of here."

The BMW seems empty without the girls in the backseat. "What's Haley doing tonight?" Eric asks.

Jordan cocks his head. "The fuck if I know. Out on a Tinder date, probably." He glances over. Smirks. "Why? You wishing she was here?"

(*No*, Eric thinks. *Exactly the opposite, actually.*)

"This isn't for the girls," Jordan says. "Not yet. This is just you and me, E."

122.

They drive up the mountain and take the highway on-ramp. Jordan puts his foot down, and the BMW's V-8 roars. It plasters Eric against his seat, and he can't help but smile as the car rockets forward, merges into traffic. Jordan slaloms around slower cars like they're pylons.

"Where are we going?" Eric asks, but Jordan's rapping along to some Drake song on the radio and doesn't answer. Eric's about to ask again, but then he notices the GoPro mounted on the dash.

"Dash cam," Jordan says when he catches E looking. "Drivers around here, you can't be too careful."

They take the highway east out of Capilano, swoop down across Memorial Bridge and into the suburbs. Jordan slows the BMW, takes the next exit, and bam, they're in Studio City, back lots and soundstages everywhere. Jordan navigates around a couple of equipment trucks, a few camera cars, and a trailer full of porta potties. He parks the BMW behind a long row of soundstages. The place is deserted.

"I wanted this to be a surprise," Jordan tells Eric, "but I can't do it by myself. Anyway, after what happened at The Room, I know I can trust you."

"Right," Eric says. "So this *isn't* for an internship, then?"

Jordan points out the window. "There's my dad's guy," he says. "Just follow my lead, okay?"

Eric looks out through the windshield as a pickup truck approaches. "Sure," he says. "I mean, fine."

123.

Jordan's dad's friend is some shaggy-haired old guy in camouflage cargo pants and a black tactical vest. He says his name is Mike, and he looks Jordan up and down as they shake hands. "You Harrison Grant's kid?"

"That's my name," Jordan sighs. *"Harrison Grant's kid."*

Then Mike looks at Eric. He doesn't look like he's sizing Eric up for an internship position. "Who's this?"

"This is E," Jordan tells him. "He's a filmmaker."

Eric blinks.

(*Follow my lead.*)

"Yeah," he says. "I, uh, make movies."

Mike looks at Eric like he doesn't believe it. Eric holds his stare and tries to look, you know, *artistic*. Finally, Mike shrugs. "So what do you guys need?"

"That's what we wanted to talk to you about," Jordan says. "Mainly, we just need to blow something up."

Eric tries to hold his poker face.

(*What?!*)

"How big?" Mike asks.

"*Big.* You're the demolitions guy, right? You can help us?"

Mike hesitates. Chews his lip. "Basically, you got a couple of choices. Obviously, you already know about nitro and TNT and dynamite. All have their pros and cons."

"What about fertilizer?" Jordan says. "That's what all

those terrorists use, right?"

"You mean ammonium nitrate. Yeah, that's an option. You go that route, you're going to need a booster, like dynamite, anyway, so unless you're planning to build a bomb in a U-Haul truck, I would steer clear."

Mike looks at Jordan like he's joking. Jordan doesn't smile back. "Okay. No fertilizer this time."

"No fertilizer. That's a start."

"We're looking for something compact," Jordan says. "This is a little, you know, top secret. Guerrilla filmmaking, you know?"

"Sure." Mike looks at Eric, who nods along, like he has a single remote clue what's going on here.

"We were going to do it in CGI," Jordan says, "but we want that authenticity."

"Fucking right," Mike says, nodding. "If you want compact, you could always go with gunpowder. It doesn't detonate so much as deflagrate, but if you keep it in a confined environment, build the pressure, you can get a hell of a bang."

"A confined environment."

"Like a pipe bomb. The more pressure, the bigger the bang."

Jordan grins at Eric. "That sounds like exactly what we're looking for." He reaches into his pocket and pulls out a wad of cash. Peels off ten fifties. "So can you hook us up?" he asks Mike.

Mike looks at the cash. Hesitates. "You kids aren't planning anything dangerous, are you?"

"Hell no," Jordan says.

Mike looks at Eric again.

"Hell no," Eric says.

124.

"What *are* we planning?" Eric asks Jordan.

They're back in the BMW, driving over the bridge and out of the suburbs and back toward Capilano.

Jordan pulls out to pass a slow-moving tractor trailer. "I would have thought that was obvious, E," he says. "We're building a bomb. We're *planning* to blow shit up."

"I mean, *duh*. But what, exactly?"

"I haven't decided yet," Jordan says. "Anyway, I don't think I can make it work in time for my next Fix. So it's going to have to wait awhile."

Eric doesn't say anything. He's thinking about the ramifications of setting off a bomb in Capilano.

He's thinking about what it will do for his FUTURE.

Jordan looks over. "Look, we're not going to start planting bombs in, like, the hockey arena, okay? Nobody's going to get hurt. I just thought it might be cool to blow something up. Can you get down with it?"

He looks over again, stares at E, steadfast, as they speed down the highway.

(As they speed toward an uncertain FUTURE.)

(Duh duh *duh*.)

Eric blinks first.

"*Shit*," he says. "Yeah, Jordan, fine, I'm with you. Just concentrate on the fucking road, okay?"

Jordan laughs. Steers the BMW back into his lane. "Excellent," he says. "This is going to be *rad*."

125.

So there. There's the bomb.

(You knew it was coming.)

And honestly, if Eric had any sense, he would probably be questioning this a little more. But Eric isn't really thinking about the bomb right now.

Right now, Eric's thinking about how he's alone in a car with Jordan Grant.

Paige isn't here. Haley isn't here.

It's just Jordan and Eric.

So you can forgive Eric if he's a little, you know, distracted.

126.

They pull up in front of Eric's house. Jordan kills the engine, and Eric knows this is the part where he's supposed to open the door and walk away, but he doesn't.

He doesn't move.

(He holds on to *the Moment*.)

Eric can see his dad's car in the driveway. He's dreading going inside. Dreading dealing with his dad's bullshit, dreading having to look some more for another internship.

(He's dreading going down to that lonely basement bedroom and thinking about making out with Jordan Grant all night. Thinking about wasting their precious moments alone.)

Eric opens his mouth to say something. He doesn't know what, exactly, but it's now or never. Make your move. Be assertive. Take action.

(BUILD a FOUNDATION for YOUR FUTURE.)

Before Eric can speak, though, Jordan snaps his fingers. "*Oh*," he says. "Shit. Right. The internship thing; I almost forgot."

Eric blinks. He *did* forget. "The internship thing. Right."

"The subtext to our meeting. The only thing I could think of to get you out of the house."

"So there's no gig?" E says. "This was all just . . . subtext?"

Jordan shakes his head. "No, there's a gig." He pulls a slip of paper from his cup holder. "Call this number. Ask for Liam. He'll hook you up."

Eric takes the paper. Jordan starts his engine.

The Moment is gone.

127.

The next morning, Eric calls the number Jordan gave him. Liam.

"I'm Jordan's friend," he says. "Jordan said to give you a call about, I dunno, an internship or whatever?"

Liam clears his throat. "Right. Yeah." Ringing phones in the background. Voices. A siren. "What's your name again?"

"E," Eric says.

"E?"

"I mean, Eric. Eric Connelly." Awkward pause. "So do you think you have anything? I'm kind of desperate."

"Eric Connelly," Liam says, like he's writing it down. "Great. You're all set."

"Perfect," Eric says. "But where are you actually located? Jordan wasn't clear on the details."

There's a pause. More voices. The sirens get louder. Liam comes back. "Pardon?"

"What's your address?"

"Two seventy-nine Hastings," Liam says. "Railtown Health Center." Angry voices. Banging and crashing. "Look, I gotta go, okay?"

"Uh, okay," Eric says. "Sure." He's about to ask Liam when he should come in and, like, start, but it's too late.

Liam's already hung up the phone.

128.

Eric drives into the city the next day. Finds 279 Hastings. It's not hard. It's pretty much the drug-addict epicenter.

(Pretty much the exact opposite of Capilano.)

Eric parks his mom's G-Wagen on a side street off the main drag, across from the Jimi Hendrix shrine and a boarded-up house. A guy with a messy beard and even messier tattoos shambles past, pushing a shopping cart. He gives the Benz a long look as he passes.

The Railtown Health Center is around the corner. It's a dirty little brick building beside a shady-looking bar and a graffiti-spattered convenience store. Eric pushes in through the front door and asks for Liam at the front desk. A harried-looking middle-aged woman points toward the back. "In the office."

Eric walks where she's pointing. Behind the front desk is an open area, tables and chairs, a coffeemaker. Then a little hallway with what looks like a couple doctors' examination rooms. There are a handful of homeless men sitting at the tables, nursing cups of coffee and eating sandwiches. They don't look up at Eric as he squeezes past them.

Liam looks surprised when Eric knocks on his open door. He's in his early twenties, maybe. He's cute, in a nerdy-hipster way. He looks busy.

"You didn't have to come down here," he tells Eric as he leads him into the office. "Jordan made it sound like I was just supposed to lie to your admissions officers for you."

The office is small and hot, and the furniture is piled with paperwork and posters. "I couldn't just not come," Eric tells Liam. "I'm pretty sure that would be unethical."

"Unethical." Liam puts down the file he's been flipping through. Studies Eric. "How do you know Jordan again?"

Eric shrugs. "School."

(*Suicide Pack.*)

Liam cocks his head. "Huh."

"How about you?"

He looks away. Kind of blushes.

(It's kind of cute.)

"I mean," he says. "How does anyone know Jordan?"

Eric looks at him. Waits.

Liam sighs. "We hooked up, I guess. He got me this job. So, you know, when he tells me I have to lie for his friend, I kind of have to do what he says."

Eric looks around the office again. At the stack of paper on Liam's desk. The top of the stack is a pamphlet about dirty hypodermic syringes.

"You don't have to lie," Eric tells Liam. "I'll stay."

"Really?" Liam says.

Out in the waiting area, one of the homeless men is yelling at somebody. Voices are raised, and something clatters to the floor. Eric thinks about Ann's office, and somehow, data entry doesn't seem so bad right now.

(*At least Liam's better-looking than Ann.*)

He shrugs. "Sure," he tells Liam. "Why not?"

129.

Liam gives Eric a stack of pamphlets. "You know what we do here?"

Eric looks around. "You're the Railtown Health Center, right? You do, like, health-center stuff?"

"Well, kind of," Liam says. "We're a needle exchange."

Eric stares at him. Doesn't get it. "What, like, for junkies?"

"Addicts, yeah," Liam says. "There's a lot of drug-injecting going on in this neighborhood. Addicts use dirty needles. Dirty needles are a serious health problem."

"So you give them clean needles," Eric says. "So they can inject their drugs?"

"It sounds crazy, I know, but it's proven to really reduce blood diseases. HIV, hepatitis, that kind of thing."

"In drug addicts."

Liam sighs. "It's not only the needles. We provide counseling, too, and addiction resources. Every little bit, right?"

Eric scuffs his shoe. "Uh, I was actually hoping for something a little more *legal*."

"We're legal," Liam says. "If that's what you mean. But I don't have any, like, *pre-law* activities for you. This is more of a volunteer position." He kind of smiles. "But, hey, it will still look good on your application, right?"

Eric opens his mouth, but nothing comes out.

(Do CONNELLY MEN work at needle exchanges?)

(*Does it matter?* Eric thinks. *You're doing good in the world, aren't you?*)

(*Aren't you* fixing *something by being here?*)

"Oh, one more thing," Liam says. He gives Eric a handful of tokens. "These are good for a sandwich at the diner down the street." He shrugs. "We find people are more willing to talk to us if we come bearing gifts."

130.

Eric walks outside in a daze. The whole street smells like piss and pot and garbage. Eric stands in the health center's doorway and looks around at the dirty sidewalk, the graffiti, the grunge.

You could be working in a prestigious—and air-conditioned— law office in freaking Capilano. Instead you're helping junkies in the center of skid row.

Some guy rolls a shopping cart past. He looks at Eric. "You want to buy a radio?"

Eric looks in the shopping cart. There's a radio in there. It's older than Eric.

Eric tells the guy no thanks, he doesn't need a radio. Holds out a pamphlet and a token. "Do you know about the resources at the Railtown Health Center?"

The guy takes the token. He ignores the pamphlet. Puts the token in his pocket and rolls the shopping cart away. Eric watches him go. Turns around and almost collides with a woman. She has her hand out. "Do you have any tokens?"

Eric gives her a token. He tries to give her a pamphlet, too, but she waves him off. Gestures to the tokens.

"Give me another one," she says.

Eric looks at the tokens in his hand. He looks back at Liam's office. "I don't think I'm supposed to do that. I'm supposed to be telling you about the needle exchange."

"Fuck the needle exchange. Do I look like a junkie?" She

reaches. "Give me another one."

"Maybe if you take a pamphlet," Eric says.

She shrugs. Takes the pamphlet. Eric gives her another token. She puts it away with the other one and walks down the street. Wads up the pamphlet and drops it on the sidewalk, doesn't look back.

It's pretty much like that for the rest of the afternoon.

131.

Eric runs out of tokens in a couple of hours. He still has mostly all of the pamphlets.

"Yeah, it's like that," Liam says, when Eric comes back to the office to re-up. "People around here aren't trying to hear sermons, you know? They're pretty set in their ways."

"Do you really think this is helping?" Eric asks. "I mean, it's still illegal to do drugs, right?"

"Yeah, and how's that working out? If people want to get high, they're going to get high. We might as well reduce the health risks."

Eric shrugs. "I guess."

"Anyway." Liam sighs. "Try to get them to take a pamphlet when you give them their tokens. We can at least *try* to get the word out."

"Sure," Eric says. "Do you have any more tokens?"

Liam looks around the office. All the paperwork, balanced precariously on every flat surface. "Listen, why don't you call it for today?"

"You mean, like, go home?"

"I wasn't really expecting you would want to actually do something," Liam says. "Come back in a couple of days, if you're serious. I'll make sure there's real work for you."

"Okay," Eric says. "Sure."

"Thanks." Liam gives him a quick smile. Then the phone

starts to ring, and Eric figures that's his cue. He's halfway out the door when Liam calls his name. "Eric."

Eric turns around. Liam's surrounded by papers and the phone is still ringing. He looks busy and tired.

(He's still kind of cute, though.)

"Thanks for coming," he says. "I guess I didn't think Jordan's friends were into this kind of thing."

Eric shrugs again.

(He's *not* really into this kind of thing, but he can't exactly tell Liam that. If he'd known not showing up was an option, he might not be here.)

"I mean, yeah," he tells Liam. "No problem."

KIK -- CAPILANO HIGH PRIVATE MESSAGE GROUP
— 07/17/16 — 11:43 AM

USERNAME: SuIcIdEpAcK
MESSAGE: My favorite cocktail is a Molotov.

132.

"His name's Allen Headley," Jordan tells them. "You've heard of him, right?"

Paige leans forward between the front seats. "The big-shot lawyer?" she says. "The guy who defended all those hedge fund managers?"

"Exactly. That guy. This is his house."

Eric peers out through the windshield into the darkness. They're up the mountain somewhere, some posh Capilano neighborhood, dark streets and big houses and, like, zero signs of life. They're parked curbside, listening as Jordan lays out his next Fix.

("Still working on that other project," he tells E, winking. "We're going to have to save it for next time.")

The house in question is massive. It's made up to look like, I dunno, some Spanish villa or something, the red clay roof and the vast expanse of sand-colored stucco. There's a wrought-iron gate across the driveway. Beyond it, a vintage Corvette sits in the driveway.

"So, what?" Haley says. "Are we fixing this guy because he defended a bunch of jerkoff investment bankers? Why not just hit the bankers themselves?"

Jordan holds up his hand. One finger. *Just wait.*

"Defending sleazy hedge fund managers, shameful though it may be, isn't old Allen's most egregious sin." He smiles. "Sit back and let me tell you a story."

133.

Jordan talks. The others listen.

"Allen Headley had a few too many Manhattans with his homeboys at the Cactus Club last October," Jordan tells them. "Then he climbed in that vintage Vette over there and tried to drive the thing home."

He shakes his head. "Allen failed. Miserably. He put dents in, like, four cars on the way up the hill. Then, about a mile from here, he ran down a poor cleaning lady named Grace Ferreira as she was getting off work. Ran a stop sign and *POW*,"—he claps his hands—"hit her, knocked her across the block. Broken hip, broken ribs, *a serious* concussion."

"Maria, our maid," Paige says. "Grace was her cousin. Maria left us to take care of her after that. She said Grace was lucky she wasn't killed."

"Allen Headley's a big-shot lawyer. He's tight with the mayor. And this town is so messed up he didn't spend one night in jail for what he did. Got off totally clean."

"That slimy motherfucker," Haley says.

"No criminal record. No fine. Not even an article in the goddamn *Capilano Herald*. As far as the world knows, Allen Headley didn't do jack shit that night."

Eric listens. Thinks about his dad and his frat buddies that night in San Francisco.

Eric sees the parallel.

"This asshole needs fixing," Haley announces from the backseat. "So what're you thinking, Jordan?"

Jordan glances into the rearview mirror. Meets her eyes, then Paige's. Then he looks over at Eric.

"Headley loves that Corvette of his," he tells them. "Paid a shitload to get it repaired. As far as I'm concerned, he didn't pay enough."

134.

Jordan might not have his bomb set up, but he has an arsenal of incendiary devices in the back of his Bimmer.

"Molotov cocktails for everyone," he says. "Tonight the Corvette burns."

Eric reaches for a bottle. The air smells like gasoline, dizzying, overwhelming. Eric's nervous again. He's feeling that electric adrenaline, that high. He's torn between puking and freaking *raging* on that Corvette, and it's not so much that he's pissed at Allen Headley for doing what he did—

(even though he *is* pissed, when he actually thinks about it)

—it's more like this is justice.

This job needs doing.

And goddamn if it doesn't feel *good*.

135.

Jordan reaches for Eric's hand, stops him.

"Not here," he says. "We'll take it up to Fincher's Bluff and burn it there. The cops will never find it."

(Fincher's Bluff is at the end of a logging road on the other side of the mountain, about as far away from Capilano as you can get. Kids go up there to get drunk, throw bonfires, shoot guns. Really *get away from it all*.)

Eric draws back, still feeling the warmth where Jordan touched his skin. "Um, okay, but how do we get the car out of the driveway? Do you happen to have the keys?"

"Keys?" Jordan says. "Nope." He reaches into the trunk again. Pulls out a pair of pliers and a long-handled screwdriver. He smiles. "YouTube."

136.

"That Corvette's a two-seater," Jordan tells the others. "So who's coming with me?"

Haley, Eric, and Paige all swap looks. Shrug. Raise eyebrows. Eric feels the adrenaline. He's bouncing on his heels.

He's thinking, *Fuck being a Connelly Man.*

"I'll do it," he tells Jordan, before Haley or Paige can talk first. "I'm coming with you."

137.

So Haley goes to work on Allen Headley's gate.

In seconds, the gate swings wide.

Haley does a curtsy and joins Paige at Jordan's BMW. "It's on you now, boys," she says. "Let's see what you got."

"Follow us to Fincher's Bluff," Jordan tells them. "But don't get caught, right?"

Haley rolls her eyes. "*You* don't get caught. We'll be fine."

The neighborhood is dead quiet. No cars. No movement. There's a light on above Allen Headley's front door, but otherwise, his cheesy villa is dark. The Corvette sits in the middle of the driveway, chrome glinting in the dim light.

It's 2:43 in the morning. Jordan claps Eric on the back. "Let's do this."

138.

The Corvette is locked.

(Duh.)

"Doesn't look like there's an alarm, though," Jordan says, peering through the windshield. Then he grins. "Guess we'll find out."

He wraps his fist in his hoodie. Looks back at Eric and winks. Then he punches the driver's-side window out.

(SMASH)

It sounds like an explosion. Like you could hear the window shattering all the way across town. Somewhere in the distance, a dog starts to bark. Eric feels his heart pounding, his palms sweating. Looks up at Allen Headley's villa again, but the villa remains dark.

Jordan has the driver's-side door open. He's bent down under the steering wheel, whole body contorted, his feet kind of kicking out. Eric can hear him muttering to himself. Can hear plastic cracking.

Eric wonders what else Jordan learned on YouTube, but he doesn't have much time to dwell on that notion, because the Corvette's engine is RUMBLING to life, throaty and loud

and

at precisely the same time

a light BLINKS on in

Allen Headley's

second-floor
window.
(*Shit.*)

139.

Jordan doesn't see the light at first.

And when Eric shows him, Jordan doesn't seem to care. "That raises the stakes, huh?" he tells Eric. "I guess we'd better bail."

"Yeah," Eric says, watching the light. "Bailing sounds like a great idea."

Then Jordan steps back from the driver's seat. Gestures to the door. "Well, go on then."

"What," Eric says. "Me?"

"Uh-huh." Jordan smiles, and his eyes are alive, luminous and hypnotic. "Let's see what you got, E. *Drive it like you stole it.*"

140.

The Corvette drives differently than Eric's mom's G-Wagen.

It's lighter.

It's lower.

It's lightning-freaking-faster.

The engine howls as Eric steps on the gas. The tires spin and chirp and the car launches forward, careens down the driveway toward the road fast—too fast—Jordan laughing in the passenger seat.

Eric eases off the gas pedal. Tries the steering wheel.

The Vette is *nimble*. It corners like it's on rails.

Eric hits the road, feels the Vette jostle over the gutter. Then he's turning down the dark street, toward Haley and Paige in Jordan's Bimmer, and the Bimmer's engine is purring and its headlights are bright, and Eric knows the girls are just waiting for him to pass them, waiting for him to lead them to Fincher's Bluff to start the *real* show,

the *real* Fix,

and Jordan's laughing, and Eric's laughing, too, because he's scared shitless, yes, but because this is freaking *fun*, too, like more fun than he's ever had in his life, and

even when

Allen Headley shows up on the street behind them—

(in his bathrobe)

    —chasing Eric and
Jordan like they just
stole his dog, Eric
doesn't stop laughing.

(Not even when he hears the sirens.)

141.

They don't sound like much, at first.

(The sirens.)

They sound like the wind whistling through the smashed driver's-side window as Eric steers the car fast through the suburbs and across the mountain toward the highway to Fincher's Bluff.

They sound like Jordan laughing, or Eric's heart pounding in his eardrums. They sound like they're coming from somewhere *far* away.

It isn't until Eric sees the lights in the Vette's rearview mirror that he kind of starts to get worried.

142.

"Shit," Eric says, his eyes ping-ponging between the rearview mirror and the road. "Dude, what do we do now?"

Jordan twists in his seat. Sees the police lights, flashing red and blue behind them. Two cars back there, now. Both of them gaining ground.

But Jordan doesn't seem to care. "Only one thing we can do, E," he says. "Lose them."

Lose them, Eric thinks. *Yeah, okay.*

(Easier said than done.)

143.

This isn't *Grand Theft Auto*; Eric doesn't lose those cop cars.

They multiply like rabbits in the rearview mirror. Block off the road a half mile from the highway, nowhere near Fincher's Bluff.

(Haley and Paige must have ditched—must be long gone, thank god.)

Eric sees the roadblock. Doesn't slow down. Grits his teeth and aims the Corvette straight down the middle of it, between the two police cars. Sees the cops tense behind their cruisers, lit up in his high beams.

Screw it, he thinks.

"E." Jordan's saying something. Eric can hardly hear him over the sound of the wind and the growl of the motor. "*Eric!*"

Eric glances across the car. Jordan's shaking his head. "We're not going to make it, E. You gotta stop the car."

Eric takes his foot off the gas. Hesitates. "You want to *give up?*"

"*Never.*" Jordan gestures to the streets on either side of the car. "How fast can you run?"

144.

Eric's never been much of a runner.

That doesn't stop him.

He slams on the brakes. The Corvette squeals to a stop. Jordan reaches for his door handle. Eric reaches for his.

"If they *do* get you, don't sweat it," Jordan says. "A trial would show the world Allen Headley never got what he deserved."

Eric freezes. "Wait, a *trial?*"

Jordan gives Eric a look. "Using our connections and wealth to avoid paying the consequences for our actions? That would make us hypocrites, E."

Then he smiles, and shoves open the door.

CAPILANO POLICE DEPARTMENT – INCIDENT REPORT

CASE FILE	56091A			DATE	07/18/16
ARRESTEE	Eric Connelly	**AGE**	17	**SEX**	Male
CHARGE(s)	Grand Theft Auto	Reckless Endangerment	Resisting Arrest		
ARRESTING OFFICERS	Seymour (Badge 120956)	Grouse (Badge 489033)			

NARRATIVE: Received report of a vehicle theft in progress in the Hollyburn neighborhood of Capilano, approximately 0300hrs July 18, 2016. Officers Grouse and myself proceeded to the 1200 block of Jefferson Avenue, where we found the complainant outside his house in a state of agitation. Complainant advised that unknown parties had just stolen his 1967 Chevrolet Corvette.

Acting on the complainant's information, we proceeded east on Jefferson Avenue to 12th Street, then south on 12th, where we observed a vintage Chevrolet Corvette driving erratically and at a high rate of speed. Attempts to instruct the driver to stop the vehicle were unsuccessful, and we continued pursuit with other Capilano PD units for approximately ten minutes, whereupon the driver stopped the vehicle at the intersection of Taylor Way and Inglewood Avenue. At this time, the driver and his passenger exited the vehicle and proceeded to run in opposite directions down Inglewood Avenue.

Officer Grouse and myself took pursuit of the driver, whom we identified as a tall white male in a black hooded sweatshirt, age unknown. We pursued the driver for approximately five minutes, until the presence of other officers directly ahead of the driver forced him to conclude the pursuit.

We apprehended the driver and advised him of his rights. The driver appeared calm as we escorted him to our squad car. He did not respond to questions on the way to the booking station.

Suspect was booked into Capilano PD headquarters at approximately 0430hrs, July 18, 2016.

145.

Jail is boring.

After the excitement wears off and the adrenaline dissipates, Eric finds himself in an empty holding cell in the Capilano PD headquarters. The fluorescent lights overhead burn bright, even though it's the middle of the night. He has fingerprint ink on his hands, and the officers who booked him took his shoelaces and the drawstring on his hoodie. The police station is quiet.

Eric sits in the empty holding cell and waits. He's pretty sure the police didn't get Jordan. After all, he's not here. And they probably didn't get Haley and Paige, either. They only got Eric.

Which sucks.

There's a pay phone down the hall from the holding cell. The guard who locked Eric in asked him if he wanted to call anyone. But Eric doesn't have Jordan's lawyer's phone number. And he sure as hell isn't calling his parents. So Eric just sits there in the too-bright holding cell and waits for the criminal justice system to process his ass.

(Why?)

Because Eric thought about it.

And Eric decided Jordan was right.

146.

Don't commit the crime if you can't do the time, right?

I mean, it's a horrific cliché, but how hypocritical would Eric be if he tried to skirt the system the same way Allen Headley did?

(A: Very.)

More to the point, how could I expect you to respect such a hypocritical protagonist?

(A: I couldn't.)

Eric got himself into this mess. He's going to deal with the consequences.

(Why?)

Because that's what people with real integrity do.[3]

---

3. The publisher made me include a life lesson or two in this book. It's like a contractual thing. Sorry to sermonize, but I gotta get paid.

147.

Eric sleeps for a couple hours on the hard holding-cell bench. Wakes up to his cell door opening. The guard again.

"Come on out," the guard tells him. "You're free to go."

"Huh?" Eric sits up. Rubs his eyes. "I didn't get arraigned or anything yet. Aren't you guys supposed to arraign me?"

"I don't know about that," the guard replies. "They just told me to come get you. So come on."

Eric follows. Feels something like vertigo, like he might be still dreaming. The guard leads him out of the holding cell area and through the police station to the front desk. There are a couple men in suits standing there, waiting. One of them looks like a Very Important Cop.

The other is Eric's father.

(WTF?)

The senator shakes hands with the other man as the guard sets Eric free. "Thanks very much, Chuck," he says. "He'll make things square with Allen Headley, I'll see to it myself."

"I don't doubt it," "Chuck" says, and both men turn to look at Eric. "Let's just hope the young man's learned his lesson."

Eric stops walking. Hears the doors close behind him, locking him out of the police area. Turns around anyway, tries the door handle. Wonders whose car he has to steal next to get himself locked back *in*.

148.

It's just past dawn. Eric and his dad are riding home in the back of Eric's dad's chauffeured Yukon SUV. Eric can smell the stink of the jail on him. He's exhausted.

His dad is the first one to speak.

"The night sergeant recognized your name on the booking sheet," the senator tells Eric. "He called his lieutenant, who happens to be a good friend of mine—woke him up, I might add—and thank god. They were ready to *arraign* you, Eric." The senator rubs his eyes. "Stealing a car? What the hell were you thinking?"

"I can't believe this," Eric mutters. "I can't believe you bailed me out."

"I beg your pardon?"

"What happened, Dad?" Eric glares at him. "What happened to all that stuff about Integrity and Honor and the Connelly Man? We're Connellys, aren't we? Aren't we supposed to *earn* everything? How does you calling in favors fit in with *everything you have ever told me since I could understand English?*"

Eric knows how he must look—wild-eyed, a little insane. He feels like his entire worldview is unraveling.

Good, he thinks. Let his father see it.

Eric's dad glances up at the driver. "Lower your voice," he says. "Do you know what it would do to our family if word got out about this? Do you know what it would do to me, publicly?"

"As if that's any excuse," Eric says. "How many secrets have *you* buried, Dad? How many times has *that* been a justification for doing the same shitty things every other asshole does?"

The senator's eyes dart back to his driver. "I think we're good here, Tom," he calls forward. "Bring the truck around back. We'll walk up the rest of the way."

The driver slows the car. Eric's dad opens his door. Steps out onto the pavement. After a moment, Eric follows.

149.

It's quiet outside. The sun is slowly rising. There's dew. Tom drives the Yukon away, and Eric and his dad are left standing there, a couple houses down from the Connelly residence.

Eric's dad waits until the Yukon disappears. Then he looks at Eric. He doesn't look mad, though. He looks a little, you know, *mournful.*

"You're getting older, Eric, and you deserve the truth. I'm sorry I waited so long to give it to you."

Eric doesn't say anything. He stares at the ground. He's still mad, and he's tired, and he doesn't know where this is going.

"But we're past that now, aren't we?" Eric's dad clears his throat. "People make mistakes, son. When you're young, you make plenty of them. I wasn't an angel; I made my share."

"So you did do it," Eric says. "You beat that guy up in San Francisco, you and your friends."

Eric's dad looks surprised. After a moment, he nods. "We'd had too much to drink. We were in the wrong neighborhood, and we were young and stupid and spoiling for a fight. I regretted what happened as soon as I sobered up."

"You committed a *hate crime.* And you paid your friends off to cover it up."

"No. It wasn't like that, I promise you. And that moment—that one terrible moment of stupidity—it would have ruined me," Eric's dad says. "It would have derailed my entire future."

"What about that guy, Roger, or whatever? What about his future? After you kicked his ass, what happened to him?"

The senator winces. "I don't know," he says. "He signed the agreement we drew up, cashed the check, and disappeared. We never heard from him again."

His dad straightens. "But after twenty-five years in political office, I'd say the good I've done more than makes up for it. And that's why you can't do things like this, son. This Corvette thing. You have too much potential."

Eric ignores this. "And Mom? Is that true too? Did you cheat on her?"

"I didn't—" Eric's dad catches himself. Glances up at the rows of houses, like he's afraid Eric's mom might be listening. He sighs.

"A moment of weakness," he says. "That's all it was. It wasn't an affair. It was hardly a *night*."

"Does Mom know?"

The senator glances at the house again. "She thinks it was a fabrication," he says. "Lies my opponents cooked up to slander my name."

"So you never told her the truth."

Eric's dad looks away. "What could I tell her? It'd have broken her heart."

"Yeah," Eric says. "I guess you're a hero, then."

He just starts walking. Down the block. Away.

"Where do you think you're going, Eric?"

"Away," Eric tells him.

"You most certainly are not. You're going to have to face *some* consequences for this Corvette thing, son. You're grounded until your mother and I decide otherwise."

Grounded.

Eric stops walking.

Looks back.

Laughs.

"Grounded," he says. "The hell I am."

150.

"So you just walked away," Jordan says. "And he didn't try to stop you?"

"What could he do?" Eric replies. "He can't control me, not anymore. Not now that I know all this dirt on him's real."

Jordan nods, his eyes wide. "I guess not," he says. "But still. That's a ballsy maneuver."

They're standing in Jordan's driveway. Haley and Paige are there, too, listening. They were all waiting out front when Eric's cab pulled up. They all listened as Eric told his story.

"Nothing you could do," Jordan says. "So long as you kept your mouth shut at the precinct, it's no harm, no foul. You didn't talk, did you?"

"Are you kidding? Not to a damn soul."

"You're not wearing a wire?"

"A wire? What the fuck, dude?" Eric draws back, kind of panicking. Relaxes when he sees the smirk on Jordan's face.

"I'm just messing with you." Jordan puts his arm around Eric's shoulder, steers him toward the house. "Get some sleep, have a shower. We have a surprise cooked for you later."

"What kind of surprise?" Eric says, but Jordan just smiles, and Eric's too tired to pursue the line of questioning. Feels like a shell of a person.

He follows Paige and Haley into the house.

151.

Eric sleeps all day. He wakes up and showers. He puts on a pair of Jordan's board shorts and a beach hoodie—

(it kind of hangs off him; he's not as built as Jordan)

—and goes downstairs and outside to the pool, where Jordan and the girls are lounging. They all look up as he comes out onto the deck.

"There he is," Paige says.

"We were beginning to think you were dead," Haley says. "Like, we'd have to send Paige up there to check for a pulse."

(Paige blushes at this.)

"Go easy on him," Jordan says. "Neither of *you* spent the night in a holding cell."

Eric smiles weakly. He's still groggy. He's still feeling a little, you know, *shaken* by the whole experience.

"Anyway, he's alive." Haley sniffs the air. "And he doesn't stink anymore."

Jordan claps his hands. Stands up from his deck chair. "Which means it's time to get cracking."

152.

They all pile into a car.

(The car is *not* Jordan's BMW.)

(It's a Tesla. Model S.)

"What's this? Where's your Bimmer?" Eric asks him.

"This?" Jordan starts the motor and the car *hums* to life. "It's my dad's, technically. Not that he ever drives it. *It doesn't sound like a real car*, he says. He likes his AMG better."

(Jordan's dad's AMG has a 6.3-liter V-8 engine. It *howls*. It also burns gas like a mother. Fuck the environment.)

Jordan drives out of the garage. The driveway gate slides open, and Jordan pilots them out onto Marine Drive. He turns left, away from Capilano.

"Uh, how far are we going?" Eric asks them. "I'm still pretty, you know, beat from last night."

Haley leans forward. Slaps Eric's shoulder. "Man up," she says. "You spent a few hours in the Capilano jail. You're not Nelson Mandela. You'll see where we're going when we get there."

"It'll be worth it, E," Jordan says. "I promise."

153.

They drive out of Capilano and up to the highway. It's dusk by the time they reach the on-ramp, the sun setting through the trees. Jordan takes the northbound ramp and points the car up the coast and into the mountains. He drives until he reaches the little dirt-road turnoff to Fincher's Bluff. Then he turns.

Gravel spits up against the Tesla's underbody, *ping-ping-ping*ing as the car climbs up the narrow logging road. The trees close in on all sides, tall and dark and imperious, and the Tesla *hums* louder as the grade gets steeper. Eric takes out his phone, watches the signal disintegrate from LTE to 3G to one bar to none. They're up in the wilderness now. Fincher's Bluff.

The road climbs for a while, and then it levels off. It widens into a clearing, marred by the remains of old fire pits and beer cans pockmarked by BB pellets and birdshot. It's almost full dark again, the stars out in abundance, something you never see in downtown Capilano. But Eric isn't looking at the sky. He's looking across the clearing, to the very middle, where Jordan's BMW is waiting for them.

Jordan stops the Tesla at the edge of the clearing. "Okay, everybody out."

The girls climb out of the back seats. Jordan's looking at Eric, waiting for him to move. "I don't get it," Eric says. "Why did you bring me here?"

"So the Fix didn't work out as planned. We're not going to let a little speed bump ruin our party, are we?"

154.

Eric climbs out of the car. Looks across at the BMW, lit up in Jordan's headlights.

"So, what?" he asks.

"We have to do something with Jordan's car," Haley says. "We can't take the chance that asshole Headley saw me and Paige drive off in it last night. It's *evidence* now."

"You did your job," Jordan says. "But we still have to take precautions. Why get caught if we don't have to, right?"

Then he smiles. "Also," he says, "my dad bought that thing for my birthday. He sent his assistant, with a credit card, to pick it out."

He pauses.

"I just want to see that fucker burn."

155.

They burn the BMW to the ground.

Jordan's Molotov cocktails work wonders, and he also brought four jerry cans of gasoline. Eric and the others drench the Bimmer inside and out with gas. Then they step back, light their cocktails, and hurl the bottles at the car.

The BMW erupts into flames. The explosion takes Eric's breath away. Instantly, the flames are devouring the car, sending choking columns of black smoke up into the night. The fire is ferocious.

Eric and Jordan and Paige and Haley step back to the edge of the clearing to watch. They're utterly alone up here; even the lights of Capilano don't make it this far around the mountain. Nobody will ever know what they've done.

It's a weird feeling, being so wild. So utterly free.

Eric is captivated.

Eric is . . . *exhilarated.*

Jordan has a joint going. He puffs twice, passes it to Haley. Then he turns back to watch the flames.

"You guys don't even know," he says, and the fire dances in his eyes. "You don't even know how far we could take this." Then: "We could fix this town forever, if we really put our minds to it."

156.

Afterward, when the flames have died down and the BMW is mostly just a smoking pile of ash and charred steel, they stand in a circle at the edge of the clearing and stare up at the stars.

And now that they've had this, well, *orgasmic* experience burning down Jordan's BMW, it's time for the real talk.

The gritty stuff.

They start having those meandering, embarrassing heart-to-heart convos you always have when it's late and you're drunk and/or high with your best friends in the world.

They start saying things they'll probably be ashamed of, but won't ever really regret.

(You know how it goes.)

Jordan starts.

"They kicked me out of town," he says, looking up at the sky, not a cloud anywhere, just a carpet of stars. "My parents. They, like, they gave me a choice: either *move*, or go to juvenile hall.

"I beat some dude up," he says. "Some shitty actor, that's why I'm here. I nearly killed this idiot."

The others don't really say anything.

"He deserved it, though," Jordan continues. "Not that I'm condoning what I did, but he wasn't even a *good* actor. Like, don't put on airs like you're king shit because you had two lines in a toothpaste commercial. You're a long way from Brad Pitt, you know?"

The others kind of nod. This is Jordan's story. Let him tell it.

"And I got off," he says. "That's the most fucked-up part of all. I should be in jail right now, but because my dad makes Hollywood blockbusters they cut a deal and I'm up here and nobody gives a shit. Like, nobody cares at all," he says.

"Hypocrites," he says.

Just the wind in the trees for a while, then—

"I tried to kill myself." Haley's staring across the clearing, and her voice is nonchalant. "This is right after I went away. I did this whole fucking urgent care thing for my, like, eating disorder, talked to some stupid shrink for an hour every day for, like, *weeks*, and then I get out and I'm actually feeling okay and I come back to Capilano and it's, like, the worst. Thing. Ever."

She shakes her head.

"Seriously, my mom and dad didn't know what to say to me. It's like they thought I was going away to, like, fat camp or something, like I would come back and suddenly know how to be perfect and skinny and beautiful. Like Tinsley," she says.

E has only ever seen pictures of Tinsley. She's smoking hot, but it's not like Haley's ugly. Compared to, like, ninety percent of the people in the world, Haley is hot as hell. But Capilano's for the one percent of the one percent. Capilano's for people like Tinsley.

"I went up on the bridge to the city one night," Haley says. "I thought I would jump off. Just, like, fall. Hit the water and break every bone in my body and die there, and that would be that."

Paige gasps. "I remember that! You posted that picture."

Haley nods. "Instagram," she says. "On top of the Lions Gate Bridge, one o'clock in the morning. I guess I wanted to see if anyone cared."

"And?" E says.

"And I got, like, twenty-three likes." Haley laughs a little, hollow. "But nobody actually *cared*."

Jordan puts his arm around her. "I do."

Haley leans into him—

(and E feels a little pang of jealousy).

"I was, like, up on the railing when he called me," Haley says. "He was the only person in the world who actually *got* it."

She doesn't say it like she's accusing anyone, but E and Paige look down anyway, look away, self-conscious.

(They knew Haley then. Where were *they*?)

"I told her it wouldn't matter," Jordan said. "I told her, if she died, nobody at Cap High would come to any, like, big, huge *epiphany* about the error of their ways. They would just think you were some weakling who couldn't cut it.

"I told her she wouldn't do anyone any good if she jumped off that bridge, but she sure as hell could teach those assholes a lesson if she *didn't*."

Haley nods. "That's why I'm out here.

"That's why the *Pack*," she says.

157.

"I guess we're all doing this True Confessions thing tonight, huh?" Paige says, after they've digested Haley's story for a while. "Does that mean it's my turn to spew?"

Jordan sparks a joint. Passes it to E. "Only if you want."

Paige doesn't say anything. She just stares across the clearing at the smoke billowing from the ruins of Jordan's BMW.

(Time passes.)

Then she looks up. "I got a job," she says. "I start tomorrow. My first day."

(Cue the record-scratch.)

Work?

"It's my dad's fault," Paige tells them. "All his money's tied up with this court case, and I need tuition money. Hence, you know, I have to work."

There's a shocked silence as the other three picture Paige in, like, Tory Burch, tagging clearance items and ringing in sales.

Paige catches their expressions. "It's not like *that*," she says. " ▮▮▮▮▮▮▮▮▮ got me a PA job on the movie he's shooting. It's actually kind of fun." Paige forces a smile. "Hey, it beats flipping burgers, right?"

An awkward silence.

"Right," Jordan says finally. "I mean, of course. *Right*."

But it's weak, and Paige sees right through it. Her smile disappears. "Oh, fuck you," she says. "Fuck all you guys. You're going to be judgmental assholes like everyone else, huh?"

"*No.*" Haley shakes her head. Holds up her hands. "It's not like that, Paige. We're just, like, surprised."

"I didn't know it was that bad," E says.

(And Paige casts him a withering stare.)

"No," she says. "*You* wouldn't."

"It's just so fucked up," Jordan says. "You were supposed to get out of here. Freaking *Yale*, right? They don't have scholarships?"

"Yeah, they do." Paige sighs. "I applied for a couple. The rest are all based on financial need. My dad's still freaking loaded, on paper."

"On paper," Jordan says.

"But he doesn't have a dime in the real world. His accounts were all frozen. Plus there's the lawyer fees and blah, blah, blah." She shrugs. "So, you know, I have to *work*. And in the meantime, everybody in Capilano knows my family's a joke."

"Fuck them," Haley says. "You don't need those assholes anyway."

"Haley's right," Jordan says. "You have *us*. You have the Pack."

Paige stares across at the smoke. "Yeah," she says. "Thank god for that, at least."

158.

E's head is swimming, and when he looks up from the gravel he sees the others looking at him, all of them, and he knows they're waiting for him to confess something, too.

(And there's one BIG, OBVIOUS CONFESSION that would be perfect for this moment.)

(*Dudes, I'm, like, gay.*)

And E knows this is the time to tell it. He knows he's part of the *Pack* now and nobody here will judge him, or laugh at him, or, like, turn on him for liking boys. He knows that . . . rationally.

But E's distracted by the way Haley's nestled into the crook of Jordan's arm, cuddled in tight. He's preoccupied by the way Paige still looks at him, talks to him, like she's still feeling betrayed and hurt and angry and she isn't getting over it anytime soon.

(And anyway, liking boys and liking Jordan are pretty much one and the same in E's mind right now, and he's kind of thinking of he'll start out with the *I'm gay* thing and then get nervous and spew the rest of it, and how awkward would that be, with Haley and Jordan so obviously banging?)

The moment stretches.

(The weed fucks with E's brain.)

The Pack stares at E, waiting for his confession.

And E studies his shoes and tries to think of the words.

And he can't.

159.

"I got nothing," Eric tells the others.

Haley shakes her head, smirking like she knew this was coming. Paige makes a face like she's hurt and betrayed all over again.

Only Jordan doesn't look fazed. He smiles. Cocks his head at Eric. "Nothing?" he says.

Eric feels his thoughts buzzing. Feels like he wants to open up and just scream about everything, every fucking conflicting feeling and emotion rattling around in his head, every repressed urge and impulse he's ever struggled with, everything that keeps him weighted down like a freaking *anchor* chained around his *chest* and chucked overboard, like he can't breathe and he's plummeting down all at the same time, and there's nobody who can even freaking *relate* to anything that he's feeling.

(It would feel so fucking good to just tell someone.)

(*These are your* friends, *dude.*)

(Do it!)

But Eric can't get it together. He shakes his head. "It's been a *day*, man. I'm too fucking high. I can't even think straight right now."

And that's where it ends.

160.

There's a brief—

(awkward)

—silence. The others look at each other, and Eric wonders if they're going to kick him out of the Pack or throw him in what's left of the fire or just shun him and never speak to him again—

(and he can't figure out which would be worse).

But Jordan's still unfazed. "That's okay," he says. "You can think on it, E. We'll revisit the topic after your Fix."

Eric blinks. "My what?"

"Your Fix." Jordan smiles, mischievous. "I did one, Paige did one, and Haley. . . . You're next on the list, champ. You're *up*."

161.

You're up.

(I mean, talk about performance anxiety.)

It's one thing to go along with this insanity. It's another entirely to conjure up some crazy yourself.

Eric thinks about it all the way home. Can't pick out anything. His mind's blank. Too much pressure.

(Like when someone tells you, "Be funny.")

(Um, could you be more *specific*?)

(What exactly do you *want*?)

162.

Anyway, we're going to leave Eric to stew for a while.

   (He has enough on his plate without us watching over his shoulder.)

   Let's change tracks for a minute.

Let's look in on Paige.

163.

Suicide Pack successes notwithstanding—

Paige Hammond is not having a good summer. Her family is imploding. Her college dreams are pretty well out the window.

Her dad's *probably* going to jail and *definitely* leaving her mom.

The house is like a war zone.

(Paige hardly ever goes back.)

She's couch-surfing now, most of the time. Her cousin Nate has a condo by the beach. He's shooting some snowboarding documentary in Chile right now, so Paige has the place to herself.

It suits her fine.

(At least there nobody's screaming.)

But Nate will be back soon. Paige's parents will still be splitting up. Her college money will still be tied up in the fraud investigation. The Hammonds will still be the laughingstock of Capilano.

And then, there's the Eric question.

(The *Connelly Conundrum*.)

The whole problem of how to feel about E.

164.

Once upon a time, Paige imagined she and Eric Connelly would grow up, get married, and grow old together.

She'd wasted time in math class being a stereotypical, like, *girl*, imagining which friends she would pick as her bridesmaids and what gown she would wear for the ceremony. She wrote "Paige Connelly" over and over again in her notebook.

(Paige isn't proud of this time in her life.)

But then Eric went away. And it wasn't like she had seen it coming, either.

First day of class, junior year, she'd come back from the family holiday in Morocco and Eric had told her, point-blank, they couldn't be together anymore.

"I just don't have time," he told her, avoiding her eyes. "I need to, you know, focus on school right now."

He'd sworn there wasn't anyone else. But Paige hadn't believed him.

(She'd been in Morocco for a month, after all.)

So she'd asked around. Done her research.

(#Stalker.)

(She isn't exactly proud of this, either.)

But everyone she talked to said the same freaking thing:

Eric Connelly's gone.

Eric's a ghost.

Eric doesn't come around here anymore.

165.

He'd buried himself in schoolwork, as far as Paige could tell. And as far as she could tell, it had paid off.

(#StudentOfTheYear.)

But now Eric is back. He clearly has some issues he's trying to deal with. And Paige is happy to see him—

(a part of her, anyway)

—but another part of her hates that E joined the Pack.

(Like, I don't care how good you are at boosting cars.)

(What happened to my apology, man?)

(What happened to, you know, *us*?)

166.

Anyway.

Paige has other things to worry about. If Eric Connelly was her only concern, she'd be laughing.

But Eric's a distant memory at the moment.

Right now, Paige is navigating a movie set. She's wearing, like, her *ID* on a *lanyard* and it is killing her. Every second.

She's looking for the catering van.

She's supposed to fetch ███████████ his coffee.

167.

███████████ is filming a movie in a studio in the city. It's a prestige picture—

(Scorsese's executive producing)

—and everyone's saying it should win ███████████ another Oscar. But ███████████ doesn't seem to care about awards, or prestige—

(or even freaking Scorsese).

All ███████████ seems to care about is chasing Paige Hammond.

168.

Paige met ███████████ at the Cactus Club, as discussed.
███████████ was there with his homeboys, a motley collection of B-list TV actors and, like, sleazeballs with money, ███████████ standing out like a Patek Philippe at the Walmart watch counter. She'd run into him on his way out of the bathroom, and he'd cornered her, chatted her up, bought her a drink—
(and Paige would be lying if she said she didn't go along with it).
(███████████ might not be as gorgeous as he was when he was twenty years old and dodging icebergs, but he's still hot.)
Long story short, ███████████ invited Paige to an after-party with his boys in his suite at the St. Regis that night.
And Paige demurred, because one simply doesn't just go to hotel suites with a group of strange men, no matter how famous they are.
But she did get drunk and spill the whole truth and nothing but the truth about the scorched-earth situation going on at her home address—
("My dad's going to jail. He embezzled a shitload of money from his real-estate partners. The government seized everything. My college fund included. So, like, you know, everything's up in the air right now. I was supposed to go to Yale. Now I'm, like, trying to learn how to make a résumé.")
And she did give ███████████ her number.
And damned if ███████████ didn't call her the next day.

169.

"It's a great opportunity," he told Paige. "People *kill* for these jobs. You're basically *living* the movies, sixteen hours a day."

Paige was unimpressed. Paige knows movie people. Paige doesn't really want to *live* the movies, sixteen hours a day.

But still . . .

"How much does it pay?" she asked █████████.

And ████████████ laughed. "Name your price."

So she did.

And now Paige Hammond is Paige the PA.

And now she's fetching ██████████'s coffee.

170.

There's a catch, though.

(There's always a catch.)

Paige knocks on the door to ████████'s trailer. Hears him shout from inside, *Come in.* She opens the door and climbs into the trailer, and as soon as she sees ████████ she can tell that coffee isn't the only thing on his mind.

"Come on in," he tells her, and it's the gleam in his eye when he says it. "Shut the door."

He's sitting on a couch along the wall of the trailer, and he does everything but pat the seat next to him as Paige brings him the coffee. He's wearing jeans and a simple white T-shirt, isn't even in makeup, and Paige has this fleeting thought like she isn't even sure ████████'s on the call list today.

Paige sets the coffee down. She can feel ████████'s eyes on her, even with her back to him, and when she turns around again, he's still checking her out.

"We never got to finish our conversation from the other night," he says. "I've been thinking about it ever since."

He slides over on the couch more, clearing a space, and Paige feels her stomach churn.

(Shit.)

(Is this what she's been reduced to? Sleeping with some asshole for a *job?*)

Paige debates this with herself for longer than she

would care to admit. Then she turns and picks up the coffee cup again.

"I forgot the cream," she tells ████████. "I'll be right back."

171.

Paige goes all the way back to the catering van. Fills a new cup of coffee for ████████. Has another PA bring the cup to ███████'s trailer—
                    (some Spielberg fanboy named Devon).
    She wanders the set for another half hour, her stomach still nerves and chaos. Then she calls E, and Gs the FO.
    (Shit.)

172.

"So you think he gave you the job just to sleep with you?" Eric asks Paige.

(They're driving home from the city, over the bridge and into Capilano. E's working at the health center and █████████'s movie is shooting in the city.)

(It's an uneasy détente, but it's better than nothing, Paige figures.)

(Anyway, she doesn't have a car.)

Paige sighs. Looks out the window as Eric drives the G-Wagen over the crest of the bridge and down toward the shore.

"Yeah, but what else is new?" she says. "Fending off sleazy older men is just part of being a girl. It's just *this particular* sleazy older man is the eighth-most-powerful person in Hollywood."

"So no pressure."

"Yeah. I did *consider* sleeping with him," Paige says. "Just for the story, you know? Something to tell the grandkids."

Eric glances over from the driver's seat. "But?"

"*But?*" She smacks his arm.

"I mean." Eric blushes. Stammers like he does when he gets embarrassed. Paige has always found it cute.

(Infuriatingly, she *still* finds it cute.)

"I'm starving," she says finally. "Are you hungry at all?"

They head to the mall across from Paige's cousin's condo. Eric doesn't want to go home to his terrible dad, and Paige is putting off being alone.

(Plus, Eric's hungry, too.)

(Hence, Subway.)

"You have to order your sandwich without saying 'um' at any point in the process," Eric's telling her. "That's the Subway Challenge. It's harder than it sounds."

Paige doesn't get it at first. Then she thinks it sounds dumb. Then she turns to the counter and starts to order a cold-cut trio on, um, Italian herb and cheese.

"*Noooo,*" she says, laughing. "That one doesn't count. One more time."

"One more time. This time it's for real, though."

Paige turns back to the counter. Makes it through the cheese question, the "Do you want it toasted?" situation. Almost messes up on the veggies issue, skates through the sauce and the salt and pepper. Then the girl behind the counter asks if she wants to make it a combo.

"Um," Paige says.

Eric claps his hands behind her. "Boom. It's over."

"What?" Paige spins. "No way, you asshole. That doesn't count. I ordered the sandwich already."

"You have to maintain control through the whole process," Eric says, smirking. "You lose."

"Technicality." Paige turns to pay. "But fine, whatever. I lose. What were we betting?"

"Pardon?"

Paige takes her change. Turns back to face Eric, and she's smiling, too. "I said, you won," she says. "So pick out a prize. What do I owe you?"

And Eric looks at her, and for a moment, it's just like old times, the summer before junior year, when they were pretty much inseparable and everything in the world was one big, secret in-joke.

And Paige is thinking, *This is it, this is how we get back to normal.*

But then Eric's smile fades.

He looks away.

"Just, like, make out, like, an IOU or something."

Paige grabs her sandwich and makes for the door. "Gah. You know what? Forget this."

173.

"Are we ever going to talk about what happened to us?" Paige asks—

(after Eric follows her into the parking lot and apologizes and whatever, and Paige doesn't know what to say, so she just shakes her head and starts walking back toward her cousin Nate's condo building, her sandwich in its little baggie, uneaten).

(And Eric is still following her.)

"Like, it's all nice and great that you're back from the dead and all," Paige continues, "but you could have at least said good-bye."

Eric doesn't look at her. He keeps walking, and he can't make eye contact, and he doesn't say anything for, like, *minutes.*

(Guys. Can't. Communicate.)

"I know," he says finally. "I'm sorry. I should have, like, talked to you. I shouldn't have just disappeared."

"Well, you're back," Paige says. "So now's your chance. Talk to me now."

Eric glances at her. Then quickly away.

And Paige holds her breath, but there's really no point.

"It's not that easy," Eric says. "I just can't."

174.

"I just can't."

(#Weaksauce.)

It rings pretty hollow.

But that's where they leave it, awkward and stilted and incapable of looking each other in the eye or even having a decent conversation.

And Paige goes up to Nate's condo.

And Eric goes away.

And for all this *Pack sticks together* bullshit, they still don't even know each other anymore.

KIK -- CAPILANO HIGH PRIVATE MESSAGE GROUP
— 07/20/16 — 07:56 PM

USERNAME: PradaMane
MESSAGE: WTF is up with the Suicide Pack?
    They got me hyped with that Molotov
    cocktail shit but no Vine? Did they
    blow themselves up, or what?

175.

Thursday night, Jordan texts Eric. *You busy?*

Eric is not busy. Eric is sitting in his room, hiding from his dad, with whom he's had an uneasy truce since their showdown at dawn.

Eric knows he should probably be doing more reading for college in the fall. Eric can't focus. He's trying—

(and failing)

—to think of a good Fix instead.

Not busy, he tells Jordan. *Bored.*

Jordan replies in thirty seconds. *Meet me at Lighthouse Park. One hour.*

176.

Lighthouse Park is on the far west end of Capilano, where the mansions stop and the forest begins. It's only a park in the sense that it isn't anything else; it's just trees and rock and a path to the little beach by the lighthouse.

Eric parks his mom's G-Wagen at the trailhead and zips his jacket up tight. It's nearly dark, and what little light is left is filtered through gloomy gray clouds. Jordan's dad's Tesla is the only other car in the lot.

Come to the picnic area, Jordan texts. *By the beach.*

The beach is about half a mile down the path. The forest is spooky quiet, only the wind in the branches and the odd raven calling. Eric is shivering, partly from fear and partly from excitement.

(Spooky's kind of sexy, when you're with the right company.)

Jordan isn't at the beach when Eric arrives. There's a Herschel bag on the picnic table, though, and Eric can hear something rustling in the bushes. "Jordan?" he calls out. "Where are you?"

There's no answer. The rustling continues. Then the bushes part, and Jordan backs out of the forest, dragging a green garbage can behind, one of those big steel drums.

"Some asshole dragged this into the woods," he tells Eric.

"There's a garbage bin back at the trailhead, Captain

Planet," Eric says. "We can't just carry our trash out like normal people?"

"Who said anything about trash?" Jordan rolls the drum toward the middle of the picnic area. "Grab me that backpack, would you? But be careful."

There's something inside the bag. Eric can feel it when he picks it up. It shifts and clinks, metallic.

"*E*," Jordan says, wincing. "I can't stress how important it is that you be really freaking careful with that backpack."

"*Okay*, geez." Eric holds the backpack like it's a baby. Carries it over to Jordan. "What's in here, anyway?"

Jordan muscles the garbage drum a little farther. He looks up, and in the last gray light of day, Eric can see the look in his eye, all mischief and bad behavior, and he figures it out, fast.

"The bomb," he says. "You actually built it."

"Exactly." Jordan sets the backpack down—gently—at the bottom of the garbage can. Then he straightens. "Okay. Here's what's going to happen."

Eric listens.

He listens intently.

(He's curious now, and apprehensive, the kind of electrifying worry like when you're waiting in line for the tallest roller coaster in the park.)

"What we have is a basic pressure-cooker bomb," Jordan tells Eric. "I've packed it full of Demolition Mike's gunpowder and rigged a detonator up to a cheap burner phone. I've programmed the burner phone's number in here—" He holds up his own Samsung Galaxy. "So when I press the send button . . ."

(He smiles wide.)

"Kablamo."

177.

Kablamo.

Eric and Jordan take cover behind a cedar tree at the edge of the picnic grounds. It's a big tree, the trunk wide enough that it shelters them both, but barely. Jordan huddles close to Eric, close enough that Eric can feel his warmth.

(Eric wonders if Jordan can feel him shivering.)

Jordan holds up his Galaxy. Scrolls down his contacts to the burner phone number. Then pauses.

"We should be filming this," he tells Eric. "The fans are getting restless. Get your phone out."

Eric aims his iPhone at the garbage drum—

(now just a shadow on the dark grass).

Jordan aims his Galaxy at the garbage drum too. Eric grips the cedar for support and ducks as low as he can. Aims his iPhone out around the trunk and wonders if it's the last he'll ever see of his hand.

Jordan grins at Eric. "Fire in the hole," he says.

Then he presses the send button.

178.

Nothing happens.

"It might take a second," Jordan says. "Cellular signals and whatnot."

Eric nods. "Okay."

"You're still filming?"

Eric shows him the iPhone. "Still rolling."

"It's coming." Jordan peers out around the cedar. "It'd *better* be coming."

179.

But there is no kablamo.

They wait two, maybe three minutes.

Maybe more.

"Do you have the wrong number?" Eric asks Jordan. "Maybe you're just calling some random."

"I have the right number," Jordan says. "I tried it, like, eight times. It should be working."

"Maybe you didn't pay your phone bill. Or, like, the coverage isn't good here."

Jordan glares at Eric. "I fucking paid my phone bill, E. Something's fucked up."

He stands and walks out toward the picnic area, still typing things on his phone.

"Wait," Eric calls out. "Don't mess around while you're out in the open. You could get blown up."

"*Thanks*, Captain Obvious. If I'd known you were going to be so much of a pussy, I would have made you wait in the car."

Jordan walks up to the garbage can, leans over, and rummages inside. "It should be working," he says. "What the shit is going on?"

"Maybe the wiring was loose, or something?"

"Or maybe you screwed it up when you jostled it," Jordan says. "I *told* you to be careful."

Jordan kicks the garbage drum. The sound resonates. It

scares Eric a couple steps backward. He's still filming with his iPhone. Jordan sees it, and flips out.

"Am I on-screen? Turn the fucking camera off," Jordan says. "For fuck's sake, E."

Eric turns off the phone.

Jordan paces.

Eric watches, and tries to figure out the right thing to say. "We can probably fix it," he says.

Jordan spins at him. "What are you, E, fucking retarded? It's fucking ruined. Wake *up*!"

He starts walking away, out of the picnic area and back toward the trail to the parking lot. Eric hurries to follow.

"Wait," he says. "Where are you going?"

But Jordan doesn't slow down. "I just can't hold your hand right now, E," Jordan says. "Just leave me the fuck alone, okay?"

He stalks toward the parking area. In the distance, E can hear his car pull away.

180.

Eric stands there, alone in the woods, for a while.

(This is not the way this night was supposed to go.)

He can't shake the empty feeling in his chest. He's never seen Jordan this way before, never knew Jordan Grant could flip out so incredibly thoroughly.

Damn.

181.

Eric walks back to the picnic area. Back to the garbage drum.

He tells himself he's getting rid of the evidence. Protecting Jordan and the rest of the Pack in case someone else finds the bomb.

That's a lie, though.

Eric knows it as soon as he lifts the bomb from the drum. He's not thinking about protecting Jordan.

He's thinking about convincing Jordan he's not a complete fucking failure.

182.

Eric and Haley and Paige were supposed to have plans with Jordan on the weekend. The weekend was when Eric was supposed to tell them his Fix. But it's Saturday now, and Jordan's bailing. He's not returning calls. He's AWOL.

(Which is partially good, because Eric still has no freaking clue what he wants to Fix.)

(But at the same time, it's bad, because the Capilano High group on Kik is clamoring for more action.)

(There hasn't been a Suicide Pack Vine since the robbery at The Room. Allen Headley's Corvette never made the highlight reels, for obvious reasons. And the Pack's fans are getting restless.)

Where the fuck is the Suicide Pack?
More more more.
Did they just bail out, or what?
We need more.
FEED US.

183.

With the Suicide Pack sidelined, Eric suddenly has a lot of free time on his hands. He should be thinking up a good Fix for the others. Instead, he's researching bombs.

This is because Eric didn't get rid of the evidence, like he probably should have. He didn't destroy the bomb.

Instead, he carried it back up the trail—

(very carefully).

He packed it into his mom's G-Wagen—

(*very* carefully).

He drove it home with him and brought it down to his room—

(also quite carefully).

And now he has the bag on his desk, and he's lifting out the bomb to dismantle it—

(more carefully than he's ever done anything in his life).

184.

It looks like, you know, kitchenware.

(It is, after all, a pressure cooker.)

There's no stew inside, though. Just gunpowder, a blasting cap, and a cheap plastic cell phone. A jumble of wires.

Eric locks his bedroom door. Opens his laptop. Sits down and tries to rebuild Jordan's bomb.

185.

It takes some looking, but Eric finds the website that Jordan probably cribbed from. It's an underground portal, ANARCHIST HAVEN, *very* deep web. There are schematics and diagrams for all kinds of effed-up shit. Eric studies them until he finds something that looks familiar. He sees the mistake right away.

(It's so simple.)

Jordan messed up the wiring from the burner phone. He crossed the wires up and hooked them in backward. It's an easy mistake.

(It's easy to fix.)

The wires are backward, Eric texts Jordan. *I fixed it, so we should be good now.*

E presses send. The message delivers.

186.

Jordan doesn't answer. Not right away.

Twenty minutes pass, and Eric closes down his laptop. Paces the room. Checks his phone obsessively.

He's just about to, like, raid his mom's bathroom for an Ambien or something when his phone buzzes.

Jordan.

You fixed it?

I fixed it, Eric says. *Good as new. Better.* ☺

A long pause. E puts the lid back on the bomb. Carries it gently to his closet and hides it behind his Givenchy high-tops.

His phone buzzes again.

Party at T Miles's tonight. I'll pick you up in an hour.

187.

Terry Miles lives up in the Properties, high on the mountain slopes overlooking Capilano. The mansions cling to the cliffsides, the roads turning and winding in switchbacks to where it gets too steep to build anything higher. Jordan drives fast, the Tesla's engine working hard to keep the speed up. Haley and Paige are in the backseat. Eric's riding shotgun. Nobody says anything. Nobody asks Jordan where he's been.

He reaches the top and slows the car and pulls into a driveway behind, like, eight Range Rovers, a couple Porsches, and a Mercedes CLS. The house is Tudor style, and dramatically lit, and when Eric climbs out of the Tesla he can look down and see the city far below, the lights of the bridge like a string of luminescent pearls.

Eric takes it in for a minute or two. Then Jordan comes up beside him. "When the big earthquake hits, all these hypocrites are going to come crashing back down to earth," he says. "And it's going to be awesome."

Then he nudges Eric. "Party favors."

Haley's holding four little pills in the palm of her hand. She takes one and swallows. Washes it down with a sugar-free Red Bull. Passes the can to Paige, who does the same. Then Jordan. They all look at Eric.

"Molly," Haley says.

"All for one, E," Jordan says. "Down the hatch."

For a moment, E has a twinge.

Of his old worries.

His old sense of responsibility.

(But what's a little recreational drug use when you've already built a bomb?)

188.

This party is a lot like the last party.

There's a bunch of kids and a bunch of red plastic cups, some crappy DJ spinning crappy hip-hop/classic-rock mashups and smiling about it, like he's the first person to think of playing Kendrick Lamar over a Hall & Oates record.

Elsewhere, people are coming out of the bathroom in pairs and threes, wiping their noses and fixing their clothes, and Terry Miles's dad—his freaking *dad*—is bopping around with his own red plastic cup and acting totally age-inappropriate, leering at the cute girls who are dancing with each other in the living room.

Jordan catches Eric gawking, slaps him on the back. "Boring as shit, right?" he says. "What a bunch of knobs."

189.

Then they're outside, on a balcony, watching a bunch of kids throw each other in the pool. Paige and Haley are down there with some girls they know from Cap, and Paige keeps glancing up at Eric and Jordan because she knows *exactly* where they are.

"I shouldn't have flipped out the other day," Jordan tells Eric. "I'm sorry. I just really wanted that bomb to work."

The balcony is nothing but shadows. The door is closed behind Eric and Jordan so the noise of the party is muted. Eric and Jordan are alone, just watching the party.

(Down on the pool deck, a bunch of juniors from the lacrosse team are trying to throw Paige and Haley in the pool.)

Jordan's leaning on the railing. He's close enough to Eric that Eric can smell the pot and whatever soap Jordan uses, something spicy and probably expensive.

(Eric likes that Jordan's close, but he wants to get closer. The pill is pushing his inhibitions away.)

(The Molly has Eric's brain swimming in bathwater, unable to focus, unable to do anything, really, but just *be*.)

"It's cool," Eric says. "I mean, whatever. It doesn't matter."

"It *does* matter," Jordan says. "We're the *Pack, right?* We stick together. I shouldn't have blown up at you." He pauses. "No pun intended."

Eric laughs like it's the funniest thing he's ever heard. Jordan laughs, too.

(They're leaning on the railing, side by side. Eric keeps looking over at Jordan, watching his mouth while he talks.)

(His lips.)

(*Snap out of it.*)

(But the Molly is kind of taking over.)

Jordan catches Eric checking him out. He smiles, sly and mischievous and intoxicating. "You bugged out at Fincher's Bluff. What's up with that? You don't have any secrets?"

Eric closes his eyes. Sees Jordan anyway, Jordan on the Sundancer, shirt off. Jordan's six-pack. And there's *so much* he wants to talk about.

"I couldn't," he says. "I can't."

"Aha. You don't *trust* us."

Eric feels another wave hit him.

"I can't," he says again. "It's, like, you and Haley are together, right? It would just make everything awkward."

The words come out before E even knows what he's saying. But Jordan only smiles again. "Someone's been feeding you incorrect information," he says. "Haley and I hook up sometimes, but we aren't, like, together. You need to stop worrying so much, E."

(Eric doesn't answer.)

(Jordan is *so freaking close* right now.)

"Just do what you want, E," Jordan says. "Live in the moment, remember?"

And that's when E decides he can't take it anymore. He leans over and kisses Jordan, quickly, suddenly, before Jordan can react. As soon as their lips touch, E's brain goes into meltdown. He pulls away, quickly, ready to apologize, duck a punch, run.

(Or all of the above.)

But Jordan doesn't yell. He doesn't gag or hit E.

He just smiles even wider, and kisses E back.

190.

It's a good kiss.

(It might just be the drugs, but E doesn't think so.)

There's a pace to it, no urgency, as if they're a couple and they've been kissing each other forever.

(As if it's the thousandth kiss between them, and not just the first.)

E closes his eyes, feels Jordan's tongue brush against his own. Then, all too soon, Jordan pulls away.

"See?" he says, grinning. "That wasn't so bad, was it?"

191.

E's beyond caring about whatever point Jordan's trying to make. He leans in to kiss Jordan again, thinking there must be a spare bedroom around here, or maybe Jordan's backseat, somewhere, anywhere, thinking:

You can't just cut me off now that you've finally blown my fucking world apart.

But Jordan puts his hand on E's chest, not unkindly. He nods down toward the pool—

(where the lacrosse douchebags have Paige and Haley cornered. They're laughing, and Paige is shrieking, and they're about to throw the girls in the pool).

"We'd better save them," Jordan says.

His hand on E's chest feels like Electricity.

"Do we have to?" E says.

Jordan smiles again, that mischievous, all-knowing smile. "Come on," he says. "Before those assholes throw them in."

192.

E and Jordan duck back into the party. There are kids everywhere, in all manner of intoxication. E can taste Jordan on his lips, and he's sure everyone can tell what they've been doing.

(E doesn't want it to be over.)

E follows Jordan through the house and out to the pool. They cut in between the lacrosse douchebags—

(who are just about to grab Paige)

(who is laughing about it, but who stops laughing and smiles wider when she sees E and Jordan)

—and E puts his arm around Paige, and Jordan takes Haley, and together all four escape from the pool area, away from the douchebags—

(who stare, mouths agape, too shocked to do anything).

(And E's thinking, now that Paige and Haley are saved, he and Jordan can wander off somewhere and continue what they started, but Haley has other ideas.)

"This party's bullshit," she says when they're almost at the back door. "I think we've done all we can here."

193.

Paige heads to her cousin's condo. The other three go back to Jordan's.

"I'm too high to sit still," Jordan says. "Let's go swimming."

They're in his backyard now, on the pool deck. The mansion is completely empty.

(Jordan's dad is in Los Angeles, and his stepmom is in, uh, Fiji? Some transcendence retreat. She's never around.)

Jordan goes into the pool house and flips a switch, and the pool lights come on, some multicolored psychedelic show that looks *amazing* with the Molly. He comes out with a bottle of Johnnie Blue. Twists open the whiskey and takes a pull, passes it to Haley. Then he takes off his shirt.

"What are you waiting for?" he says. "Strip."

Haley and E look at each other.

"No time for bathing suits," Jordan says. "Are we swimming, or not?"

E takes a sip of the whiskey. It burns going down and sits warm in his stomach. He passes the bottle to Haley, and unbuttons his shirt.

They drink in silence, peel off their clothes until they're all three of them in their underwear, their skin glowing pale candy colors from the lights from the pool, the night a blanket all around them. Jordan takes a last drink of whiskey and puts down the bottle and grins.

"Last one in is guilty of a seditious act of terrorism," he says, and then he's jumping in the pool, diving down deep and swimming underwater toward the shallow end. E doesn't wait for Haley. He dives in and swims after Jordan.

194.

Haley jumps in behind E. Surfaces, laughing. Shrieking. She and E follow Jordan to the shallow end.

The night air is cool around them. E sits low, so only his head is above the water. Haley and Jordan do the same. They look at each other.

"The Pack is *back*, bitches," Haley says, giggling, and she slides back down in the water until she's completely submerged, and then swims, pulling and kicking, for the other end of the pool.

And it's at that moment, while she's underwater, that Jordan slips in beside E and kisses him again.

195.

(HALEY)

Haley swims to the far wall. Bursts to the surface, gasping for air, then dives down again and swims back to the shallow end. She comes up again in the shallow end, panting, grinning like a maniac. Wipes the water from her face, the hair from her eyes, and there are Jordan and E, making out.

Haley watches them as she catches her breath. It's actually kind of sexy, if a little, you know, surprising. Jordan and E are both hot, and the pool lighting and the water on their tanned skin isn't hurting, either. *What the hell*, Haley thinks, *why can't I enjoy this little show?*

(Still, it's hard not to feel left out.)

(#ThirdWheel.)

Haley's standing there in the shallow end, wondering if she's supposed to keep swimming or, like, go inside while Jordan and E get it on, or what. Then it's as if Jordan reads her mind. He breaks the kiss off with E and looks over at her. Gives her his sexy/cocky smile.

"Come here," he says, and the meaning is clear.

Come be with us.

Both of us.

Haley considers this. It wouldn't be the craziest thing she's ever done. But then Haley catches the way E's holding

Jordan, cuddled in close. There's conflict in the way he's watching her—fear and jealousy and something darker, too—and Haley realizes this isn't just a game to E; no, he's actually, like, *into* Jordan, wrapped up in Jordan's spell. And Haley can see that he's not into sharing.

So Haley shakes her head. "Thanks, but no thanks," she tells Jordan—

(and sees E visibly relax when she does).

"Maybe another time."

Then she sinks down into the water again, does a mermaid turn and swims to the far end, the deep end, finds the ladder and climbs out and pads across the deck to the mansion, shivering in the cool night air. She slides the back door open and walks into the kitchen, thinking she'll maybe brainstorm her next Fix before she goes to bed.

And when she turns around to slide the door closed again, E and Jordan are making out in the shallow end of the pool, completely taken with one another, and it's like they haven't even noticed she's gone.

196.

(E)

E hears Haley close the door, and he knows he's alone with Jordan again.

(*At last.*)

And then Jordan's kissing him, and his skin is slick and wet, and his muscles are hard, and E can feel himself shivering, like literally *shaking* with excitement, as he kisses Jordan back.

But even though E's drunk and high and utterly fucked up on Jordan's voodoo, some small part of him knows he should be proceeding with caution. He knows he should be worried about . . . something.

(But who gives a shit about that, anyway?)

E knows he should be thinking this through, examining what impact it will have on HIS FUTURE.

Figuring out how it jives with everyone's EXPEC-TATIONS.

But as E follows Jordan out of the pool and into Jordan's house and up the front stairs to his bedroom, he's not really thinking about any of those things.

He's not BEING RESPONSIBLE.

He's not THINKING about HIS FUTURE.

The only thing E's thinking—

(as he follows Jordan into his bedroom)

—is how this is just as good as
  he always imagined
          it would

                      be.

197.

It's lunchtime. Eric and Paige are walking through the city, Hastings Street, the East Side, dodging stares from homeless people and junkies.

Paige is PAing on ███████████'s movie a few blocks away from the Railtown Health Center, so she texted E and asked if he wanted dim sum. And here they are.

"I'm sorry." E's blushing. "I didn't want you to hear it from anyone but me."

"I just feel bad." Paige hands E her coffee cup. Fumbles with a package of Belmonts. "I'm not *against* the idea of you liking boys. I'm just . . . really surprised."

"Yeah," E says. "I was too."

Paige walks for a little while without saying anything. "I guess I was kind of imagining that you and I would get back together, now that you've crawled out of your cave and you're being social again. I never really understood why we broke up in the first place."

"My dad, mostly," E says. "He didn't think a Connelly Man should be spending time on a relationship when I could be BUILDING A FOUNDATION for my FUTURE."

"Right. And then there's the whole 'you like boys' thing."

"Right."

"I turned you gay," Paige says. "I always thought of myself as a pretty good girlfriend, but now I have to live with the fact that

I turned you off women entirely."

"It wasn't you," E says quickly. "I just didn't really know. And I mean, I wouldn't say *entirely*. . . ."

Paige gives him a smile. "I'm just messing with you." They wait for a light to change. Paige doesn't say anything until they're on the other side. "I'm not going to pretend, though. I really liked what we had together. It hurt when you disappeared."

"I'm fucked up," E tells her. He knows he's an asshole for bailing on Paige without an explanation. For leaving Paige to put the pieces together alone.

"I'm not mad. I just don't want to lose you again." Paige flicks her cigarette butt to the curb. "Not, like, as a boyfriend. Just as a *friend*."

"I'm not going anywhere."

"It's just, I could use a friend lately," Paige says. "My mom and dad are having freaking World War Three over this divorce, and I feel like my whole life is falling apart."

"That's what the Pack is for, right?"

She glances at him. "The Pack stuff is fun, yeah, but it's like a Band-Aid. At the end of the day, my life's still a shithole. It scares me sometimes, what we're doing. Like, where does it end?"

E shrugs. "It ends when we say it ends. When we get sick of fixing things."

"You think? You really believe we're all just going to walk away from this one day?"

E doesn't know what to say. Joining the Pack was the best thing that ever happened to him. He doesn't want to think about what happens when the Pack ends.

"You're really into Jordan, huh?" Paige asks, after a beat.

"I mean, yeah," E says.

Paige doesn't say anything. She just kind of frowns down

at the sidewalk like she's thinking. "Just promise me you'll be careful," she says. "You know?"

E stops. "What's that supposed to mean?" When Paige doesn't answer, he continues. "Like, it's all good when I'm robbing The Room, but hook up with Jordan and suddenly you're concerned?"

"Gah, I don't know, Eric," Paige says. "It's just a lot of big changes. All at once. That's all."

(Cue more awkward silence.)

Then E checks his watch. "I gotta get back."

Paige exhales, relief, like the conversation has gone sideways and this is the out they've been looking for. "Me too," she says. "███████████ probably needs me."

They walk to the next intersection.

Paige hugs him good-bye.

KIK -- CAPILANO HIGH PRIVATE MESSAGE GROUP
— 07/30/16 — 06:57 PM

USERNAME: SuIcIdEpAcK
MESSAGE: My new bikini is the bomb.

198.

It's bathing suit season. For most kids in Capilano, this is cause for celebration.

Not for Haley Keefer.

(I already told you about Haley's older sister, Tinsley. Tinsley is twenty-one. She's an actress—a *real* actress. She moved down to L.A. and had a story arc on *Grey's Anatomy*. Tinsley is what you would call "conventionally beautiful.")

Haley isn't. At least that's what her mom tells her—

(*"You'd be almost as pretty as Tinsley, sweetheart, if you could just lose a few pounds."*)

Consequently, Haley spends a lot of time looking in the mirror. She spends a lot of time feeling like she's ugly. Or fat. Or not good enough.

She hears her mom chiding her every time she eats a French fry.

(Haley doesn't eat many French fries.)

Haley starves herself, but it doesn't solve the equation. Her mom just cocks her head and clucks at her, tells her she looks emaciated and should be working out more.

Haley hates working out. It makes her feel fat and lazy.

Everything makes her feel fat and lazy.

Everything makes her feel not good enough.

(Except the Suicide Pack.)

199.

School always came easy for Haley.

(She's *smarter* than Tinsley, not that that counts for anything. She's probably the smartest of our four main characters—even E.)

Haley's mom and dad don't really care about smarts, though. Her dad is a washed-up old rock star who dropped out of high school for his first world tour senior year. Her mom is her dad's second wife, a former swimsuit model he met at the Viper Room in Los Angeles.

(Haley's mom is always talking about how she could have been a supermodel if she hadn't quit the game to follow Haley's dad on tour.)

(She's probably wrong, but anyway, she had Tinsley and now the whole question is moot.)

Haley's mom didn't get much of an education either. Now that her modeling days are behind her, she spends her time living vicariously through Tinsley and designing outrageously expensive bikinis to sell at Côte d'Azur, the boutique Haley's dad bought her in downtown Capilano.

Haley's parents don't really understand their youngest daughter. And the reverse is also pretty much true.

200.

How This All Ties In with Haley's (Second) Fix:
Short answer: It's bathing suit season.

Long answer: Tinsley is in Los Angeles shooting a speaking part in the new Sofia Coppola movie, and Haley's mom needs someone to test-model this year's line of outrageously cut and ridiculously priced bathing suits. She barges into Haley's room, wakes Haley up from a nice, relaxing marijuana-and-Houellebecq-induced nap and drags her downstairs to her workshop. And that's when the nagging begins.

("Your butt, sweetheart—have you thought about using the StairMaster more?")

("Maybe if we got you a personal trainer, you could finally lose that little bit of baby fat around your tummy.")

("For *god's* sake, honey, why can't you smile more? Like Tinsley?")

It's when Haley's mom mentions Tinsley that Haley's had enough. She bolts, still trussed up in this hideous paisley print haute couture bodysuit her mom's trying to get her to model. Makes it up to her room, her high all but freaking vanished, pulls on a pair of cutoffs and a tank top, steals the keys to her mom's Porsche Boxster, and burns rubber for Jordan's house.

201.

(She studies herself in the Porsche's rearview mirror as she drives. Hates herself for doing it, but can't stop. Picks out every flaw she can find as she waits at a stoplight.

(She knows them all by heart, anyway.)

Nose too big.

Cheeks too chubby.

Gap in her front teeth too wide.

Hair a perennial disaster.

And a pimple starting to show on her cheek.

Haley knows her mom keeps a stack of Tinsley's headshots in the glove box, just in case she needs to brag to the other Capilano moms. She pulls one out now and looks it over, and yep, Tinsley is still perfect, still so sunny and blond it's unbearable. And even though Haley has seen enough of her sister to know where the picture is touched up, it doesn't help.

Tinsley is practically perfect.

Haley is flawed.

Those are the facts.)

202.

Jordan listens as Haley vents. Jordan calls Paige and E, and pretty soon they're all listening.

"I just want to fuck up my mom's swimsuit store sometimes," Haley tells them. "I want to trash the place, all of it, every last bodysuit and bikini bottom and picture-perfect poster of my picture-perfect sister.

"I just want to burn that motherfucker to the ground," Haley tells them. "Is that so wrong?"

The others swap looks. Jordan and E exchange a mysterious glance.

"I think we might be able to help you with that," E says.

And then he tells Haley and Paige about the bomb.

203.

"Wait a second," Paige says. "You built a *bomb*?"

Jordan's smiling his shit-eating smile. "I mean, I built a *crappy* bomb. E perfected it."

Paige spins to look at E. "*You?*"

E just shrugs. "Found instructions online."

"Where is it?"

"My bedroom closet," E says. "I hid it behind those Givenchy Tysons Haley swiped." He pauses. "I mean, it's not very big."

"But it *would* fuck up the Côte d'Azur," Jordan says. "I can promise you that."

Haley thinks about it. "You guys would do that . . . for me?"

She looks at E. "This is *your* Fix. Are you sure this is what you want to do with it?"

E feels relief flooding his veins like he just took a pill.

"Hell yes," he says. "Let's blow the joint. Suicide Pack sticks together, right?"

"Damn right," Jordan says.

Haley mulls it over. She's thinking about the poster that hangs in the window of her mom's obnoxious boutique. Tinsley in a bikini, photo-shoot style. Tinsley's stomach is better than flat. Her butt doesn't sag. Her blond hair is flowing in the breeze.

(No way in a million years will Haley look anywhere near that good.)

Haley imagines that poster blown up to shreds. The

whole fucking boutique in pieces.

(Houellebecq is writing about terrorist bombs and sex resorts. Haley kind of digs the nihilistic vibe.)

"Fuck it," she tells the others. "Let's do it."

204.

The next few days are unbearable.

"You have to go home," Jordan tells Haley. "Make peace with your mom, succumb to her demands for a week or two. Be the perfect daughter for a while."

(*Be Tinsley*, Haley thinks.)

"Then, when she thinks everything's perfect, we hit her," Jordan says. "Kablamo."

Kablamo.

205.

So Haley goes home. Walks through the front door and it's like her mom didn't even notice she was gone.

"Hi, sweetheart," she says, a big plastic smile on her face. "What are you doing today?" Then she frowns, leans in closer. "Your face looks dry. Have you been moisturizing like I showed you?"

Haley sighs and puts down her bag. Remembers what Jordan said about being good. "I guess I haven't been doing it right," she tells her mom. "Can you show me again?"

206.

Haley endures.

She endures her mom's beauty suggestions. Her mom's weight-loss tips. She tries hot yoga with her mom, and the Stair-Master. She even tags along to the gym to see *Johan*, her mom's lecherous twentysomething 'roid-monkey personal trainer.

Johan spends the whole hour fondling Haley while pretending to show her how to "refine her technique." Haley fends him off as best she can while maintaining a sunny disposition, for her mom's sake.

("Don't smile too wide, sweetheart. You'll get laugh lines.")

As the week progresses, Haley begins to gain a deeper understanding of her mom's life. She notices how desperately her mom clings to what remains of her beauty, how obsessively she works through her skincare routine morning and night, how she dresses to flatter, how she forces herself to smile small, avoid sunlight, eat smaller portions.

Haley also sees how her dad ignores her mom when she's talking. She sees how her mom tries to keep his attention, make him laugh, engage in conversation. How her dad barely looks up from his magazine, or his phone, when she's speaking.

Haley sees how her mom could feel, you know, marginalized. She's lived her whole life in a world where beauty is her only currency, and now her fortune is slipping away.

It's sad.

Pathetic, really.

And it explains why Haley's mom nags Haley so incessantly about her own looks. About her weight. About her appearance.

Haley realizes that her mom isn't a bad person. She means well. She's like E's dad, probably. She wants what's best for her children. She's just clearly incapable of imagining a world where beauty isn't the only quality that matters. But that's not her fault, is it?

Eventually, Haley begins to feel sorry for her mom. She begins—amazingly—to feel empathy.

She starts to feel like maybe . . . maybe she should think of a new Fix.

Haley's trying to figure out a way to inform the Pack she needs a little more time. Then her mom tells her she has a surprise.

207.

"No peeking!"

Haley covers her eyes in the passenger seat of her mom's Boxster. Resists the urge to sneak a look. She's been hiding her eyes ever since they drove over the bridge, trying to enjoy the moment, smiling despite herself—

(just not too wide).

(Haley hasn't spent this much time alone with her mom since, like, *ever*.)

So Haley sits in the passenger seat, a dumb grin on her face, feeling silly as she hides her eyes behind her hands, but feeling happily curious, too. Her mom hasn't given any hints, just came into Haley's room this morning with a huge smile on her face and announced they had a big day together. She'd practically dragged Haley out to the Boxster, the smile never wavering—

(so much for the laugh lines)

—and giggled like a little girl, all the way to the bridge. Now, Haley's pretty well given up trying to guess where they're going. She just sits there and listens to her mom sing along to the radio, feels the warmth of the sun on her skin and the wind in her hair and feels, you know, happy.

Her mom drives for fifteen or twenty minutes. Stopping and starting, turning left and right, until Haley's half convinced her mom's taking detours just to confuse her. But then she feels the Porsche slow and turn into a driveway. Her mom kills the engine.

"Okay, sweetheart," she says. "You can open your eyes now."

Haley lowers her hands. Blinks in the sudden sunlight. They're in a parking lot south of downtown, near the general hospital. They're at a private medical clinic, Haley sees. Her heart sinks.

DOCTOR RICCARDO MILANI, the sign out front reads. COSMETIC PLASTIC SURGERY.

208.

"She told me I could have whatever I wanted," Haley tells the others. "A nose job. A boob job. Botox. Lip injections. Whatever I wanted, like I would *finally* be beautiful."

The others make general sounds of disgust. "She's clearly insane," Jordan says. "You're smoking hot."

"You're just, like, *alternative*," Paige says. "I don't see why that's a bad thing."

"You definitely don't need plastic surgery," E says, awkward as ever.

Haley stares out at her mom's boutique through Jordan's Tesla's windshield. It's dark, after midnight, and Main Street is deserted. "Whatever," Haley sighs. "It's just the last fucking straw."

209.

What Haley doesn't tell the others:
>   She was tempted.
>>   And that's probably what pisses her off the most.

210.

"So that's the lengthy preamble." Haley gestures out the window. The Côte d'Azur, abandoned for the night. "And now we're here."

"Amen," Jordan says. "So let's bomb some shit."

211.

They're dressed in all black, as usual.

Black shoes.

Black pants.

Black shirts.

Black hats.

(Bank robber *chic*.)

Haley and Paige and Jordan and E sit low in the Tesla, three or four storefronts down from the Côte d'Azur. The bomb's in the trunk; Haley helped Jordan and E sneak it out of E's house.

(It looks like a cartoon bomb, just kitchenware and bare wires. It doesn't look dangerous at all. But Jordan swears it will *seriously* fuck up the store.)

Haley's heart is pounding. She's surprised she feels so nervous. She's pretty much over getting stressed out for Fixes. There's the adrenaline rush, sure, but there's never any fear anymore.

Trashing some shitty tabloid's office is a lot different than blowing up your mom's pride and joy, though. And even Allen Headley's gated driveway seems a lot easier to infiltrate than Main Street Capilano, even if the street is deserted.

Jordan catches her eye in the rearview mirror. "Yes or no," he says. "Go or no-go. It's your call."

Haley closes her eyes and sees Milani again. Sees the

light in her mom's eyes as she talked with the doctor.

(*Finally* beautiful.)

(*Finally.*)

"Let's just do this already," she says, before she pussies out.

212.

Jordan stays behind. Aims his phone at the storefront.

"I'll keep the engine running," he tells the others. "Pick up some B-roll. You deliver the package and get out of there quick."

"Yeah," Haley says. "We're not sticking around."

She and Paige follow E out of the Tesla and around to the trunk. E picks up the bomb as Haley reaches for the tire iron Jordan stashed beside it.

"For the window," she tells E, who is looking at her funny.

"Why couldn't you just steal a key?"

"Because the *police*," Paige says. "They would know who could get their hands on a key, right?"

Haley nods. "Exactly."

E carries the bomb. Haley and Paige walk beside him, three figures in black, one holding a tire iron, another carrying a GoPro, and the third a bulky backpack. Not suspicious at all.

The store is a couple doors down. Haley stops in front of the picture window. The store is shadows, but Haley can see the silhouettes of racks and displays, stripes and crazy patterns, halter tops and bikini bottoms, straps everywhere. Tiny swaths of fabric with ridiculous price tags. And Tinsley, everywhere, her model pout and perfect body plastered on the wall and the aisle ends, her poster propped in the window.

Haley studies her sister's face. Hefts the tire iron and

aims square at Tinsley's pretty button nose.

(SMASH.)

No alarm sounds. It could be a silent alarm, or it could be that Haley's mom just doesn't think bathing-suit-related crimes occur in Capilano. Either way, Haley doesn't plan to stick around to find out. She sweeps the tire iron across the remains of the window, clears the broken shards. Then she takes the GoPro from Paige and climbs into the store.

"Come on," she tells the others. "We'll put it by the cash register."

E follows Haley into the store. Paige stays outside, playing lookout. The glass crunches under E's feet. Haley leads him into the gloom, down the aisles to the cash register. She knows this place by heart, but it's still weird to be in here in darkness.

Haley steps aside so E can walk past her. He lays the bomb at the base of the sales counter. Haley surveys the store one last time. Films the stillness, the shadows.

Then she and E book it back outside to Paige and Jordan and the Tesla.

213.

E opens the passenger door as Haley and Paige slip into the back seats. The street is still dark and empty. No cars have passed. Nobody's out walking.

E slides into the passenger seat and closes the door with a *thud*. The sound seems to echo off the storefronts. Haley peers over his shoulder at the front of the Côte d'Azur.

(She can hardly tell the window's broken, from here. The store is dark. It looks like normal. It looks like they could just drive away and nothing would have changed.)

(It's all going to change, though. Very soon.)

Jordan glances at Haley in the rearview. Haley meets his eyes. "Let's do this." Jordan nods and shifts the car into gear, pulls out halfway into the street. Hands his phone back to Haley.

"On my signal," he says. "E, you're on camera duty."

E points the GoPro at the Côte d'Azur as Jordan pulls out into the driving lane and stays there, the car aimed toward the boutique, a few storefronts down. Haley takes the phone, her heart pounding, aims it toward her mom's store like a remote.

"You don't have to point it like that—" E starts to tell her. But Jordan cuts him off.

"Go," he tells Haley.

Haley presses the send button. There's a brief pause, while the signal transmits. Then the entire front of the Côte d'Azur disappears in a burst of light.

214.

The blast is LOUD.

The explosion breaks the window in the Côte d'Azur's door and the windows in the neighboring storefronts.

The Tesla *rocks* from the force of it. Car alarms go off immediately, a whole chorus. Smoke billows out through the empty picture window, and brightly colored bathing suits drift through the air and land on the pavement, strappy one-pieces and skimpy bikini tops, some of them torn ragged, but most of them whole, blown out of the boutique like shrapnel.

Haley searches the smoke as Jordan steps on the go pedal, but she can't see Tinsley's face anywhere.

215.

Jordan reverses down the street, away from the smoke and the storefront and the bathing suit carnage. Executes a quick three-point turn so the Tesla is facing west, toward Marine Drive and Jordan's dad's mansion. Haley twists in her seat to watch the Côte d'Azur disappear in the distance, just a thick cloud of gray smoke against the black sky. She can hear the sirens now. Jordan's driving too slow.

Faster, she thinks. *Drive this freaking car faster.*

But of course Jordan has this all thought out, and if he drives like a maniac, they'll probably get pulled over. So Jordan drives normal, just four kids on their way home from something totally innocent.

(Just don't ask why they're wearing all black.)

Jordan drives away from the town center. The road loops into the forest and along the shoreline, and the lights of the first mansions appear between the trees. A police car screams past, red and blue lights piercing the darkness, and Haley doesn't breathe until it's around the next corner.

Jordan finds her eyes in the rearview mirror again, and Paige and E turn to look at each other too, and they all kind of exhale and laugh a bit, and Haley is glad the others were as freaked out as she was.

They keep driving until they reach Jordan's house. They pass more police cars, but none of them slow down. Jordan reaches his driveway, hits the clicker to open the gate. The gate slides open, and then it slides closed behind the Tesla, and Haley follows E and Paige and Jordan out onto Jordan's driveway, and it's so quiet out here that they can still hear the explosion, ringing in their ears.

216.

CAPILANO POLICE RULE FOUL PLAY IN CÔTE D'AZUR EXPLOSION

The explosion that ripped through the popular swimwear boutique Côte d'Azur two nights ago was caused by a bomb, a Capilano Police detective announced this morning.

"This was a professionally constructed bomb," Detective Tom Dawson told the *Herald*. "A textbook IED, designed for destruction. Whoever did this knew what they were doing."

Dawson would not comment when asked if the department has any leads in the case, nor would he speculate as to whether the bombing bears any connection to other seemingly random acts of destruction that have occurred in Capilano this summer.

"We're exploring all possibilities," Detective Dawson told the *Herald*. "The department won't rest until these cases are solved and the perpetrators brought to justice."

217.

"'Professionally constructed,'" Jordan reads from his phone. "'Whoever did this knew what they were doing.'" He grins across the Tesla at E. "What do you know, E? We're bona fide terrorists."

E sips from his Fiji water and reaches for Jordan's phone. "Eyes on the road," he says. "You may be a terrorist, but you can't text and drive."

"Who's texting?" Jordan hands the phone over. "I'm just reading the news."

"Whatever," E says. "I still think you overdid it with that Vine."

It's Monday morning, and E has a killer hangover. He and Jordan saw Calvin Harris at the Roxy on Saturday night, and then Jordan knew a guy who was throwing a warehouse party somewhere by the docks. E can't remember much about what happened after, except that he drank a lot and wound up tangled in Jordan's sheets this morning.

(Haley skipped the party. She went home the morning after the bomb—

"Went to be with her family," Jordan said. "It would look pretty damn suspicious if she just disappeared right now, don't you think?"

—and Paige begged off after the Calvin Harris show. She said she had to get up early to work on ███████'s movie, but she's been kind of *weird* since the bomb went off, anyway.)

Now E and Jordan are heading to E's house. E needs fresh clothes, and probably a shower. He's already running late for his volunteering thing. And he's worried about the Pack's latest Vine. The Côte d'Azur bombing.

Jordan made Haley post it. As far as E's concerned, it's borderline incriminating. It's sure as hell not fun and games. A close shot of the bomb. GoPro footage of the Côte d'Azur. Close-up on Tinsley Keefer's face.

And then the blast.

Haley's laughter.

The Pack logo.

The tagline: "Beauty is in the eye of the bomb holder."

218.

"It's too obvious," E tells Jordan as they drive. "They're going to suspect Haley. If the cops see that Vine, they'll know for sure. It's her mom's store, after all."

Jordan speeds through a yellow light. "What kind of crazy person would blow up her own mother's store?"

"Well, Haley, apparently."

"Yeah, but the police don't know that. Haley's been the perfect daughter all week. Right now she's probably, like, agreeing to get a boob job just to cheer her mom up. No one's going to suspect her."

Jordan rounds a corner too fast, and E winces from the g-forces. His head throbs. "So who do you think they'll investigate, then?" he says. "They have to have some kind of theory."

Jordan shrugs. "They'll probably pin it on some crackpot. Some nut they've been looking for an excuse to arrest—but not us."

E thinks about it, and he decides Jordan's right. Still, it's hard not to worry. A bomb is a pretty big deal.

Jordan slows for a stop sign. "You have to stop worrying so much," he says, reaching over to rest his hand on E's upper thigh.

(His fingers trace circles, and E leans over to kiss him, but Jordan draws back a little bit, teasing.)

"You just have to trust me," Jordan says. "Everything's going to be fine."

(There is a voice in E's brain that doesn't completely believe Jordan.)

(But E's getting pretty good at ignoring that voice.)

219.

Jordan parks the Tesla at the curb across from E's driveway, and E leads him into the house. Down the stairs to his bedroom.

It's dark down there. It's a lot smaller than Jordan's bedroom. E's self-conscious of everything as Jordan stands in the doorway, looking around.

"Wow," Jordan says, studying the dusty trophy shelf, the bookcase, the one piece of art on E's walls—

(a framed print of his grandfather's campaign poster his dad gave him for Christmas one year).

"So this is where the Connelly Man prepares for a life of greatness."

E looks around, trying to see the room the way Jordan sees it. His academic achievement medals and trophies on the shelf. A couple of old rugby awards, because his dad lettered in rugby at Stanford. A collection of cast-off legal textbooks on the bookshelf, a couple of old comic books and the odd novel E's never had time to read. His cluttered desk, his messy closet. The twin bed he's had since he was, like, eight.

(Jordan has a walk-in closet, a private bathroom, and a private sunroom. He has a king-size bed, and his walls are decorated with framed, limited-edition Japanese language posters for his dad's movies, and fliers and art by big-name artists who Jordan knows personally.

Jordan's room is a castle.)

"I'm sorry you have to see this place like this," E says, digging through his closet for a clean shirt. "My dad thinks a Connelly Man should know hardship, apparently."

Jordan scoffs. "Like your dad knows anything about hardship. He probably had a team of personal servants growing up."

"A maid," E says. "That's all I need."

Jordan grins that wicked grin. Puts down the Student of the Year plaque he's holding and comes across the room to E.

"I'll send mine right over," he says, his hand on E's chest. "Or maybe you should just move in with me."

He has that look in his eye, the mischievous sexy look that more or less guarantees trouble. He pushes E back onto the bed, straddles him. The frame groans, and E opens his mouth to protest, fend Jordan off. "I'm going to be *so* late for work."

"Forget work," Jordan says, pressing his mouth against E's. "Liam's not like those pricks at HH&B. He won't care."

E's about to protest, thinking, *Liam might very well care, and anyway, I don't want to be a dick to him*, but then Jordan's pushing his tongue into his mouth, and E realizes he doesn't possess the power to tell Jordan to stop, so he shuts up and kisses Jordan back instead.

220.

Jordan has E's shirt off when the floorboards creak upstairs. E freezes. *Shit.*

(Nobody's supposed to be home right now.)

Jordan catches the look in E's eye. Lets him sit up. "What's wrong?"

"Someone's here," E says, looking around for his shirt.

"Yeah, I heard that. So?" Jordan arches an eyebrow. "You're almost eighteen, E. You're not twelve."

"As if that matters." Footsteps upstairs, but E can't tell if they're his dad's or his mom's. "They don't know about us. They don't know I'm, you know . . ."

"Gay?" Jordan laughs. "You're such a dumbass. We're adults. We use condoms. Why should it matter who we're fucking?"

Footsteps on the *stairs* now, coming down to the bedroom, coming in hot.

(E can't find his shirt anywhere.)

Shit. Shit. Shit.

"Roger Dodger," E tells Jordan. "My dad freaking *beat up* that gay guy in San Francisco. What do you think he'll do to us?"

"He isn't going to do shit. Calm down."

"I can't calm down." E exhales. *"Where in the hell is my shirt?"*

The footsteps stop outside E's door. The house goes quiet. Jordan reaches behind himself and fishes out E's T-shirt. Hands it over, but E's barely paying attention.

(It's like the whole house is listening, now.)

Three knocks at the door, loud, sharp, authoritative. Then E's dad's voice booms from outside. "Eric," he says. "Are you in there?"

221.

Jordan's still smiling like this is the funniest thing in the world.

Shit.

E can *feel* his dad waiting for an answer. "I'm here," he calls back. "Just give me a second."

E pulls his shirt over his head. Stands and crosses to the door. Collects himself.

"Dad, hey," he says as he pulls the door open.

"Senator Connelly," Jordan says from the bed. "How's it going?"

E's dad looks past E and into the bedroom. Takes in the mess, the rumpled bed, *Jordan.*

(His dad is dressed for travel, holding an overnight bag.)

"Going on another trip?"

E's dad frowns. "Honolulu," he says. "I'm speaking at a convention. Just stopped by to pick up my luggage." He pauses, and his brow turns into canyons again. "What are you doing home? Shouldn't you be at your internship?"

E fakes a cough. "I'm not feeling so good."

(This isn't exactly a lie, but E knows a hangover isn't going to get him any sympathy points.)

"I'm going to make up the missed time tomorrow."

(This isn't technically a lie either. E *could* stay late.)

"I'm working on stats problem sets instead. Jordan just dropped by to make sure I'm not, you know, dying."

(Okay, now *this* is a lie.)

"Honolulu, huh?" Jordan says. "That's rad. Do you think you'll have any time for, like, surfing?"

"Surfing." E's dad looks at him like he's insane. "No, I won't be doing any surfing. This isn't in any way a vacation."

"Oh," Eric says. "Too bad."

E's dad studies him. Disapproving, like anyone who stays home sick is the same kind of monster who would go to the beach in Hawaii—

(definitely no Connelly Man).

"I should get back to it," E says, a big, cheesy fake smile on his face. "What time does your plane leave?"

"Hmm?" his dad says. "The flight's in an hour and a half." He looks past E again. Takes a long hard look at Jordan. Then his eyes go back to E, and his forehead goes all Mariana Trench.

"Eric, your shirt is on inside out," he says. "And if you think I don't see your friend trying to pull his socks back on, you're both kidding yourselves." He looks at E, hard. "What's really going on here?"

E feels his face flush. "It's not what you think," he tells his dad. But he can tell from his dad's thundercloud expression that it's pointless to even try.

222.

"You were fooling around down here," E's dad says. "You haven't been home in days, but you brought your friend over to have *sex* in *my house*. And now you have the gall to lie to my face about it."

"So what?" E replies. It's out of his mouth before he knows he's saying it. "Are you actually going to stand there and judge me? You're not exactly, like, a paragon of virtue."

His dad's face is turning angry red. "We don't raise Connelly Men to be morally bankrupt," he says, his voice trembling. "I've put up with a lot of bullshit from you this summer, Eric. But I will *not* tolerate this kind of perversity."

E can't think of an answer that won't get him disowned. It doesn't matter. Jordan butts in.

"So what are you going to do, *Senator?*" he asks. "You going to kick his ass like you beat up that *faggot* in San Francisco? Are you going to teach him a lesson?"

E's dad spins at Jordan, furious. "You did this. *You* did this to my son."

"I'd say we did it to each other, but whatever turns you on." Jordan winks at E as he stands up from the bed. "We were going to fuck around in E's bed like a couple of big gay homos, but you had to come down and cock-block us. I guess we'll have to take this party somewhere else. Wouldn't want you to have to commit another hate crime."

E's dad does look ready to unleash another beating. "*Get. Out.*"

"What did I just say? I'm leaving." Jordan sidles in close to E. He has his arm around E's waist before E can react. "But I'm taking your son with me."

(*Dude! Shut the fuck up!*)

E's dad makes a move toward them, and E thinks, *This is it, Roger Dodger redux—*

(*or maybe he'll just murder me first*).

"Do it," E says, stepping in front of him. "Go on and hit him, you hypocrite. And then watch how I tell Mom what you're really about."

But his dad stops himself. He's red all over and, like, shaking with rage, but he doesn't hit anybody.

"Don't come back, Eric. I won't have this filth in my home."

E's legs are jelly. He feels numb. He lets Jordan push him away from his dad and out to the hallway. Up the stairs.

"You should try practicing this filth sometime, *Senator*," Jordan calls back. "Maybe then you wouldn't be such a douchebag."

223.

E follows Jordan.

He follows Jordan out through the back door and across the backyard, and down the alley and around the block to the curb where his Tesla is parked. He climbs in the passenger seat, and Jordan drives away, and E doesn't look back at his house or his dad; he doesn't really look anywhere.

He just sits in the car and lets Jordan drive them somewhere, while he tries to figure out how he's supposed to be feeling right now.

224.

"That was shitty, what happened with your dad," Jordan says. "I'm sorry he caught us."

Jordan and Eric are sailing up the coast in the Sundancer, north of the city. They passed Lighthouse Park a few hours ago, and they're still going. There aren't many boats on the water. The land is mostly forest and rock, a few stubby islands. They're almost completely alone.

Eric has calmed down, a little bit. He's kind of, maybe, a little bit *happy*, actually. A little bit *relieved*. His mom was going to find out eventually, and his dad was never going to like it.

Still, though.

"I can't ever go home again," Eric says. "He won't let me back in the house."

Jordan rolls his eyes. "Why would you actually *want* to go back there? You want to live with that guy? He's an asshole."

"What else would I do?" Eric says. "He's my dad."

"You're almost eighteen. You'll officially be an adult soon. You can do whatever you want."

"Not all of us are as freaking loaded as you. I don't exactly have access to unlimited funds."

"So you stay with me for a while. Figure out what you want. You don't have to go back there."

"And what about law school?"

"There are, like, hundreds of law schools, E. You're a

smart human being. If you really want to go to law school, you'll get in. You don't need your dad for that."

Jordan disappears into the galley. Comes back with a drink. "Here," he says, handing Eric the glass. "Look around. We're in paradise, just you and me. We have enough fuel, drugs, and groceries to last us for days."

He settles in beside Eric. Pulls him close. "Do you really want to spend that time thinking about your dad?"

225.

Jordan and E are away for three days.

(It's actually really nice.)

E gets over the stuff with his dad. He pushes it away and tries not to think about it. Jordan helps. He's a good distraction. They drive the boat into some inlet in the middle of nowhere, drop the anchor, swim, cook food, and fool around, and repeat the process.

"It's just you and me," Jordan tells E as they're sunning themselves on the front of the boat. "Haley and Paige are important, too—they're integral, obviously—but when it comes down to it, E, we have to decide who we can trust."

"We can't trust the girls?" E asks.

Jordan purses his lips. "Haley's probably cool," he says. "She's a ride-or-die chick. But Paige is already bugging out; have you noticed?"

E nods. He has noticed.

"It's like she doesn't believe in the cause anymore. Like she's having second thoughts. Would you agree?"

E's pretty sure Paige *is* having second thoughts. In fact, she's practically told him this.

"Sooner or later, the day's going to come when we have to decide," Jordan says again. "We have to decide who we can trust."

"We can trust Paige," E says. "She's not going to, like, snitch on us or anything."

Jordan lies back. Stares up at the cloudless blue sky. "I just think we should be careful. We've made so much progress so far, but the best is yet to happen. And when it comes down to it, E, I need to know you're with me."

"I'm with you," E says.

Jordan props himself up on his arm. "You swear it? You're in this to the end?"

"To the very end," E says. "I swear."

Jordan sits back down again. "Good. That's all I needed to hear."

226.

(It should be obvious that this is going to turn out to be A VERY BAD DECISION.)

227.

To the end.

It sounds good when Jordan says it. It has a nice ring to it. E lies there on the deck and closes his eyes and thinks about how good life could be, if it really were him and Jordan. If they could go out like boyfriends and be a couple in public, maybe move in together and, you know, play house.

They could still go to shows and warehouse parties and do crazy things, but at the end of the night, they would be alone together, just the two of them. And E would feel safe, and he could live in *the Moment*, without ever having to worry that he was fucking things up.

(And maybe E would be good for Jordan, too. He could help Jordan figure out what he's going to do with his life, and, you know, work through the Suicide Pack stuff, and the stuff with *his* parents.

Maybe they could be good for each other.)

The sun is starting to drift down over the islands to the west. The sky is starting to turn purple and gold. E rolls over on his towel and looks at Jordan until he looks back.

"What?" he says, lowering his Wayfarers. He's smiling, a little bit. E leans over and kisses him.

"Nothing," E says. "I just think I'm falling for you."

228.

E and Jordan tie the boat up at Capilano Marina three days later.
They're sunburned and salt-encrusted and tired. Their phones are
full of missed calls. Texts they've ignored. Messages on their voice
mail.

There are, like, eighteen missed calls from E's home
number—

>(Must be his mom, E figures, because his dad would
>see calling as a form of weakness. He would expect E
>to come crawling back.).

There's a missed call from the Railtown Health Center, a
voice mail from Liam asking E how he's doing—

>(he'd called in sick from the Sundancer).

There are a few texts from Paige and Haley, too, but
nothing serious. E puts his phone away. Debates turning it off
again. He isn't ready to be back in the real world, not yet. He's
wishing they could turn around and sail away on that boat again.
He's kind of wishing he and Jordan could just sail away together,
like, permanently.

Like, forever.

KIK -- CAPILANO HIGH PRIVATE MESSAGE GROUP
— 08/06/16 — 01:44 PM

USERNAME: Anonymous-9
MESSAGE: Ooh, scary terrorist bombers. Let's
    see how tough the Pack is when they
    can't hide anymore. It's only a matter
    of time . . .

229.

There are about a hundred new replies on the Capilano High message group. Nearly all of them are from kids badgering Anonymous-9 to give up what he/she knows about the Pack.

"Fuck that guy," Jordan tells E. "He's trying to steal our fucking fame for himself."

"It has to be someone from Cap, though," E tells the others. "He's in the school message thread, whoever it is."

"So who the hell knows us?" Haley says. "Who wants beef with the *Suicide Pack?*"

They think about it, all four of them. There's one obvious answer.

"Callum Fulchrest," E says. "You guys stole his dad's painting. You publicly shamed him. If he figures out it was you, he could be getting revenge."

Haley shakes her head. "Callum's in Barcelona. Anyway, he's a chump. This isn't his style."

"But what if it is, though?"

"Whoever it is, they sound pretty cocky," Paige says. "Maybe we should tone it down for a while. Lay off the Fixes."

Jordan gives E a meaningful look.

"Or the Vines, anyway," Haley says. "The last one was pretty obvious. Maybe we don't need to be *so* freaking bold."

Jordan doesn't respond. He doesn't say anything. He makes the others wait until he's sure they're listening.

"We're not letting this loser push us around," he says. "We're doing this town a service. If this asshole wants to interfere, he can face the consequences."

E and Haley and Paige kind of look at each other.

(Like, *What are the consequences?*)

"Let's watch this guy close," Jordan says. "Maybe we can fix him, too."

230.

You probably already figured it out, but that last chapter?

Total foreshadowing.

Sooner or later, E and the rest of the Pack are going to come to a reckoning with Anonymous-9. You know it, and I know it.

We just don't know how.

231.

E goes back to the Railtown Health Center on Monday morning. It's the first time he's been back since, well, the Côte d'Azur bombing.

"Must have been some kind of food poisoning," Liam says when E walks into the office. "And look, you even got a *tan*."

"I fell asleep in the backyard," E tells him. "It was the first time I slept all week. I was, like, *out*."

Liam gives him a look, like, *Yeah right*.

"Anyway, I'm feeling a lot better now. So what do you need me to do?"

Liam shuffles some papers. "I had this whole big project lined up for you. Something big and fun and, like, *meaningful*. But then you got sick and bailed on me and now I don't really need it done anymore."

"Crap," E says. "Okay. So what should I do instead?"

"Instead?" Liam shrugs, looks around. "I guess you could make a pot of coffee."

232.

So that kind of sucks.

Liam has E on grunt work. Menial tasks. Intern shit:

Making coffee.

Photocopying.

Picking up lunch from the diner down the street.

Cleaning the bathrooms.

Taking out the trash.

(*Bitch work.*)

But whatever.

Liam was ready to give E a solid reference letter without him even walking into the health center. If he wants to be mad that E took off for a week, so be it. Let him hate.

E has other things to focus on.

Better things.

Like Jordan.

233.

Life is good.

E and Jordan celebrate. They party. They live in VIP, in penthouses and lofts, in warehouses and shitty dive bars down by the docks. They take Jordan's Sundancer out to Wreck Beach again, and they bump Y.G. *loud* and piss off the naked hippies. They tan. They drink. They fall asleep by the pool.

(E loses himself in Jordan.)

It never gets boring.

It never gets old.

The police don't come looking. The phone calls from home stop. E's free of EXPECTATIONS. Free of his dad's PLAN.

(Free to be his own CONNELLY MAN.)

They party with Haley and Paige, sometimes, and sometimes they don't. But Jordan and E always go home together.

Always.

(This is paradise.)

E's happy.

He's really freaking happy.

234.

Meanwhile, Haley's just about ready to move out herself.

It's been almost two weeks since the Côte d'Azur bombing. Haley's mom hasn't quit crying since. Haley's dad tolerates it, for a couple of days. Then he gets bored.

"The insurance will cover the damages, Monica," he says. "We'll rebuild the store even better than before."

But Haley's mom isn't having it. "It isn't about the money," she tells Haley, after her dad has checked out and disappeared somewhere. "I put my *heart* and *soul* into that place. And that someone would just destroy it for no reason, it's just—"

She starts crying before she can finish. Haley rubs her back, tries to tell her it's okay.

Tinsley can't come home from Los Angeles. She's stuck doing reshoots on that Sofia Coppola movie. It's on Haley to bring her mom Kleenex and coffee, try to convince her to eat something.

(*For god's sake, grow up,* she's thinking the whole time. *It's just a freaking store.* ~~It's not like I died.~~ *It's not like* Tinsley *died.*)

"At least I won't get fat," her mom says, after refusing Haley's latest offer to, like, make her a sandwich. "But maybe you could fix me a drink, sweetheart."

A couple police officers show up at the house. Detectives, a man and a woman. Haley answers the door, brings them into the kitchen to wait for her mom to come down from her bedroom.

The detectives both look like they're seven feet tall. Every time they look at Haley, she's sure they can tell what she did.

"Do you want some coffee?" she asks. "Or maybe a sandwich?"

The man cop—his name is Dawson—says yes to a ham sandwich. The woman—Richards—only takes coffee. She's tall, but not fat. Haley wonders if she's trying to keep her figure, too.

(#BikiniSeason.)

"I'm sure my mom could get you a discount on a nice swimsuit," she blurts out, before she even knows what she's doing. The cops frown at her, eyebrows raised. "You know, for helping to solve the case."

The cops swap glances. "We haven't solved it yet," Dawson says.

"I know," Haley says. "But, like, if you do."

There's an awkward pause. "I don't think we're allowed to take presents," Richards says finally. "But that's very nice of you to offer."

"Sure," Haley says. "No big deal."

They all go silent again, and Haley listens for her mom but can't hear her. The cops are looking at her some more. "So, do you have any leads?" she asks them. "I guess you guys must be looking pretty hard."

Dawson doesn't say anything. He's just studying Haley. But Richards shakes her head. "No leads yet. We're still waiting on lab reports, canvassing for witnesses, all of that. But you're right; this case is a high priority for us."

Haley nods.

"This may seem like fun and games to the perpetrators, but someone could have been seriously hurt by that bomb,"

Richards continues. "We just want to find these people before they put anyone else at risk."

"And we will," Dawson tells Haley. "We'll catch up to whoever set that bomb. Mark my words."

235.

Jordan and E drive back to Studio City to pick up more explosives. "I blew our whole stash on Haley's Fix," he tells E. "Gotta prepare for my turn, though."

"One bomb wasn't enough?" E replies.

Jordan shakes his head. Downshifts and pulls out into the passing lane. "The Côte d'Azur was just a test run. I had to make sure the bomb actually worked."

"It works," E says. "So what's your target?"

But Jordan just smiles. "Fixes always stay secret, E; you know that. You'll have to wait and see."

236.

They're supposed to meet Mike behind the same studio as last time. Except he's not there when Jordan and E arrive.

Jordan parks the Tesla. Looks around. Pulls out his Galaxy, punches in a number.

"Hey," he says. "It's me. Where are you?" Pause. "No, we're here. Same place as before." Pause. "Mike, I told you it's no problem. Don't make me come over there."

He listens. "Good. We'll be waiting." Then he ends the call.

"Something wrong?" E asks.

Jordan shakes his head, pockets his phone. "He's just being a baby. He'll be here in twenty minutes."

237.

Mike shows up forty minutes later. He pulls up in an old Ford SUV, sits in the truck and doesn't climb out right away. Jordan and E watch him from the Tesla.

"Come on," Jordan mutters. "Don't be such a pussy."

Then the Ford's door swings open, and Mike steps out. He looks smaller than last time, like he shrunk or something. E doesn't have much time to look at him, though, because Jordan's reaching for his door handle and stepping out onto the gravel.

E and Jordan stand in front of the Tesla and wait for Mike to close the distance. He stops maybe ten, fifteen feet away, like he's afraid to come any closer.

"Did you bring the stuff?" Jordan asks him.

Mike doesn't answer.

"The powder," Jordan says. "I told you, we need more of it. Did you bring it?"

Mike seems to be fighting something. He doesn't make eye contact. Finally, he spits on the ground. "I told you, I can't do this anymore. I can't help you boys."

"Why," Jordan says. Flat. It's barely a question.

"That bombing on the North Shore, that bathing suit store. You think I don't know that was you?"

"I don't know what you're talking about," Jordan says.

"You ask me for a couple thousand dollars' worth of explosives. Soon as I give it to you, your neighborhood starts blowing up. Now you come to me wanting more, and you think you're going to get it?"

He doesn't look like he's going to play nice. E's starting to get worried. This guy could sell them out, after all. He could tell the police what he knows.

But Jordan doesn't look worried at all. "First of all, we're not setting off any bombs. We're filming a movie, and we *hate* CGI."

Mike spits again. He doesn't look convinced.

"*Second*, even if we were setting off bombs, what the fuck does it matter? You're still getting paid, aren't you? You still have your job. It would really suck if Grant Studios had to find a new demolitions expert, though, you know?"

Mike laughs. "You can try to threaten me, son, but something tells me I won't be doing a lot of demolitions work for your dad if I'm locked up in jail, either."

"You don't want to go down this road," Jordan says. "You're not going to like where it takes you."

"I believe that." Mike's already turning back to his truck. "Sure seems to have brought me nothing but bullshit so far."

He walks back to the old Ford. Calls over his shoulder at Jordan and E.

"Sorry, boys," he says. "You'll just have to get your kicks some other way."

238.

"He could fuck us over," E says as Jordan speeds the Tesla back toward Capilano—

> (and I mean, like, triple digits, engine humming, lock-you-in-jail speeding).

"He could totally tell the cops that he sold us explosives."

Jordan drives, his jaw set, his right foot to the floor. "He's not going to fuck us over, E. He'd be just as fucked. He sold gunpowder to teenagers. How do you think that would play in court?"

E doesn't say anything. He holds on to the armrest as Jordan slaloms through traffic.

"My dad's Harrison Grant," Jordan continues. "Harrison Grant can afford a better lawyer than some piece-of-shit draft dodger, and Mike knows it.

"He's not going to pull anything," Jordan says. "Ergo, we'll be fine."

239.

"So I guess you have to change your Fix, huh?" E asks Jordan. "Now that we're screwed out of gunpowder."

Jordan glances at E. Downshifts and pulls out to pass some trophy wife in her Lexus. "I'm not changing the Fix."

E blinks. "Wait, what?"

"I'll get the explosives," Jordan says. "One way or another, I'm going to pull this thing off, and it's going to change our freaking lives."

240.

Even E can admit that that's kind of a worrisome comment for Jordan to make. And if E were, you know, in a different headspace, he might be inclined to look more critically at what's going on here.

But E's in Jordan's headspace.

E's living in the Moment.

It's like E's the iron fillings, and Jordan's the magnet. Or maybe E's the moth and Jordan's the flame, and E's drawn to Jordan even though, somewhere deep down, he knows he'll probably get burned.

That's a pretty apt metaphor, actually.

Let's go with that.

241.

Anyway, that's just a speed bump. A minor glitch in *the Moment*. Life remains good.

Even Liam seems happier.

"Wow, you really must be feeling better," he tells E, after E's been back at the health center for a week. "It's like you actually *want* to be here."

"I'm just trying to put the work in," E tells Liam. "Anything I can do to help."

Liam watches as E sweeps the floor. Rubs his chin like he's thinking about something. "Forget about the broom for a second," he says finally. "Come on into my office."

242.

"That project I mentioned the other day," Liam says. "You still want in?"

E cocks his head. "What, the really important one?"

Liam nods. "You've been busting your ass since you came back. It's kind of a waste to only use you for lunch runs."

"I don't mind," E says. "But if you have something else you want me to do . . ."

"We need to raise money. It's a hard sell right now. Giving clean needles to drug addicts isn't exactly the most popular cause in the world."

"Yeah, I kind of noticed."

Liam shuffles some papers. "People don't understand. They hear 'needle exchange' and think we're just enablers. They don't see the other stuff we do here, the counseling and the detox resources we offer. So we don't get the funding we need."

E nods. "I get it. So what do you want me to do?"

Liam reaches in his desk. Pulls out a digital camera, some fancy DSLR, the kind that shoots video. "The director wants me to make a fund-raising video. You can help by interviewing people who use the exchange. I'll put you in contact with some of our success stories. We can quote science to politicians all day long, but someone needs to show the reality. We need to show the public that we actually help."

He slides the camera across the desk. "So what do you think? Are you in?"

243.

E takes the camera. Wanders out through the health center in search of subjects.

It's not as easy as it sounds. Most of the health center's clients are pretty scary. They're dirty and they kind of smell funny. Some are very obviously mentally ill. They all look like they'd rather be left alone.

E gets shot down, like, four or five times. A couple people swear at him. Somebody spits.

"Don't worry about it," Liam says. "This stuff always takes time."

244.

E finds his first interview subject that afternoon. She's a stringy-haired lady about his mom's age, sitting on a milk crate next door to the health center. She's been into the center a couple of times, E remembers. He introduces himself, shows her the camera. She tells him she'll talk if he gives her a dollar.

E finds a couple of bills in his pocket and hands them to her. She takes them, crumples them into her own pocket.

"What do you want to know?" she says, her voice chain-smoker ragged.

E looks through the camera's viewfinder. Makes sure it's recording. "I guess I'm just supposed to ask you your name, and whether you like the health center or not."

The woman's name is Jill. She's forty-three, and she was born back east, in Gloucester, Massachusetts. She wound up on the West Coast because it's warmer than the east, and she's been here longer than E's been alive.

"I've seen you in the health center a few times," E tells her. "We're trying to film a video to show people that it's useful. Is there anything you can say to convince them?"

Jill shrugs. "I don't really know much about the place. I go in when I need a clean needle."

"Do you think it's worthwhile to have a needle exchange in Railtown?" E asks.

"Well, sure."

"Why's that?"

Jill looks at E like he's stupid. E motions to the camera. "For the general public," he says.

Jill laughs, ragged. "Shit, I would have thought that was obvious." Then she looks at the camera, looks out into the street. "I had two friends die of AIDS they got from dirty needles." She looks at E. "How's that?"

"Great," E says. "Uh, who were your friends?"

"Bud Traverse and Casey Z. This was a couple of years ago, before your little center came along." Jill looks out into the street some more, so long that E thinks she's, like, zoned out or something. Then she blinks.

"There's been less people dying since that center opened," she says, pushing herself to her feet. "And that's about all I know about that."

245.

E feels okay about the interview footage.

It's pretty decent stuff, he figures.

(Maybe it's even doing some good in the world.)

Liam seems to like it, anyway.

"This is perfect," he says when E shows him the footage. "This is exactly what we need, Eric. Simple, stark, and *real*. Good job."

"Thanks," E says, even though he really didn't do anything. He's heading back to his car when his phone buzzes—Paige. Calling, not texting.

"Hey, can we talk?" she says, her voice halfway between crying and mad. "I just lost my fucking job."

246.

The Pack convenes at the Cactus Club, on Capilano Beach. They get a four-top in the lounge, show the waitress fake IDs. Order a round of the club's signature drink.

(The Sunset Beach, a vodka soda with peach Slurpee. *Perfect* for those endless summer nights.)

Then Paige lays out the story.

"It's ███████████," she tells them. "He got me that PA job on the movie he's shooting."

The others nod. Yeah, they know this. Get to the juicy bits.

"Anyway, it was all going fine. He's, like, flirty or whatever, but I didn't really think anything of it. He has a fiancée back home in L.A. and stuff."

"Like that ever stopped anyone," Haley says.

Paige rolls her eyes. "Exactly. I met him here about a month ago. We hit it off, I guess, and then he got me this job, and my first day on set, he called me to his trailer and tried to hook up."

The drinks come. Paige waits until the waitress is gone again. She sips her Sunset Beach, and then continues.

"So, I kind of avoided him after that. But today, I got called to his trailer. ████████████ was in there, all by himself. He tried to give me a back massage, and when I told him no, he said if I didn't play along, he would get me fired."

"So what did you do?" Jordan asks.

Paige looks at Jordan like he slapped her. "What the fuck do you think? I got the hell out of there. And, like, ten minutes later, the AD pulled me aside and told me he had to let me go."

She downs the rest of her drink. "So, here I am. Last week of summer and I'm officially too broke to pay for college. Yay me."

247.

"That's bullshit," E says. "Can't you, like, file a complaint?"

"With who?" Haley says. "The police? It's his word against hers. And he's freaking ████████. He's untouchable."

"Anyway, it was pretty under-the-table," Paige says. "I didn't exactly fill out any tax forms. I was working illegally. Nobody's going to take my side."

"Except us," Jordan says.

They all turn to look at him. Jordan gives them that devil-may-care smile. "Well?" he says. "This is *perfect*. It's Paige's turn for a Fix anyway."

"No way," Paige says. "This is not a Fix situation."

"Why not? This is tailor-made. One of the best things about these Fixes is we can solve problems we couldn't solve otherwise, right?"

Paige looks at Haley. "Tell them what you told me."

Haley shakes her head. "It's really not a big deal."

"Tell them."

"*Fine.*" Haley sighs. She looks around the Cactus Club, and leans across the table. "Look, the police came by my house the other day. That detective from the papers, Dawson or whatever. His partner, too. They wanted to know if I knew anything about the bombing."

"And?" E says.

"And I told them I didn't know shit. What do you think?

It's not a big deal, like I said. They obviously don't know anything. I don't even know why I told Paige."

"We still have to be careful," Paige says. "The police have those composite sketches from the Room thing."

"Which don't even look like us," Jordan says. "No one's going to suspect us. And even if they do, who gives a shit? We're actually changing this god-awful place. Aren't you proud?"

"Tell me you don't want to get this sleazeball back for what he did to you," Haley says. "Tell me no part of you whatso-ever is itching to burn this douche with your Fix. Tell me you're fine letting him go on filming his shitty movie while you're out of a job and can't pay your tuition, because you wouldn't be his, like, concubine. Go on, Paige. Tell me."

Paige doesn't say anything. She looks around the table. Her eyes find E's. She studies him for a moment. "What do you think?" she asks. "What should I do?"

E knows what Eric would say.

Eric would preach caution.

Eric would tell Paige to wait until the heat dies down. He would point out that the Capilano police are already sniffing around, that there are Vines out there that could incriminate the whole crew. He would suggest that now might not be the right time to try anything too, you know, *visible*.

Eric would tell the others to THINK about THEIR FUTURES.

(But Eric hasn't been around for a very long time. And *E*, well, he's on a whole different wavelength.)

"This guy sounds like an asshole," E says. "Let's torch him."

248.

They order another round of Sunset Beaches. The mood is celebratory. They lean in close to one another and start to hash out a plan.

"███████████ has this limited-edition Ferrari he *adores*," Paige tells them. "Like, obsesses over. He won't even fly his fiancée up from L.A., but he made the producers pay to have his car sent here."

"That's our target," Jordan says. "Haley can boost it."

Paige shakes her head. "He keeps two security guards posted beside it whenever he's on set. That's, like, their only job, to watch that car. Anyway, it's kitted out with an alarm and an immobilizer. You need the actual key to override the alarm."

"How do you know all this?" Haley says.

"Because ████████████ never shuts up about it. The whole time I was in his trailer he blabbed about his stupid million-dollar car. I could probably tell you the VIN if I thought hard enough."

"Well, he's not on set all the time," Jordan says. "Maybe we just go to where he parks it at night, bring Molotov cocktails, and trash the Ferrari where it stands. No need to drive the piece of shit at all."

"It's parked in the basement of the St. Regis hotel," Paige says. "A private garage, accessible only by room key, and monitored by a parking attendant."

"Security's tight at the St. Regis," Jordan says. "I tried to swipe a fork from the restaurant at Easter brunch and they nearly had me arrested."

"So maybe the Ferrari isn't the answer," E says. "Is there anything else we can try?"

"Nothing as good as trashing his pride and joy," Paige says. "Nothing as *fun*, either."

"The Ferrari is definitely the target." Jordan thinks for a moment or two. Another round of drinks arrives and is consumed. Then Jordan claps his hands.

"Okay," he says. "I have a plan."

249.

Jordan lays out his plan.

It's audacious, obnoxious, stylish, and cinematic. (Dangerous, too.) It's everything a Suicide Pack Fix should be.

"It's a twist on the honey pot," Jordan tells the others. "A little femme-fatale action. Paige tells ███████████ she wants her job back. She's willing to meet him in his room at the St. Regis. She'll do *whatever it takes* to convince him." He pauses. "Of course, the little pervert will know she wants to sleep with him. He'll jump at the chance, because he's a piece of shit."

Haley makes a face. "Gross."

"But what's better than one smoking-hot Capilano girl?" Jordan looks around. "*Two*, obviously. So Paige will bring Haley along. She really, *really* wants her job back."

"Great," Haley says. "So I have to meet this douche, too."

"Once you ladies are in the room, you'll swipe ███████████'s room key, and the keys to the Ferrari. Then you'll get the hell out of there, and—"

"Wait," E says. "I feel like you're glossing over a really important step here. *How* exactly are they supposed to take the keys without ███████████ seeing?"

Jordan looks at E like he's dumb. "There's two of them, E. I'm sure they can come up with a way to distract a sleazebag with one thing on his mind."

E doesn't look convinced.

"Shit, if all else fails, they slip a roofie in his drink. Knock him out cold. Lift the keys, easy, while he's snoring away."

"I have another question," Paige says, raising her hand. "Won't ███████████ figure out pretty quick who stole his car? I mean, we come up there and then his car disappears. And we didn't even sleep with him?"

"I'm *not* sleeping with him," Haley says.

Jordan holds up his hands. "He'll know exactly who stole his precious Ferrari. But he won't do a damn thing about it."

They all stare at Jordan, waiting for the punch line.

"Why not?" E asks.

"Because Haley's seventeen," Jordan says. "And because you'll have pictures. TMZ will build a shrine to us—"

> (*FAMOUS MOVIE STAR CAUGHT IN*
> *UNDERAGE THREESOME!!!*)

"His fiancée will leave him. His reputation will be shot. He'll know it was us, but he won't do a damn thing about it."

250.

They all kind of sit and stare at Jordan in silence for a minute. Another round of Sunset Beaches appears.

"Uh, okay," Haley says. "So after me and Paige grab the keys and skedaddle, what happens next? We just get in this guy's car and drive away?"

Jordan shakes his head. "You rendezvous with E in the lobby. Hand the keys off."

"Wait," E interrupts. "Why me?"

"You look kind of like ███████████," Jordan says. "Same height and build, similar hair color." He blows a kiss across the table. "You're much cuter, of course."

"Younger, anyway," Haley says.

"Gee, thanks," E says.

"You'll be wearing a hat to conceal your true identity. You and Paige will take the keys down to the garage. Drive away in the Ferrari. It will be dark, and the parking attendant will be looking into your high beams. He won't get a good view before he's eating your dust.

"You get the hell out of there," Jordan continues. "Go for a joyride. Meet Haley and me up at Fincher's Bluff." He winks. "We'll bring the Molotov cocktails."

251.

So that's Jordan's plan.

    That's how Saturday night is supposed to go.

(You can probably figure out that Saturday night doesn't quite go as planned.)

KIK -- CAPILANO HIGH PRIVATE MESSAGE GROUP
— 08/20/16 — 08:31 PM

USERNAME: SuIcIdEpAcK
MESSAGE: Wherefore art thou, Romeo?

252.

Saturday night. Jordan and E drop off Paige and Haley outside the St. Regis. They park Jordan's Tesla in the public beach parking lot next door to wait for the signal.

("Text us when you have the keys," Jordan tells Haley and Paige. "Text us '911' if anything goes sour.")

It's a beautiful Capilano summer evening. The last of the sunset is just disappearing behind the islands to the west. The city skyline is a bright wall to the east. And ahead, in the bay, freighters lie at anchor, their lights shimmering off the black water.

"It's kind of romantic out here," Jordan says, grinning at E. "You want to fool around while we wait?"

"What, now?" E frowns. He's not exactly, like, *in the mood*. He's too busy trying to rehearse the plan, hoping he doesn't get recognized, wishing he didn't have wear this goofy fedora.

Jordan laughs. "Relax," he says. "I'm just messing with you."

E relaxes as much as he's able. His feet tap a rhythm on the Tesla's plush carpet. He checks his reflection in the mirror, realizes he looks as stressed as he feels. He stares out at the water, tries to calm his breathing. Waits for Jordan's phone to buzz.

253.

Paige and Haley enter the St. Regis through the side entrance. They're wearing sundresses and big floppy hats. They look like normal Cap girls—apart from the duffel bag.

(It doesn't matter. Nobody sees them.)

There's a ladies' restroom beyond the bank of elevators. They skirt the edge of the lobby and hurry toward it. They keep their heads down, the hats covering their faces. Haley checks the restroom to make sure it's empty. It is. They both disappear inside.

They emerge, new women, twenty minutes later. Haley's in Balenciaga, Paige Alexander McQueen. Hair impeccable, makeup to the nines. They're bombshells, traffic stoppers. They're dressed to *kill*—

(hold that thought).

They keep their heads down as they wait for the elevators. Eyes downcast. The elevator dings. The doors slide open. Haley and Paige walk inside.

████████████ has a top-floor suite. It's a long way up. Haley and Paige check their reflections in the mirrored door. They fix their hair. They meet each other's eyes. Haley smiles and squeezes Paige's hand.

(*"This is going to be awesome."*)

The elevator dings again. The doors slide open. Paige squeezes Haley's hand back. Then they walk out to the hall.

254.

███████████ is shorter than he looks in the movies. Older. He's not quite as hot, either, without the magic of Photoshop and an army of hair and makeup artists.

(*E actually* is *cuter*, Haley thinks.)

███████████ is wearing, like, sweatpants and a Prada hoodie. He's leaning against the doorframe. He leers at Paige and Haley as they walk off the elevator.

"So glad you made it, babe," he says. "Does your friend want a job too?"

Haley stifles the urge to throw up.

"She doesn't need a job," Paige tells him, her voice all syrup and seduction. "She's just here to help me convince you to hire me back."

"What a great friend." The movie star holds out his hand to Haley. "And beautiful, too. I'm ███████████," he says. "Please, come inside."

255.

It plays out like it's supposed to, at first.

██████████'s suite is vast. Multiple bedrooms, minimalist furniture, floor-to-ceiling windows with a sweeping ocean view.

(Somewhere, hidden speakers are playing The Weeknd at an unobtrusive volume.)

Haley spots the keys to the Ferrari immediately. They're hard to miss. They're sitting on the coffee table in the living room area, directly in front of Haley and Paige as ██████████ ushers them to the couch.

(Paige thinks she sees a room key on a side table by the door.)

(Perfect.)

The movie star sits down opposite Paige and Haley. Leans back and studies them both like they're candy. "*So,*" he says. "Convince me."

Paige launches into some spiel about how she really needs her job, and she'll do anything to get it back.

(Haley kind of tunes her out.)

The spiel goes on and on, Paige looking remorseful and desperate and, like, vulnerable, the asshole pervert movie star lapping it up. Then he holds up his hand to stop her. "You didn't come here to *talk*, did you?"

(*BARF.*)

He picks up a remote, and The Weeknd gets louder. Paige and Haley look at each other. "I need a drink," Haley tells ████████████. "Will you make us a drink?"

Paige stands. "And I need to go freshen up. I'll be right back."

The movie star doesn't look pleased, but he rolls with it. "Drinks," he says, standing and walking to a wet bar in a corner. "What's your poison?"

Haley eyes the car keys on the table. Eyes ████████████. Can't think of a way to swipe them without him noticing.

On to Plan B.

"Vodka soda," she tells ████████████. Pastes a smile on her face. "And make mine *strong*."

256.

The movie star is just setting the drinks on the coffee table when Paige calls his name from the bathroom. She pokes her head out. "Can you help me with something in here?" she asks.

█████████ smiles. There's nothing in the world he'd like better. He hurries over to Paige. Paige and Haley lock eyes, and Haley reaches for her handbag.

(Plan B is a little concoction Jordan cooked up. "Just like a roofie, except faster," he told Haley and Paige. "It should knock him out cold in, like, five or ten minutes."

"Five *or* ten?" Haley said. "How accurate are your estimates? I don't want to be stuck with this asshole longer than I need to be."

"Ten minutes, tops," Jordan assured her. "You can handle yourself for that long, right?")

Haley pours Plan B in █████████'s vodka soda. Stirs it around until the powder dissolves clear. Picks up her phone and texts Jordan.

Go time.

257.

This is where things start to go sideways.

For starters, the movie star doesn't touch his drink. Not even once. He comes back and sits down and makes small talk for a minute, and then he looks at Paige and Haley with that sick smile again, like, *Put up or shut up.*

And Haley tries to stall by pretending to be distracted by the, like, *amazing* view, and ███████████ takes the bait and stands behind her and points out the city landmarks, his hand on her hip in the grossest way possible.

(And he still hasn't touched his drink.)

And Haley tries to stall some more, wanders around like an airhead, admiring the art on the walls and the furniture and, like, the freaking *fridge*. And ███████████ plays along, but he *still* never touches his drink.

And finally, Haley's out of ideas, and the movie star has her cornered, and he calls Paige over.

"No more bullshit," he says.

258.

Paige and Haley look at each other.

███████████ leers at them.

Haley wonders how far Paige is willing to go for this Fix.
(Not much further, it turns out.)

Paige shakes her head. "I can't do this," she tells Haley.

███████████ laughs a mean laugh.

"Just what I thought."

259.

"There was a room key on that end table," ████████ tells Haley and Paige. "Which one of you took it?"

Haley and Paige look at each other. Paige's eyes go wide. *Play dumb*, Haley's thinking. *Deny everything.*

████████ walks over to Paige. "I'm guessing it was you. Probably on your way to the bathroom, am I right?"

"I don't know what you're talking about," Paige says. "I didn't take your room key."

"Bullshit." ████████ reaches for Paige's handbag. "Let me see that purse."

Haley starts to interject. ████████ stops her with his hand. "You stay right there," he tells her. "I'll deal with you next. I'm *dying* to know what you put in my drink."

He smiles at Haley, a cold smile, and beyond him, Haley can see Paige is panicking. Shit.

"You thought I didn't notice?" The movie star laughs. "Try again. Now, do I have to call security, or can we settle this ourselves?"

He leers at Haley, and then he turns and leers at Paige, so smug and self-satisfied it makes Haley sick.

She telepathically screams at Paige to distract the little pervert. Reaches into her purse for her cell phone.

260.

E is in the lobby of the St. Regis when Jordan comes through the front doors. He crosses the lobby quickly, and from the look on his face under his snapback, E knows something's wrong.

E starts to stand up from the lounge chairs where he's been pretending to read a newspaper—

(Sample story: *CAPILANO POLICE STILL STYMIED IN CÔTE D'AZUR BOMBING.*)

—ready to follow Jordan, but Jordan catches the movement and turns and shakes his head slightly. *No.* E sits back down. Watches Jordan disappear onto the elevator. Tries not to worry about what's going on upstairs.

261.

The next few minutes are ugly.

████████████ grabs Paige's arm, rough. Paige screams. Haley reaches out, tries to stop ████████████. ████████████ pushes her away with his free hand, sends her sprawling to the floor.

"This could have been easy," ████████████ is telling Paige. "Now it's gotta be hard."

He's pushing her toward a bedroom. Haley picks herself up off the floor. Scrambles for her phone. Texts Jordan again. *911. 911. 911.*

Jordan texts back immediately. *Open the door.*

Haley hurries to the door. Can hear Paige fighting ████████████ behind her. She opens the door, and Jordan's on the other side. He pushes past her and across to where ████████████ is struggling with Paige. Grabs him by the shoulders and wrenches him back. ████████████ spins, smirks when he sees Jordan. "Who are you supposed to be?" he says. "The knight in shining armor?"

"Something like that," Jordan says. He swings at ████████████. The movie star ducks it, does some martial-arts bullshit that leaves Jordan on the ground.

"Good thing about making movies," ████████████ says, smirking. "Plenty of opportunity to learn new skills."

He turns back to Paige, pushes her, drags her. Fends

Haley off with one hand as she fights him. He's *laughing*, the bastard.

"Just forget it," Paige is saying. "Just call the cops, Haley. Just forget the Fix."

"Bullshit," Haley tells her. "It's three against one."

She launches herself at ███████████ again. ███████████ swats her away. Haley's just about to stand up and attack the sucker again, maybe aim for his balls this time, when—

Jordan rushes past her with authority. He's holding, like, a gigantic stained-glass vase, and, as Haley watches, he lifts it high in the air and brings it down

hard

on ███████████ 's head.

262.

Maybe it's the way ██████████ falls.

Maybe it's the way his head bounces off the hardwood.

Or maybe Jordan's just that strong.

Either way, ██████████ goes down.

He doesn't get up.

263.

"Holy *shit*." Paige is kneeling beside ████████. "Jordan, what did you do?"

The movie star is lying on the floor, facedown, not moving. "Did you check for a pulse?" Haley asks. She kneels beside Paige, puts her hand on ████████'s neck for a beat. Then she shakes her head. "Geez, you guys, I think he's *dead*."

The word hangs in the air. The penthouse suddenly seems small, claustrophobic. The movie star still hasn't moved.

"Wipe down everything you touched," Jordan tells them. "*Everything.* Think hard. Don't leave any fingerprints."

Paige looks up at him. "What are you talking about? We need to call an ambulance."

"And tell them what?" Jordan says. "We were trying to steal this guy's amazing Ferrari and we accidentally killed him? We need to get out of here, now. And we can't leave any evidence behind."

"Oh my god." Paige stares at Jordan. "*No.* That's not what we're doing. We can't just abandon him here."

She looks to Haley for support. Haley just shrugs. "I don't really want to go to jail for this asshole. I'm just saying."

"CPR," Paige says. "We need to do CPR." She straddles ████████'s body. Starts attempting compressions.

Jordan rolls his eyes. "*Paige.*"

Paige doesn't answer. Jordan motions to Haley, *Get her*

off him. Haley stands, puts her arm around Paige. Ushers her to the side.

"We don't have time to waste on stupid shit," Jordan says. "Sooner or later, someone's going to check on this douchebag. We don't want to be here when that happens. So think back to everything you might have touched, and wipe that shit down. Then we get the fuck out of here."

Paige is breathing heavy. She's practically hyperventilating. She stares at Jordan like he's just admitted he tortures small animals.

"Come on, Paige," Haley says. "This guy was a creep. You really want to risk the rest of your life to save him?"

Paige doesn't say anything, but she lets Haley pull her to her feet. She doesn't look behind her, where ███████████ lies, unmoving.

"Good," Jordan says. "Now what did you touch?"

264.

E can't take it. There's been no sign of Haley or Paige or Jordan. He's been lurking in the lobby of the St. Regis for way too long.

E puts the newspaper down and goes to the elevators. Presses the up button and rides to the top floor. The hallway is quiet when the doors open. No security guards. No police. No screaming.

That's a good sign.

E walks down the hall toward ███████████'s suite. The door is closed. Locked. E knocks on the door.

There's a long, pregnant pause.

Then the peephole goes dark. A moment later, the locks click and the doors open. Haley peers out, her face ashen. "What are you doing here? You're supposed to stay in the lobby."

"I saw Jordan," E says. "I thought it was *911*. What the hell is going on?"

He tries to peer past Haley into the room. Haley blocks him. "You don't want to come in here, dude," she says. "You really, *really* don't."

(But when does that ever work?)

"Uh, yeah," E tells her. "I really think I do."

He pushes past her and into the room. Down the little hallway into the vast living area, the expensive, minimalist furniture, the kitchenette with its granite countertops, the living area with its floor-to-ceiling ocean views.

And the movie star lying dead on the mahogany floor.

"*Holy fucking god,*" E says. "*What the hell happened?*"

Jordan comes out of the bedroom. "Never mind what happened. Just don't fucking touch anything, okay?"

E stares at the body. "Is he—?"

"Sure is," Haley says.

"Oh my *god.*"

Jordan comes over. Takes E's face in his hands. "There's no time for '*Oh my god.*'" He gestures to Paige. "We're already full on our freak-out quota. What I need is for you to help me get us out of here as quickly as possible. Okay?"

E looks past Jordan to the body. Jordan moves so E's looking at him. "*Okay?*"

"Holy shit," E says. "I mean, yeah. Okay."

265.

Jordan and Haley wipe down the whole suite. Anything any of them could have conceivably touched.

Paige just silently freaks out in the corner. E tries to comfort her without touching anything.

(███████████ just lies there.)

Finally, Jordan's satisfied. "Good," he says. "I think we're in the clear. Now we just have to get out of here."

E points to the body. "We're just going to leave him?"

"You want to wrestle a famous movie star's body out of a five-star hotel?" Jordan shakes his head. "We're leaving him. Let the cops try to put it together. We're clean."

He's still in control. After this, after all of this, he still knows what he's doing. He's not stressed at all.

"We just have to get out of here," Jordan says. "And we can't let anybody see us, okay?"

"Yeah, okay," E says. "But how do we get out?"

Jordan points to the door. "Use the fire escape, dummy."

He ushers the Pack out of ███████████'s suite. Hangs back for a long moment, lingers inside the suite while the others wait out in the hall. Then he's out.

"Had to make sure we were clean," he tells them. "Let's go."

They sneak down the hall to the emergency fire stairs, Jordan in the lead, then E, then Paige and Haley. Nobody comes out as they're sneaking. Nobody sees them. Jordan disables the alarm. They hit the fire stairs and Jordan pushes the door open, and they start the long descent to ground level.

They don't say anything. They go slow and cautious and as fast as they dare. Their footsteps echo through the stairwell as they descend. They listen for doors opening, or anyone who might see them.

The drop takes forever. Then they reach the ground floor. There's a fire door to outside. Jordan pushes it open. E and Paige and Haley follow him out to the night.

They're in an alley. There's a hedgerow opposite. On the other side is the public beach parking lot. Jordan leads them up the alley, toward the front of the hotel. He sticks to the shadows. He doesn't make a sound. E creeps behind him and tries to emulate what he's doing. Tries to forget the sight of ██████████'s dead body.

They reach the front of the hotel, the end of the hedgerow. Jordan circles around to the other side, the beach parking lot. It's nearly deserted, at this hour. His dad's Tesla sits in the shadows.

E follows. Nobody sees him. Haley pushes Paige around the edge of the hedgerow too. Goes to follow her, and doesn't notice the curb in between the two lots. Sees it too late and falls flat on her face.

The others are already halfway to the car. Haley pulls herself to her feet, feeling stupid. Looks back at the hotel, for god knows what reason, and stops cold.

A kitchen worker, a sous chef or something. He's coming out of a service entrance like, thirty feet away. He's lighting up a cigarette. He stops when he sees Haley. He stares right at her. His eyes lock on hers for an interminable length of time.

Then Haley shakes it off and keeps going.

266.

"This is not a catastrophe," Jordan says.

They're all in the Tesla now, a couple miles from the St. Regis, cruising west on Marine Drive toward Jordan's mansion. The roads are mostly deserted. No police cars. No sirens. Nobody knows what they've done.

(Yet.)

None of the others reply. Paige is having a freak-out in the backseat of the Tesla. She keeps mumbling things that none of the others can understand. Haley keeps trying to get her to calm down. It's not working.

"Paige, listen to me," Jordan says. "All of you. Listen up."

There's something in his voice E's never heard before. Something hard and maybe mean.

"Nobody was supposed to get hurt," Paige says. "That wasn't the fucking *Fix*, Jordan. *Nobody was supposed to get hurt.*"

"It was an accident," Jordan says. "I didn't mean it. But he was a piece of shit, Paige. I would do it again if I had to."

Paige looks like she's ready to cry.

"I'm not saying this is an ideal scenario," Jordan says. "But it isn't the end of the world. Everything's going to be fine."

E looks at Jordan, and he can't tell if Jordan's lying, or if he really believes it. E's pretty sure *he* doesn't believe it. E's thinking they're screwed.

"That piece of shit," Haley says. "Why couldn't he just

drink his fucking roofie?"

"It's over," Jordan says. "What's done is done. That guy was a creep, and he had it coming. It sucks that we killed him, but we didn't get caught."

"Dude," E says. "It's great that we didn't get caught and all, but we just *killed* a guy."

Jordan exhales. "I know you're scared, E. But if you don't want to spend the rest of your life in jail, you're going to need to man the fuck up a little bit. Like, now."

E doesn't say anything. He doesn't exactly like Jordan's tone. It's like E's part of the problem. That's not what E wants.

Jordan keeps driving. They're almost at his house.

"Nobody panic," Jordan says. "We're going to be fine."

267.

E and the others bag up their black clothes and hide them in Jordan's pool house. They change into sweats and hoodies and go back into the mansion and bring pillows and blankets down to the theater room and turn on the TV. There's nothing on the news yet. It's too early in the morning. Nobody's broadcasting.

There are a couple of lines on the internet, though. Twitter is picking up the story. It's all rumors and conjecture at this point. There's nothing about the Suicide Pack.

They divide up the blankets and the pillows and the couches. Jordan mutes the TV and turns the lights low. E lies there in the darkness and the quiet, trying to fall asleep, trying to erase the dead movie star from his brain.

Eventually, he drifts off. But ███████████ isn't going anywhere. He haunts E's dreams until morning.

268.

E wakes up. The TV is off, and Paige and Haley are still asleep. Jordan's gone. E sits up and wraps himself in the blanket.

He wanders out into the mansion and finds the nearest bathroom. As he comes out afterward, he hears a door close. He follows the noise.

Jordan's in the kitchen. He has croissants from Artigiano and four coffees. He looks pretty well rested. He doesn't look like he stayed up all night worrying about ███████████.

(E has a series of thoughts as he walks into the kitchen.

The thoughts are as follows:

Jordan bought coffee from Artigiano.

Artigiano is not at all close to Jordan's mansion.

(It's all the way over by Capilano Marina.)

(There are multiple coffee shops closer.)

So why Artigiano?)

Jordan looks up when E walks in. "Morning, sunshine." He slides E a coffee and the bag of croissants. And an iPad with a video loaded on the screen. "Check this out."

He shows E the iPad. Presses play.

And E watches in absolute horror.

269.

What E sees:
    A slow pan across ██████████'s penthouse suite.
    The city skyline out the windows. Drinks on the coffee table.
    Pan across to ██████████'s body, lifeless on the floor.
    (Cut to black.)
    Then the Suicide Pack logo.
    Then the punch line.
    ROMEO MUST DIE.
    (Cue Robo-Haley's maniacal laugh.)

270.

"*What in the actual fuck, dude?*" E stares at Jordan. "*What did you do?*"

Jordan smiles like the sphinx. "It's our latest Vine, E. It's going to break the internet, right?"

"No." E grabs the iPad. Fumbles with the touch screen. "You have to delete it. You can't post that shit."

"Too late," Jordan says. "It's already posted." He gestures to the bag of croissants. "Try a croissant, E. They're delicious."

But E isn't thinking about eating.

E's thinking about the freaking electric chair.

"*What the fuck are you thinking?*" he's saying.

"Will you quit with all the drama? We're going to be fine. We were careful last night. The plan was a good one. The only witness is dead. Nobody even knows we were at the St. Regis. You kept your head down so the cameras wouldn't see your face, right?"

"Yeah, okay, but what about the other Fixes?" E asks. "Paige had connections to the movie star. Haley's freaking *mom* owned the Côte d'Azur. And what about Mike? He knows we bought explosives. He already suspects we set that bomb."

"Don't worry about Mike," Jordan says. "Mike's a nonfactor."

"How do you know that?" E's running his hands through his hair. E's feeling like he might, you know, *faint*.

Jordan sips his coffee. Bites into a croissant. Takes the iPad back and fiddles with it. "Take a look, E," he says, handing the iPad back. "They *love* us."

E looks at the screen.

He's in the Capilano High message group.

(And it looks like a freaking piranha feeding frenzy.)

271.

OMG.
OMFG.
Is this fucking real?
How the fuck did they get this footage?
Can anyone trace this?
Hoax? Y/N
Why the f would they post this?
Why the f would they kill him?
Meh.
I never liked his movies anyway.

[Etc.]
[Etc.]
[Etc.]

272.

"We just have to act normal," Jordan says. "Nobody knows it's us. You guys need to relax, okay?"

They're back in the theater room. E's feeling like his brain is oozing out his ears, and Haley and Paige look about the same. Paige's makeup is smudged; she's been crying. Haley can't take her eyes from Jordan's iPad. She keeps shaking her head and muttering something E can't hear, but it's probably profane.

Jordan holds out a coffee and the bag of croissants. "Eat up, you guys," he says. "Everything looks better on a full stomach. I promise."

Haley looks at him like he's insane. "I don't have an appetite."

"Have some coffee at least. Perk up a bit."

"I don't want *coffee*, Jordan." Haley's voice is menace. "What I *need* is to understand what you were thinking, posting this Vine."

Paige curls up, hugs her knees to her chest. "We have to tell the police," she says. "They're going to find us anyway. We have to get ahead of this and just hope they'll be lenient."

E feels a brick in the pit of his stomach. Sees law school disappearing before his eyes. Sees a long life in prison instead.

He looks over at Haley and sees the same fear in her eyes. But Jordan sits down on the couch beside Paige. "Look at me," he says.

Paige doesn't answer. She doesn't look at Jordan. She hugs a pillow to her chest and stares across at the wall.

"We're not going to the police," Jordan says. "We're not confessing shit, either. We're the *Suicide Pack*. We don't let anyone in this town mess with us."

"We fucking *killed* a guy, Jordan," Paige says. "And it's still just a freaking *game* to you?"

Jordan looks at her, hard. "It isn't a game. It was never a game. It sucks that ███████████ had to die, but he was a total fucking sleazeball. This is just the universe paying him back."

"I still don't get why you had to post that freaking Vine, though," Haley says.

"Nobody's going to trace it to us. No one ever has to know. As long as we act normal, we're totally fine. And if not?"

He grins.

"I have a six-point-eight-million-dollar trust fund," he says. "If that won't keep the heat off us, it will at least get us somewhere far away, fast. Okay?"

He looks around the room. Nobody answers.

"*Okay?*"

Weak nods. Feeble shrugs.

Jordan shakes his head. Sets down the bag of croissants. "You guys should really drink that coffee," he says. "It's like a *morgue* in here."

273.

And that's that.

    Paige promises to keep quiet. They *all* promise to keep quiet. They drink coffee and eat croissants and spend the day in the theater room, watching the news.

    Their faces never show up onscreen.

    The police never knock at the door.

    (*Holy shit*, E thinks. *We might actually get away with this after all.*)

274.

Paige leaves the mansion the next morning.

"I just need to get out," she tells the others. "Clear my head a little, get some space."

She catches the way Jordan and Haley and E look at her. "I'm *not* going to sell you guys out, okay? I just need to be alone for a while."

"I should get home, too," Haley says. "Check on my mom and, like, try to act normal, I guess."

"Keep your mouths shut," Jordan tells them. "Anyone tries to talk to you about this, you let me know ASAP, okay?"

Paige and Haley nod.

"We're going to be fine," Jordan says. "Just everyone trust me."

KIK -- CAPILANO HIGH PRIVATE MESSAGE GROUP
— 08/22/16 — 11:58 AM

USERNAME: Anonymous-9
MESSAGE: Another bat-shit crazy Suicide
    Pack production. Bravo. As if murdering
    Gatsby makes you all heroes. I know
    you're on here. I know you can see what
    I'm writing. Well, tick-tock, losers.
    Destiny is about to catch up with you.

275.

There's a For Sale sign on Paige's front lawn when she gets home. No cars in the driveway, a lockbox on the front door.

(She hasn't been home since forever, due to the divorce and the acrimony and the constant stress. Couch surfing has been a much less uncomfortable living arrangement.

But right now, Paige needs her own space.)

She unlocks the back door and walks into the house. The air is still. The place is unnaturally clean. There's a stack of brochures on the kitchen counter, a real-estate agent's smiling face, a bunch of professional photographs of the house.

(There's nothing in the fridge but fucking Perrier.)

Paige pours herself a glass of water. Downs it, and leaves the empty glass on the counter, beside the brochures. Then she hauls her bag upstairs to her room.

Her room is different, too. Someone messed with her stuff. Her books are all hidden and her stuffed animals rearranged. Someone threw out her old journals, or moved them somewhere. Paige sets the bag down on the floor, kicks off her shoes. Pulls out her laptop and tries to connect to the internet, but she can't get a signal.

Even the freaking Wi-Fi is gone.

276.

Paige lives like a squatter in her own home. She buys cookies and chips and soda from the little family-run convenience store down the hill, a box of stale Cinnamon Toast Crunch. She studies the case on TV.

(Or, rather, the *cases*.)

(*Her cases*.)

The murder. The bombing. She combs the newspaper's website.

███████████ died from massive head trauma. There were recreational drugs in his toxicology report. No signs of forced entry into the suite. Capilano PD is reviewing the St. Regis's security tapes now.

(No suspects yet in the Côte d'Azur bombing either.)

Rumors abound.

But no one in the real world is talking about the Pack.

(Yet.)

277.

There's something else in the news besides bombing coverage. A little article, barely four paragraphs long: *MISSING MAN CON-FOUNDS POLICE, FAMILY.*

Paige doesn't know why she clicks through. Boredom, maybe, or just morbid curiosity.

The missing man is a sixty-five-year-old Vietnam veteran. He now works as a special effects technician for Grant Studios—Jordan's dad's company. He hasn't been seen in almost a week.

(He disappeared the day after Paige's Fix went awry.)

There's a picture beside the article. A man with white hair and a big, shaggy beard. Tattoos. He looks like an old biker thug. The article says his name is Michael McDougall. He'd worked with movie kingpin Harrison Grant for nearly twenty years.

Police don't have any leads.

278.

A couple days later. Paige is sleeping late when she hears something outside in the driveway. Voices, two of them, a man's and a woman's.

(At first Paige thinks it's the real-estate agent. He's been coming around now and then, showing the house off to prospective buyers. He always looks at Paige with a mixture of pity and, like, desire.

Paige tries to stay out of his way.)

The doorbell rings.

(The real-estate agent has a key.)

Paige goes to her window and looks out at the driveway. Sees the unmarked police car parked by the front door.

It's not the real-estate agent this time.

It's the cops.

279.

Two cops, in particular. Plainclothes detectives.

(You know who they are.)

Dawson and Richards. They badge Paige at the door. Ask if they can come in. Paige lets them in. She has nothing to hide—

(here).

The detectives leave their shoes on. They follow Paige into the kitchen. Dawson picks up a brochure from the counter. "Your parents selling?"

"Divorce," Paige tells him. "My dad's in some legal trouble at the moment."

"So why's your mom leaving? Because he's getting locked up, or because the Feds froze his bank account?"

Richards gives him a look, and he holds up his hands, grinning a little. There's something mean about him that sets Paige on edge.

"You heard about the murder at the St. Regis," Richards says. She smiles a little nicer, playing the good cop. "██████████, the movie star. We're running the case."

"We're working that bombing, too," Dawson says. "The bathing suit store down on Main Street, the real trendy one. What's it called?"

"Côte d'Azur," Paige says after a moment.

"That's right. Your friend owns it."

"Her mom." Paige's mouth suddenly feels very dry. "My friend Haley's mom. It's her store."

"*Was* her store," Dawson says. "Ain't much of a store anymore."

"Have you seen Haley lately?" Richards asks. "We went by her house, but she wasn't around."

"No, I haven't," Paige says. "Why are you even looking for her, anyway?"

"There was a witness at the St. Regis," Dawson says. "A busboy on his smoke break. Said he saw a girl outside the hotel on the night in question, about the time the medical examiner figures ██████████ breathed his last."

Paige feels her heart rate jump to double time. She tries to hide it. "I didn't hear anything about any witnesses."

"We withhold information from the media," Richards tells her.

"Can't keep our suspects *completely* in the loop," Dawson says.

Richards reaches into her jacket, pulls out a piece of paper. "The thing is, Ms. Hammond," she says, unfolding the paper, "the busboy's description sounds uncannily similar to *this* girl. And *that* girl looks a lot like your friend Haley Keefer."

She slides the paper over to Paige. It's the composite sketch of Haley from the Room spree. When it showed up in the newspaper, Paige couldn't see the resemblance. Now, looking at it again, all she can see is Haley.

"Wait, what?" Paige says, hoping she looks shocked. "You think Haley killed ██████████ *and* robbed The Room? *And* bombed the Côte d'Azur? Is she a suspect in the nine-eleven attacks, too?"

"Not just Haley," Dawson says. "She brought three friends to The Room, remember?"

"And, what? I haven't seen them, either, if that's what you're asking."

The detectives swap another look. Richards takes the picture back. "You knew ██████████, didn't you? You guys were kind of an item?"

"We went out for drinks once or twice. He got me a job on the movie he was shooting. It didn't go further than that. He had a fiancée in Los Angeles."

"What I hear, that never stopped him," Dawson says.

"You lost that job, though," Richards says. "A week or so before the murder. What happened?"

"How should I know?" Paige says. "The AD came up to me one day and told me they didn't need me anymore, so I went home. That's it."

"Just like that, huh?" Dawson says. "No cause given?"

"What are you suggesting?"

"You're a pretty girl. That's all I'm saying."

"There were three cocktail glasses in ██████████'s room when security found the body, Paige," Richards says. "One had been laced with a pretty powerful sedative."

"You guys are just trying to solve every crime in town at once, huh?" Paige says. "No offense, but this sounds like a stretch."

"That's what we thought, too," Richards says. "Believe me, this wasn't the first theory we came up with. But then . . ."

She steps aside for Dawson, who holds out his phone to Paige. Onscreen, the ██████████ Vine is playing, an endless loop.

"What do you know about the Suicide Pack?" Dawson asks her.

280.

Paige forces herself to stay calm.

"I think I should probably have my lawyer around if you want to keep asking questions," she tells the detectives. "I don't think she would like what you guys are insinuating."

Dawson points at Richards. "She's insinuating. I'm outright telling. I think you and your little friend murdered ██████████. And you blew up that store, too."

"You'll have to talk to my lawyer," Paige tells him. "And until then, you have to leave."

Richards pretends to wince. "This isn't the way to do this, honey. If you get yourself out ahead of this thing, we can keep you out of jail."

Dawson says, "Play the lawyer card one more time and we'll throw the book at you."

Paige stares him down. Hopes she looks brave. "I don't know what you're talking about," she says. "I already asked you to leave. Do I have to call in your badge numbers?"

Richards and Dawson look at each other. "Have it your way," Dawson tells Paige. "I'm just saying, keep that lawyer on speed dial."

281.

Richards hands Paige a business card as she walks to the door.

"Listen, you're still young," the detective says. "This isn't serious yet, but it could be. You get nailed for this, you do heavy time. Do you really want to throw your life away?"

My life is already garbage, Paige thinks. *You can't help me.*

"You decide you want to talk, give me a call," Richards says, pressing the card into Paige's hand. "Just remember, it's a limited-time offer."

282.

Paige calls Haley as soon as the cops are gone. "Where are you?"

"Jordan's," Haley tells her. "There's, like, some slip-and-slide in the Properties later. I guess it's like a hundred feet long. We were thinking about going."

(*To a slip-and-slide*, Paige thinks. *Now?*)

Haley picks up on the vibe. "Look, I know what you're thinking. But we have to get out, act normal. Jordan's right. The more we act guilty, the more attention we attract."

"Yeah," Paige says. "About that."

She tells Haley about Dawson and Richards. "They know you were at the St. Regis that night. They think I was there, too, and we killed him together."

"But that's bullshit," Haley says. "We were so careful."

Paige tells her it doesn't matter. Tells her about the busboy on his smoke break. About the Room composite. The three cocktail glasses, the roofie in ███████████'s drink. About Jordan's Vine.

"Those cops were really scary," Paige says. She pulls Detective Richards's business card from her purse. Studies it. "Richards gave me her card. She said I should talk to them now, get ahead of this. She said she could help me."

"She's bluffing. Remember the rules? Don't tell them anything without your lawyer present. If they really had anything, they would have arrested you already, right?"

"Right," Paige says.

(But that doesn't make her feel much better.)

She stays silent a beat or two. "There is one other thing," she says finally. She tells Haley about Michael McDougall.

283.

Haley listens to the whole thing. How McDougall worked for Jordan's dad. How he disappeared the morning after the murder.

"It can't be a coincidence, can it?" Paige says.

"Yeah, but what are you saying? Like, Jordan *disappeared* this guy because he knew too much about what we're doing?"

"Jordan killed ██████████, didn't he?"

"We *all* killed ██████████. Anyway, Jordan was just defending us. There's a big difference between killing someone in self-defense and killing someone on purpose, isn't there?"

Paige doesn't say anything.

(*Was it* self-defense?)

She's really not sure.

284.

Haley tells Paige she'll talk to Jordan.

"He probably just paid that guy off," she says. "Bought him a plane ticket to, like, Fiji or something. Got him out of the way for a while."

Paige isn't convinced. But she tries to be.

"I just need to know we're not, like, serial killers. I don't want anyone else getting hurt."

"Just relax," Haley tells her. "I'll talk to Jordan."

KIK -- CAPILANO HIGH PRIVATE MESSAGE GROUP
— 08/24/16 — 10:33 PM

USERNAME: Anonymous-9
MESSAGE: Who's ready for answers, Capilano
    kiddies? Isn't it about time we find
    out the SUICIDE PACK's true identity???

KIK -- CAPILANO HIGH PRIVATE MESSAGE GROUP
— 08/24/16 — 10:36 PM

USERNAME: Anonymous-9
MESSAGE: Tick-tock.

285.

"She said those detectives came to see her," Haley tells Jordan. "They got to the Vines, and now they know about the Pack. Plus some busboy at the St. Regis gave the cops my description. They've seen me before, after we blew up my mom's store. I guess they remembered."

Jordan rolls his eyes. "Somebody snitched on us. Big surprise. No one has any honor in this town."

"Did you really think it was going to stay a secret? This whole thing escalated when we killed ███████████. It's, like, a whole other level of crazy." She hesitates. "And did you read those posts from Anonymous? Whoever that guy is, he's talking like he knows us."

"He doesn't know us. It's a bluff; he's just messing with us."

"Okay, but why, though?"

"Who knows? Maybe he's jealous that we're getting so freaking popular. Maybe he wants the attention to himself. Or maybe it really *is* Callum Fulchrest, and he's playing some revenge game."

Haley looks at him. "So what do we do?"

"We wait it out, duh," Jordan says. "We play the game back until we figure out who he is. Then we teach him not to mess with the Pack."

286.

"There's something else, too," Haley tells Jordan.

Jordan stops pacing. Looks back at her, waiting.

"Paige read a news article. Some guy at your dad's studio is missing, some special effects guy? She's scared it has something to do with us."

Haley expects Jordan to look confused or surprised, or maybe deny everything. But he just purses his lips. "Shit," he says. "Paige is going to sink us all."

"Jordan?" Haley hears a little alarm start to go off inside her head. "What happened to the special effects guy?"

Jordan ignores her. "We need to have a team meeting." He walks to the back door. Pokes his head out to the deck, where E is tanning by the pool.

"Go get Paige," Jordan tells him. "Take my car and meet us down at the boat."

287.

First thing E notices when he drives up to Paige's place is the For Sale sign on her front lawn.

(The place looks deserted.)

E parks in the empty driveway and goes up the front stairs to the door. He rings the doorbell, and nobody answers. He knocks, and it's the same story.

He texts Paige. *Hey. Let me in.*

There's a pause. Then those ellipses show up on screen and she's typing something.

Whoa, she writes back. *One sec.*

E waits. He looks around the neighborhood, up and down the block. It's a beautiful day. The sun's shining out over the water, shimmering gold and blue. It's a great day for a boat ride.

The door unlocks and swings open. There's Paige. She's not wearing any makeup. She's wearing a hoodie. She looks like she was maybe asleep.

"Uh, Jordan wanted me to get you," E tells her. "We're supposed to have some kind of team meeting. On his boat."

Paige's eyes go wide. She steps back and disappears into the house. The door stays open. After a moment, E follows her inside. The house is very clean. It looks like nobody lives there.

"Where did everyone go?" E asks Paige. "Are you the only one here?"

Paige is in the kitchen. The kitchen looks lived-in. There

are piles of dirty dishes in the sink. An empty box of Cinnamon Toast Crunch on the counter.

"My mom's in Italy," Paige says. "My dad's just gone. These days, it's just me and the real-estate agent."

"When did they put the house up?"

Paige shrugs. "Sometime between the Room spree and ███████████, I guess. I haven't exactly been home in a while."

E doesn't say anything. E just kind of watches the dust hanging in the beams of sunlight coming through the kitchen windows. He waits for Paige to say something, but Paige doesn't say anything either.

"So, uh, it kind of sounded important," E says finally. "This team thing, or whatever. We're just supposed to meet at the boat."

Paige leans against the kitchen counter. Crosses her arms over her chest. "Haley told you guys, didn't she? She told you what I know about Michael McDougall, and now this is happening."

"*What's* happening? Who's Michael McDougall?" E frowns. "I didn't talk to Haley at all. She and Jordan were talking, and then Jordan told me to come get you. That's all I know."

Paige pulls out her cell phone. "Michael McDougall," she says, typing something. "Special effects technician at Grant Studios. Missing since last Thursday, the day after we killed ███████████."

She hands E her phone. Onscreen is the news article. E looks at the picture and puts the pieces together. Feels something cold and scary start to gnaw at his insides.

"You know this guy?" Paige asks.

"Demolitions Mike," E says. "That's who we bought the explosives from to make Haley's bomb."

"I *knew* it." Paige looks triumphant. "It's Jordan, E, don't you get it? He's tying up all his loose ends."

"What is this, a mob movie?" E shakes his head. "Listen to yourself, Paige. Jordan wouldn't do that."

"Wouldn't he? He built a bomb for fun, Eric. He seems *proud* of the fact that we *murdered* a movie star. You really think we're dealing with someone with a strong moral compass?"

(E feels that frustration growing again. There's no reason for Paige to be such a goddamn *drama queen*. Of course Jordan didn't kill Mike. Everything's blown out of proportion.)

(Except there's a little voice in E's head, reminding him of how Jordan bought coffee from the coffee shop by the marina the morning after Paige's Fix. How he seemed so confident that Mike wouldn't sell them out.)

"On second thought, don't answer that," Paige says. "You're so drunk on Jordan's Kool-Aid, you probably don't know which way is up anymore."

(That does it. E's little voice of reason is suddenly drowned out by his *frustration*.)

"Oh, fuck you," E tells her. "You're just jealous because you're still in love with me, and I'm happy with Jordan."

"You think I'm doing this because I'm *in love with you?*" Paige laughs, even though nothing's funny. "I'm *worried* about you, Eric. This whole thing is spiraling out of control, and you're too caught up in your little bullshit fairy tale to even notice."

"It's not bullshit. We're in love."

"In *love?* You're his fucking sidekick. Wake *up.*"

E's phone starts buzzing in his pocket. It's obviously Jordan. Paige lets out a long, frustrated breath.

"Look, whatever," she says. "Do what you want. But if you think I'm going out on that boat with you guys, you're crazy."

288.

Jordan and Haley are waiting on the dock when E pulls up. Jordan frowns when he sees E is alone. "Where's Paige?"

"I couldn't find her," E lies. "She didn't answer her texts, and her house was, like, deserted. I don't think anybody was there."

(E isn't sure why he's lying. But it has something to do with that little voice in his head.)

Jordan doesn't say anything. E can practically see his brain working. "She's in hiding." Jordan starts pacing. "Shit. I was afraid this would happen."

E doesn't say anything. Neither does Haley. They're just waiting for Jordan to decide what to do.

(*You're his fucking sidekick.*)

(*You're drunk on his Kool-Aid.*)

Abruptly, Jordan stops walking. He straightens. Smiles. "Let's get out on the boat," he tells E and Haley. "Let's figure out what we're going to do."

289.

Nobody says anything until they're out past the bay. They go ten, fifteen miles from the city, almost halfway to the islands that lie to the west. It's windy on the water, and the waves are pretty choppy. The boat rocks back and forth in the swell.

There's nobody around, not this far out. They're miles past the pleasure boats and the cargo ships anchored in the bay. There's nobody to see them. Nobody to listen.

Jordan powers down the Sundancer. Turns the boat into the waves and jogs along, pretty slow. It's quiet enough to talk now. Jordan breaks the silence.

"Paige is a liability," he says. "It's only a matter of time before she sells us out."

"We'll be okay, though, won't we?" E asks him. "You said you could get us out of anything."

"Yeah, *us*. I said if we stuck together we'd be fine. If Paige goes rogue on us, we're like a table with only three legs. We fall over."

"It's the stuff about the effects guy that's freaking her out," Haley says. "I don't even think she cares about ▮▮▮▮▮▮▮ anymore. She just wants to make sure no one else is getting hurt."

Jordan doesn't say anything. He's leaning against the front of the cockpit, between the controls and the stairs into the cabin. He's looking out over the water like he's thinking about something.

"I think we can get Paige back on board," E says. "We just have to figure out once and for all what happened to Mike."

"*Mike.*" Haley frowns. "You knew him?"

"We bought the explosives from Mike," Jordan says. "He was my dad's demolitions guy."

Haley's face kind of drains of color. "Oh."

"Mike was getting scared. That first bomb we set off had him freaked. Just like Paige. He wouldn't play ball anymore."

"So what happened?" E asks, even though he doesn't really want to know. "Did you pay him off or something? What did you do?"

Jordan looks at E, and he's serious now. "What did I do?" he repeats. "I did what I had to do to protect us. To protect the Pack."

(I guess this isn't a surprise. You must have seen this coming. But E didn't—and there's really no way to adequately prepare for when your best friend-slash-boyfriend springs you with this kind of news.)

"You killed him. You *killed* him? *Shit*, Jordan."

"This is all going to be fine." There's something really strange in Jordan's voice. It's sickeningly calm. "We're going to make it out of this, I told you. You just have to trust me."

Haley stands. "So you just fucking *killed* somebody else, Jordan? You didn't think that was something we would maybe, like, want to *talk over*, first? *What the* fuck *were you thinking?!*"

Jordan ignores her. He's looking at E. "That day on the boat. You said you were with me. Did you mean it?"

"I mean . . ." E hesitates. "Dude, I'm just trying to process—"

"Yes or no, E. It's not a hard question."

(It's not exactly an *easy* question, though. Not with Haley losing her shit in the back of the cockpit, and Jordan so spookily calm, and E's head spinning.)

"*E. Do you trust me to get us out of this?*"

(I mean, what do you say? E can't exactly tell him *no*, can he?)

"I trust you," E says, fast, before he can stop himself.

Jordan nods. "Good. Then I'm sorry this next part has to happen."

"Wait, what?" E shakes his head. "No. What are you doing?"

Jordan reaches into the cabin. Comes out with a long piece of wood with a spike on the end, like for fishing—

(a *gaff*).

"I'm sorry," Jordan says, and it's not clear who he's talking to. "I'm doing this for us."

Then, before E can react, Jordan takes two steps across the cockpit toward where Haley's standing in the stern. He swings the wood like a baseball bat and catches her in the midsection. She stumbles, and he hits her again.

The second hit knocks her off the back of the boat.

290.

E kind of blacks out.

(He's pretty sure he's screaming.)

E starts scrambling. Haley's splashing in the water and yelling for help, and E's looking around for a life preserver or a life jacket or some kind of live-saving device, a rope, anything to help her get back on board.

He's thinking this is a joke, or some weird demonstration, that's all, and now that Haley's learned her lesson they can all go back to Capilano and, like, get stoned or something.

(He's still not really registering what's going on.)

There's a life preserver on the sundeck, at the front of the boat. E's crossing to the stairs to get it when Jordan stands in his way. "Leave it."

"What? But we can't just leave her out here."

Jordan doesn't move. "I said leave it." He reaches for the controls. Pushes the throttle higher. The engine gets louder and the boat picks up speed, churning white water behind.

"What the fuck are you doing?" E tries to reach around Jordan for the throttle.

(Behind the Sundancer, Haley is still splashing, still shouting. Every time a wave comes, she disappears behind it. She's coughing and sputtering. There's nobody around.)

E makes another grab at the throttle. Jordan blocks him, shoves him down to the deck. E scrambles back to his feet.

(The Sundancer is like forty, fifty feet away from Haley now, and putting in distance. Haley's hard to pick out in the waves.)

Jordan pushes E backward again. "Don't test me, E."

His voice is still calm. Way too calm. It makes E even more desperate.

He gathers all of his strength. Launches himself at Jordan, knocks him into the control panel. His back hits the throttle and pushes it to full bore. The boat surges forward. E and Jordan are both knocked off-balance.

Jordan recovers first. Pushes himself to his feet and picks up the gaff hook. Waves it around like he's the leadoff batter. "I told you not to fuck with me," he says.

Then he swings.

291.

E's thinking three things as that gaff connects:

    1. *Haley is going to die,*

    2. *I'm going to die,* and

    3. *This might not actually be a love story after all.*

292.

But Eric doesn't die.

He wakes up in the cockpit of the Sundancer. Jordan's at the controls. The engine is howling. The boat's slicing through the water.

They're racing the waves back to Capilano.

Eric is alive.

Haley is gone.

293.

Eric throws up.

He retches and pukes all over himself, and then he rolls over and pukes some more. He can't stop seeing Haley in the water. Can't stop hearing her scream.

"Oh, for god's sake, E, grow up."

This is Jordan. He's still standing at the controls, but he's looking back at Eric, his features are hard.

"Pull yourself together, dude," Jordan tells him. "We're almost back in town, and we have some serious shit to cover before we get there."

Eric sits at the back of the cockpit and stares at his shoes, and tries not to puke any more. Tries not to think about Haley. Jordan slows the boat to an idle and ducks into the cabin, and Eric's afraid he's coming out with the gaff again, but he just hands Eric a bottle of Fiji water.

"We had to do it," he continues. "You get that, right? The police were onto Haley. They have her *picture*. If they tied her to █████████'s murder, they know she's part of the Pack. And that makes her a liability." He looks at Eric, his eyes wide and earnest.

"I couldn't let her lead them to us, E," he says. "There's too much at stake here. We're not finished yet. You understand that, right?"

Jordan motions to the Fiji water, tells Eric to drink up,

but all the designer water in the world isn't going to make Eric feel better. He cranes his head above the side of the boat. They're a few hundred yards from the entrance to the Capilano Marina. The city is spread out before them, the lights twinkling on as the day comes to an end, the mountains behind it turning purple in the evening sun.

(It still looks like paradise.)

"I did this for us," Jordan's saying. "I know it seems crazy, but I need you to trust me. If we stick together, we can fix this whole fucking town."

294.

(As if that makes Eric feel any better.)

295.

Haley's mom's Porsche is parked in the shadows at the back of the marina lot.

"These next few minutes, hours, they're important," Jordan says. "We need to be smart, and we need to move quickly."

Eric doesn't answer.

Eric's thinking, *I don't want to do this anymore.*

But Jordan reads his mind. "I need you here, E," he says. "And you need me, too. They'll burn you for the movie star just like they'll burn me. And then the Pack will be finished and this town will be fucked."

"But that's bullshit," Eric says. "I didn't kill anyone."

"You think that matters? You were in the room when ▬▬▬▬▬▬ died. You were part of the plot to cover it up. Nobody's going to care that you didn't swing the vase. And let's be honest, there's no real proof that you didn't."

Eric doesn't say anything.

"You were there with Mike, too," Jordan continues. "You really want to face down two murder charges alone?"

E feels numb. This isn't happening.

(Haley's dead.)

(*You're his sidekick.*)

"First thing we need to do," Jordan says, "is ditch this car. Follow me in the Tesla."

He holds out the keys. Eric hesitates. Jordan takes Eric's hand and presses the keys into his palm.

"Hey," he says. "Just do what I tell you and everything's going to be fine."

296.

Jordan drives the Porsche out of the marina. Turns east through Capilano and takes the bridge over the bay and into the city. Eric follows in the Tesla, up the arc of the suspension bridge and then down the other side, into the giant park that marks the city gates. It's nighttime now, full dark, and as they cut through the black forest, the Boxster's brake lights are the only thing Eric can really see. Eric follows the brake lights. There's nothing else he can do.

Jordan drives out of the park and into the city. Bypasses the financial district, and drives toward Railtown. Eric follows him up Hastings to Main Street, where he turns south, just before the Railtown Health Center. They drive a couple blocks, and then Jordan signals right and pulls into an alley across from the bus station.

He stops the Porsche in the shadows. Eric waits in the Tesla. He watches the brake lights extinguish, and then he watches Jordan wipe the steering wheel clean with the sleeve of his hoodie. Jordan wipes the rest of the car down too, the inside and the door handles. Then he steps out. Looks around once, drops the keys down a sewer grate. Walks back to the Tesla and climbs in.

"They'll think she hopped a bus somewhere," he says. "By the time anyone finds her, she'll be unrecognizable."

Eric's stomach turns. He doesn't want to think about Haley this way.

"They'll all think she's the bomber," Jordan says. "As long as Paige doesn't spoil it for us, we should be golden."

He reaches across the car, takes Eric's hand, squeezes. "So let's go make sure Paige doesn't spoil it."

297.

Paige. Shit.

Eric drives. He's pretty much on autopilot right now. His head is throbbing from where Jordan hit him with the gaff hook. Plus, it hurts to breathe. He might have a broken rib. And he's probably in shock. The events of the past hour are still sinking in.

Jordan doesn't seem worried at all. He turns on the radio. He looks out the window and watches the city go by, cranes his neck to look at a cargo ship passing under the bridge.

Paige is still alive. E told Jordan she was gone, but that was a lie. She's probably still at home. She has no idea what happened to Haley.

She has no idea what's headed her way.

Jordan picks up on Eric's vibe. He squeezes Eric's hand again. "I know this is hard for you. Haley was a good person. She died for the Pack. That's the ultimate sacrifice, and we should respect it."

(*Run, Paige. Charter a fucking jet and fly to, like, Fiji. Get out now.*)

"Paige is a liability," Jordan says. "She's a threat. For all we know, she's the freak who's been threatening to out us online. We can't let that fly, E. We have to deal with her."

Eric drives up the mountain. Turns onto Paige's street. Creeps the Tesla down the block until they're in front of her house.

There's a light on in the upstairs window.

(*RUN, PAIGE. GET OUT OF THERE.*)

"Keep going," Jordan says. "Park out of sight."

Eric idles the car forward until they're in front of the next house, hidden by a tall overhanging tree.

"Perfect. Kill the engine."

Eric does.

298.

Jordan climbs out of the car. Eric climbs out too. He kneels down on the pavement and pretends he's tying his shoe.

He takes out his phone.

(He could call the police right now. 911. Save Paige's life. He could get back in the Tesla and drive until the battery died, leave Jordan here to get burned.)

(But if Jordan gets burned, Eric gets burned. And it's all fun and games playing martyr to the cause when you're facing a criminal mischief charge, but murder? No thanks.)

(Eric isn't calling the cops.)

He finds Paige's number. He texts her—

(*RUN. OUT THE BACK DOOR. RIGHT NOW.*)

—and presses send just as Jordan peeks his head around the front of the Tesla.

"What's taking so long?"

"Shoelaces," Eric tells him, sliding the phone underneath the front tire. "Be ready in a second."

"Well, hurry up," Jordan says. "We can't afford to waste time."

299.

CUT TO: PAIGE

>. . . who is trying to Google lawyers on her phone when she gets Eric's text.

>*RUN. OUT THE BACK DOOR. RIGHT NOW.*

>Then she hears the voices in the driveway.

>Shit.

It's too dark outside to see who it is. The driveway lights are off, and there aren't any streetlights. All Paige can see are shadows. She crouches as far away from the window as possible, and listens.

The voices come up to the front door. Then the doorbell rings. It's LOUD in the silent house. Paige feels her heart jump.

(*If it's the cops, Eric can go screw himself.*)

But it's not the cops.

Paige figures this out quick.

(Just as soon as she hears the front window shatter.)

300.

Jordan breaks the front window with a patio stone. He reaches in and fiddles with the lock. Then he tries the doorknob. The door swings open.

"Let's hope they didn't set the alarm," he says.

"Yeah, let's hope," Eric says, as loud as he can without sounding loud. "That would really be a shame."

Jordan gives him a funny look, and then he disappears into the house. The front hall is dark. The whole house is silent. Eric listens, strains his ears for signs of life, praying he doesn't hear any. He doesn't, thank god.

(Eric's not sure what he'll do if Jordan really does find Paige. He's hoping he can convince them both to stay calm, take it easy. Hoping he can:

a) keep Paige from finding out about Haley,

b) keep Jordan from killing Paige, and

c) keep Paige from calling the police.)

(Good luck.)

"Paige?" Jordan's voice breaks the stillness. There's no answer. Not a sound. Jordan pokes his head into the empty living room. "Guess they really did bail on this place, huh? Come on. Let's check out the upstairs."

He starts up the front stairs. Eric reluctantly follows.

(*Run, Paige, run!*)

Jordan and Eric reach the upstairs landing. They're at

the end of a long hallway. Doors on either side, bedrooms. Paige's bedroom is the second on the left.

(Paige's room is where the light was coming from. Eric knows this, but he doesn't tell Jordan.)

Jordan creeps down the hall. Eric follows. He tries to act like he's being quiet, but he keeps bumping into things. He steps on the creaky floorboard. He even tries to breathe loud.

Jordan looks back. "*You gotta be quieter,*" he whispers.

Eric shrugs and tries to look apologetic.

(Sometimes it pays to be a perennial screwup.)

They reach Paige's bedroom door and pause. The door is half open. Eric fights the urge to scream something, give the game away.

(*You warned her. If she's still here now, it's her own fault.*)

Jordan looks back at Eric, checks that he's ready. Eric nods. Jordan pushes the door open.

(Eric holds his breath.)

(*RUN!*)

Then Jordan swears. "*Damn it.*"

Paige's bedroom light is on, but the room is empty.

Paige is gone.

301.

Paige can hear Eric's voice behind her as she hurries down the back staircase. Can't make out the words, but she knows damn well it's him. And that means Jordan's probably with him, and maybe Haley, too. From the tone of Eric's text, Paige is pretty sure why they're here.

To keep her quiet.

Shut her up.

Maybe even kill her.

(*They're your best friends, dummy. They're not going to kill you.*)

But Paige thinks about Michael McDougall. And she thinks about Eric's text. She hurries down the back staircase and into the kitchen. Creeps across the dark room as quietly as she can. Unlocks the back door and slips out into the yard, slides the door closed behind her.

She's on the deck now, her heart pounding. Can't hear the voices anymore. She hurries across the deck, down the little stairs onto the grass, and across the grass toward the back alley. Toward safety.

She's almost there when she collides with something. Something dark, something hard and metal. It clatters away with a sound like a gunshot, startling the neighbor's dog into a barking frenzy. Paige trips and falls, scrapes her knee. Her fucking mom's garden furniture, a table and chairs. The real-estate agent pulled it out for the viewings.

Shit.

It's wrought iron and solid. It really freaking hurts. Paige touches her leg, feels the rip in her pants, the skin raw underneath. Then a light comes on behind her, the kitchen light. There are lights for the backyard, too. If they come on, Paige is toast.

She has to get out of here.

Paige half crawls, half stumbles to the back fence, the gate. Pulls it open and slips through, closes it behind her as quiet as she can. Staggers down the alley with her heart threatening to rip through her chest.

302.

CUT TO: JORDAN AND ERIC.

"What the hell was that?" Jordan peers out at the back-yard. "Did you hear a noise back there?"

"Probably just a raccoon or something," Eric replies. "Maybe, like, a skunk."

Jordan frowns. "Sounded pretty loud to be a skunk. Let's check it out."

Eric opens his mouth to argue, but Jordan's already halfway out the door. Eric follows him onto the deck. They look around. It's dark, no moon in the sky. A dog barking next door, a car horn down the block.

"What's back here?" Jordan says. "I can't remember the last time I was at Paige's house."

"Just a backyard. There's some grass and a garden."

"And behind that?"

Eric hesitates. "The garage. And the alley."

"Let's go."

They cross the backyard. Make the fence, and the gate. Jordan pulls the gate open, and he and Eric peer out into the alley. They can't see anything. They can't hear anything. "Let's try the garage," Jordan says.

They check the garage. There's nothing in there but boxes and Paige's dad's motorcycle. The light from the open door casts a beam over the backyard, though, and Eric sees what caused that huge crash.

Garden furniture. A table and chairs, antique metal, pretty ornate. The table lies on its side, midway between the house and the back gate. It's way too heavy for a skunk to knock over.

Jordan's still checking out the garage. Eric edges over to the table. Bends down and lifts it, gets it upright just as Jordan comes back out to the yard.

"Anything?" Eric asks him.

Jordan looks around. Looks at the garden furniture. He shakes his head. "Nothing. Let's go back in the house."

303.

Eric and Jordan poke around Paige's house for another hour.

   ("Maybe she left, like, an airline receipt or something," Jordan says.)

   They don't find anything.

   (An empty box of Cinnamon Toast Crunch, and a stack of brochures.)

   Paige is gone.

304.

They drive back to Jordan's house. Jordan pulls into the driveway and stops. Leaves the Tesla running.

"First thing tomorrow," Jordan says, "I'll call my lawyer. Let him know our ex-friend Paige Hammond and her partner, Haley Keefer, might be spreading malicious lies about us to the police." He glances at Eric. "And don't worry, E. My guy is the best. Even if the cops do come for us, he'll make sure we get to tell *our* side of the story."

Eric doesn't say anything. He doesn't know what to say.

(His head is still spinning.)

(What is "*our* side of the story," exactly?)

(He might have a concussion—or maybe he's been over-dosing on Jordan the past couple of weeks.)

"Right now, though, we need to cover our asses," Jordan says. "And that means—"

(He hits the garage door opener on the Tesla's visor. The garage door rumbles open, revealing Jordan's garage, empty save for three brand-new pressure cookers and a couple telltale coffee cans in the corner.)

"—we need to move these explosives to a secure location."

Eric stares in at the garage. "You built more?"

"They're not finished yet. But yes," Jordan tells him.

He gives Eric that smile.

"It's my Fix, remember? And I'm telling you, E, this one is going to change your life. Like, forever."

305.

I mean . . .

You had to figure there was some kind of big, climactic showdown brewing, right?

That's always been the direction this was headed.

E isn't about to hop a Greyhound and bail and leave all the dramatic stuff to the cops.

He isn't flying away to some desert island with Jordan.

That would be cheap. It wouldn't jibe with the thematic demands of the genre—or the HERO'S JOURNEY.

E has to learn a lesson.

He has to, like, *do* something, and it has to symbolize how he has, you know, *changed*. Grown. Evolved.

Whatever.

(Plus Paige is on the run now, so we kind of have to resolve that.)

My point is, I hope you're not surprised that Jordan has more bombs. And I hope it doesn't piss you off if I tell you—

[SPOILER ALERT!]

—those bombs are going to have to explode.

Just not yet.

306.

Jordan picks up the pressure cookers, and carries them back to the Tesla.

"What the hell are you talking about?" Eric asks him. "What are you planning, Jordan?"

Jordan places the pressure cookers in the Tesla's trunk. Turns around and goes back for the gunpowder. "I can't tell you the target. It's a *surprise*." He glances back at Eric. "We're going to be famous, though. I can promise you that. We'll be household names when we finish this Fix."

Jordan places the twin cans of gunpowder in the back of the Tesla. "And it won't even matter about Paige and the police, because we'll be gone, E. We'll pull off this Fix and bail out of this shitty town, and we'll be fucking free for the rest of our lives. And anytime anyone mentions Capilano, *anywhere*, they'll say our names with it. That's how famous we're going to be."

Eric's not exactly wavering, but his mind's testing out the possibilities. Jordan's dad has a shitload of money. Therefore, Jordan has money. Jordan could buy them first-class tickets to a non-extradition-treaty country, and they could spend the rest of their lives on the beach, living in *the Moment* together.

(Just like those three days on the boat, except forever.)

(To the very end.)

"You want to do this," Jordan says, tearing the cell phones out of their cases. "You know you want it. Your mind just can't accept it, because you've trained it to worry so much. You focus on the worst-case scenarios."

Eric doesn't say anything. He *is* worried. But he's starting to see Jordan's point, a little bit, like the first hint of sunrise in the morning.

"Luckily, you've got me to show you another way," Jordan says. "So, your family's disowned you. Paige ran away. There's a very good chance you're already a fugitive." He looks at Eric with those hypnotic eyes. "What, exactly, is keeping you in Capilano? More to the point, why would you *stay* in this broken place?"

He holds Eric's gaze.

He waits for an answer.

Eric shifts his weight and looks around the driveway.

"Shit," he says.

307.

Eric almost gets in the car with Jordan.

    Almost.

    He's *thisclose* to buying what Jordan is selling.

308.

It all sounds so easy.

> (And yet.)

> If Eric goes along with this . . .

> Maybe he didn't actually murder the movie star, or Mike McDougall—

>> (or *Haley*)

>>> —but he's not stopping it.

>>> He's condoning the crimes.

>>> He's an accessory.

>>> Guilt by association.

>>> (He's Jordan's *sidekick*.)

> Eric doesn't want to be Jordan's sidekick; he wanted to be Jordan's *boyfriend*, but suddenly the idea doesn't have the same appeal.

> He may not want to be president, but he *definitely* doesn't want to be a murderer.

> So.

> Jordan's halfway in the driver's seat of the Tesla. He's watching Eric over the roof. "No time to waste, E. Let's go."

> Eric thinks about Mike McDougall. About ███████████. About freaking *Haley*.

>> (He thinks about Paige.)

> "I can't do this with you," he tells Jordan. "I won't."

309.

Jordan doesn't blink. Jordan isn't fazed.

"Fine," he says. "Be a pussy, if you must. I'll just fix this town by myself."

(And something triggers in Eric.)

"I can't let you do this," he tells Jordan. "This isn't cool anymore."

But Jordan just smiles. It isn't a nice smile. "Oh yeah?" he says. "And, what, Eric, you're going to stop me?"

310.

What follows is a very short struggle.

(You couldn't even call it a fight.)

It ends with Eric on the ground in Jordan's driveway, holding his bloody nose as Jordan drives off in the Tesla.

It ends with the Tesla's brake lights disappearing around a curve on Marine Drive.

It ends with Eric lying there alone.

311.

Eric pulls himself to his feet and wipes the blood and snot from his face. Stands in the driveway in front of Jordan's dark, empty mansion, and doesn't have a clue what to do.

A part of him is wishing he'd climbed in that car with Jordan. A part of him believes Jordan's the only way out of this mess. Commit to the Suicide Pack. Stick together forever. Follow Jordan to the ends of the earth.

But Eric's sick of *following*.

He's sick of Jordan's Fixes.

Eric's starting to feel like Jordan isn't really in the Pack to fix anything at all. He's starting to suspect that maybe Jordan just likes to watch the world burn.

And that kind of makes Jordan the biggest hypocrite of them all.

312.

Liam picks up on the third or fourth ring. His words are like one big, weary sigh. "What do you want, Eric?"

"I need your help," Eric tells him. "Jordan's planning something crazy. Something, like, *big*. And I can't stop him by myself."

There's a long silence. Eric runs through his list of other people he could call. Other people who could possibly help him find Jordan.

(Paige isn't answering her texts.)

(It's a short list.)

(It's pretty well nonexistent.)

Then Liam lets out his breath.

"You'd better have a good story," he says. "Where are you?"

313.

Liam drives an old Hyundai. The backseat is littered with paperwork. He leans over and pushes open the passenger door. Eric climbs inside. Liam looks at Eric and flinches.

"My god," he says. "You look like you got attacked."

Eric pulls down the visor and studies himself in the mirror. His face is scratched from the gravel in Jordan's driveway. His nose is still bloody. He has a black eye, too, and a welt on his forehead.

"That's from Jordan," he tells Liam. "We kind of had a difference of opinion."

Liam frowns when Eric says Jordan's name. "You really have to explain what's going on," he says. "I hope you didn't call me all the way out to Capilano because you had a lovers' quarrel."

"It's not a freaking lovers' quarrel," Eric says. "I told you, this is big."

314.

So Eric explains everything.

315.

"So you *didn't* kill ███████████," Liam says when Eric's done. "It was all Jordan and those girls, right? You weren't even in the room."

Eric shakes his head. "I was part of the team. The Pack. I knew what was happening. I helped them get away."

"But you didn't kill him. You didn't kill the special effects guy, either, or your friend on the boat. It was all Jordan. *You're* not actually a murderer."

Eric doesn't say anything.

(He *is* a murderer.)

(He's part of the Suicide Pack.)

"There isn't anything in the news yet," Liam says, checking his phone. "Your face isn't, like, on a Wanted poster or anything. Jordan's, either. So maybe your friend didn't go to the cops."

Eric wonders where Paige is.

(He hopes she's really far away.)

"You think we should call them?" Liam asks. "The cops? Like, if Jordan's really running around with a bunch of bombs, shouldn't we—"

"We can't," Eric tells him. "Not yet. If the police know for sure that Jordan killed ███████████, they'll know *I'm* in the Pack, too. And then my life is over."

Liam stares at him. "You're willing to risk lives to protect yourself?"

Eric avoids his eyes. "Let's hope it doesn't come to that," he says. "I just need you to help me find Jordan, okay?"

316.

But Liam isn't much help. "We only dated for a few months. And to be honest, we mostly just fooled around here, or on his dad's boat."

(Eric flashes back to those three days on the Sundancer. Pictures Jordan and Liam doing the same thing, having the same conversations, watching the same sunsets. It hurts like a stab wound.)

(He shakes the image from his mind.)

"Think," he says. "*Please.* Anywhere you can think of that he might have gone. Anything in Capilano that he actually *hates*, something he would use as a target."

"I'm thinking," Liam says. "I'm just really not sure."

KIK -- CAPILANO HIGH PRIVATE MESSAGE GROUP
— 08/27/16 — 08:46 AM

USERNAME: Anonymous-9
MESSAGE: Good morning, Cap kiddies! I hope
    you're excited! You've all been waiting
    SO patiently to know the identities of
    those destructive fanatics who call
    themselves the SUICIDE PACK, and I'm
    happy to tell you TODAY'S THE BIG DAY.
    That's right, I know the identities
    of every member of the PACK (all four
    of them), AND I WILL REVEAL THAT
    INFORMATION TONIGHT, IN AMBLESIDE PARK.
    Come one, come all! Fun for the whole
    family! Tell a friend!

317.

"Eric, wake up."

Liam shakes Eric out of a restless, fitful sleep. Eric rolls over. Rubs his eyes. Checks his watch.

It's quarter to ten in the morning.

(Eric never meant to fall asleep, honest. But yesterday was kind of a crazy day, with the whole Jordan-killing-Haley thing and then the Jordan-trying-to-kill-Paige thing and all the times Jordan, like, kicked Eric's ass . . .

He was kinda exhausted.

So he slept a little.

Sue him.)

Liam's standing over Eric. He's holding Eric's phone. "This thing's been blowing up for, like, a solid hour," he says. "I thought maybe it had something to do with what's happening."

Eric takes the phone. Kik notifications, and tons of them. He swipes his phone unlocked, opens the app. The Capilano High message board is on fire again. Eric scrolls up.

And up.

And up some more.

He scrolls up a half hour, and then he sees the new message from Anonymous-9.

"Son of a bitch," Eric says. "I know where Jordan's planting the bombs."

318.

So, here's the thing:
Jordan's final target—
(and thus the climax of this book)
—has to be something symbolic. It has to be something crazy dangerous. It has to, you know, *raise the stakes* higher than anything we've experienced before.

And what higher stakes than if THE WHOLE TOWN's at risk?
What better way to rid Capilano of all the hypocrites than by setting off bombs
at the *Capilano*
Summer's End
Ball?
(Kablamo.)

319.

(Rich people stories always end with ridiculous parties.

It's, like, *required*.)

320.

A brief digression about this *particular* ridiculous party party:

Every August, the Capilano elite throw a tremendous party in Ambleside Park, by the beach. It's called the Capilano Summer's End Ball, and it's technically some kind of charity event for, like, Africa or something, but it's really just an excuse for the whole town to get dressed up like it's the Oscars and pay a couple thousand dollars a plate to feel like they're doing good in the world. Everybody who is *anybody* will be there. And they'll bring their kids with them.

Eric knows a little bit about the gala, because his mom is on the board of directors. Eric knows, for instance, the gala is tonight. He knows his dad is supposed to give a speech.

And he knows everyone in Capilano will be there.

(Well, naturally.)

321.

In case you missed it, here's the key to the whole saga:

Jordan is Anonymous-9.

He's been building buzz for the Pack under a secret identity.

(The oldest trick in the book.)

And Jordan's BIG REVEAL tonight isn't just, like, a speech.

The people want the Suicide Pack. They're going to get the Suicide Pack. They're going to get more Suicide Pack than they know what to do with.

(And in this instance, Suicide Pack = chaos and burning and a lot of explosions.)

322.

Eric and Liam find a pay phone outside a 7-Eleven, and Eric calls Capilano PD. He tells the desk sergeant that the guy who killed ███████████ is planning to blow up the Capilano Summer's End Ball.

He tells the desk sergeant that Jordan Grant is the guy planting the bombs.

"How do you know this?" the desk sergeant asks.

"Never mind how. Just get your officers to Ambleside Park. Do it now."

Eric hangs up the phone. Walks back to Liam's Hyundai and gets in the passenger seat. "Okay, drive," he tells Liam. "The cops are going to come looking. And we don't want to be around when they get here."

323.

Eric calls home with his cell phone. Gets the machine.

(*Damn it. Pick up.*)

He calls his dad's cell phone instead. His dad answers. "Senator Connelly."

"*Dad.*" Eric realizes he's yelling. Tries to keep his voice calm. "Dad, it's me. Dad, you need to stay home today."

"Eric? Where are you?"

"It doesn't matter. I just need you to listen to me. You can't be at the gala today, okay? You have to get out of there. Mom, too."

Eric's dad laughs, scornful. "Your mother is with her sister in San Francisco, Eric. *You* drove her there, and after all of the planning she put into this event. Though I'm certain San Francisco's not far enough to escape the shame."

(Eric checks the time on his Omega. It's already twelve fifteen. The gala starts at six.)

"Dad, there's a bomb," Eric says. "Jordan's going to blow up the gala. You can't be there when it happens."

"Is this some kind of a joke? Are you on drugs?" Eric's dad's voice is hard. "You need to come home before you damage your future any—"

"Fuck my future," Eric says. "Just stay home, okay? *Please.* Go somewhere and hide out until this is over."

"I *will not* stay home," his dad replies.

(Click.)

324.

"Well?" Liam says.

Eric puts down the phone. "He basically told me to go fuck myself."

"So what do we do now?"

Eric looks around. Looks at his watch. "I guess we find out if the police believed me."

325.

Ambleside Park is situated by the water on the west side of town. The symphony does performances there every Sunday in the summer. People get married with a view of the ocean.

(It's *Capilano's crown jewel*, if you believe the brochures.)

Eric and Liam park a couple blocks over from the west end of the park—

(the most isolated entrance).

They can hear music wafting through the trees,

the string quartet rehearsing

(or something).

(Rich-people stuff.)

"You don't have to come with me," Eric tells Liam. "It will probably get crazy in there. You should probably walk away."

Liam stares out the window. "What if I drive away from here and the police don't defuse the bombs?"

"I mean, I can still probably stop him."

"But what if you can't?" Liam shakes his head. "People could die. I can't just bail now."

Eric looks at him. "Well, thanks."

"You don't have to thank me." Liam kind of laughs. "It's not like I *want* to be here."

326.

Eric and Liam sneak into the park. Creep toward the gala, the red carpet, a big tent, and the aforementioned string quartet. There's a valet stand out front, a parking lot.

(There's an army of police officers, too. They're everywhere.)

Eric and Liam hide in the trees at the edge of the parking lot. They hide for a long time. They watch the cops guarding the tent, and the workers scurrying in and out, and they listen to the string quartet rehearse the same goddamn Vivaldi number, like, eight million times.

And as the afternoon turns to evening, the party begins. Luxury cars fill the valet parking lot. Rich people in designer clothes line up outside the tent, posing for pictures on the red carpet.

Eric and Liam scan the arriving guests for any sign of Jordan. Search the valet lot for Jordan's dad's Tesla.

They don't see Jordan.

(But they do see . . .)

327.

Eric grabs Liam's arm. *"Over there,"* he says, pointing. *"That's Paige."*

Liam frowns. "Oka-ay?" he says. "Who's Paige again?"

Eric gives him a look.

"Oh," Liam says. "One of the girls. You think she's here with Jordan?"

Eric doesn't know why Paige is here at all. He doesn't know why Paige isn't, like, a thousand miles away from here.

"You need to get her out of here," he tells Liam. "Take her somewhere safe until this is over. I'll watch the tent."

"You want *me* to talk to her?" Liam says.

"I can't go out there. What if the police know about me? I can't take the chance."

Liam just watches as Paige crosses the lot to the line outside the tent. She looks around the park, once, and then joins the line.

"Go," Eric says. "Before she's inside."

Liam pauses another beat. Then he swears and climbs out of the bushes, shaking his head.

328.

Eric watches as Liam hurries across the valet lot to the line. He watches Liam approach Paige, tap her on the shoulder. He watches Paige frown as she turns and sees Liam. Watches her features darken as Liam says something.

Paige shakes her head.

She gestures emphatically.

She doesn't look like she wants to go anywhere.

Liam glances back at the bushes. Eric screams at him telepathically. *Do not. Let her. Go into that tent.*

Liam turns back around to Paige. He says something else. Paige looks past Liam. She looks directly at the bushes where Eric's hiding.

She steps out of the line, and starts walking toward Eric.

329.

Paige is in the bushes before Eric can react.

(She's tearing her Badgley Mischka, but she doesn't seem to care.)

"Give me one good reason why I shouldn't call the cops," she says. "I'm sick of this bullshit, Eric. I'm done."

"I know," Eric says. "I'm sorry. You were right, about everything. But you can't be here right now, Paige. It's too dangerous."

"Yeah, I *know*. Haley said you and Jordan went crazy. She said you're going to destroy Anonymous-9 before he can tell them about us tonight."

There's so much to unpack in that statement that Eric short-circuits for a moment. "Wait . . . Haley?"

"She texted me just after Anonymous dropped his last message. Told me to meet her at the gala." Paige glares at him. "We're ending this, Eric. This *Pack* bullshit is like a million miles out of bounds already, and—"

"Haley's dead," Eric says.

Paige blinks. "What?"

"Haley didn't text you this morning. I saw Jordan kill her last night. She's dead, and she doesn't know anything about the gala, Paige. That was Jordan texting you from her phone."

"But—" Paige's face goes slack. "How do you know?"

"Jordan has three more bombs," Eric tells her. "He wants as many people here as possible before he sets them off. So he invented Anonymous-9 to make sure they all came."

Paige's mouth moves. She doesn't make any sounds, though. She looks down at the ground and plays Eric's words back.

"Haley's dead," she says.

"Yeah," Eric says. "I'm so sorry, Paige. I totally fucked this all up."

Paige looks ready to reply. She doesn't get the chance. Because just as she starts to speak, the first bomb explodes.

330.

The explosion doesn't come from the gala. It sounds like it came from far away, the other end of downtown probably, by the mall. It's muffled, but it's for sure a bomb blast. It sounds just like the bomb that destroyed the Côte d'Azur, the first bomb—

(Jordan's bomb)

(E's bomb).

"What the hell?" Liam says. "I thought you said Jordan's target was the gala."

Eric's mind is racing. He's trying to figure this out. Outside the bushes, the Capilano PD is mobilizing. Cops are running to their cruisers. They're hollering into radios. They're slamming doors and whooping sirens, peeling rubber toward downtown.

"What's over there?" Paige says. "What would Jordan want to target?"

"The St. Regis. The marina. Tory Burch." Liam thinks. "Anthropologie? Nordstrom Rack? *Starbucks?*"

The last of the police cars screams out of the parking lot. Its siren fades into the distance. A stillness descends. Dead quiet.

(And then Eric gets it.)

"It's just a diversion," he tells Liam and Paige. "He's getting the police out of the way."

Liam peers out of the bushes at the line of confused rich people and handful of rent-a-cops who are lingering in the wake of the PD's mass exodus.

"Looks like it worked," he says.

KIK -- CAPILANO HIGH PRIVATE MESSAGE GROUP
— 08/27/16 — 06:08 PM

USERNAME: Anonymous-9
MESSAGE: If you're not at the gala, kiddies,
     you're missing one epic party. Who's
     ready to know THE TRUTH???

331.

Across the parking lot, outside the tent, everyone under the age of nineteen checks their phone at the same time.

>(Eric can literally *see* the moment when Jordan's message hits.)

Kids start texting. Typing. They look up and chatter to the person next to them. Everyone's excited. Everyone's trying to get back in the tent.

>The cops are forgotten.

>The Pack's more important.

>Eric has one focus—find Jordan.

332.

"I'm going to stop him," Eric says. "Liam, come with me. Paige, you stay here."

"Wait, what?" Paige frowns at Liam. "I don't even know this guy. How come he gets to go and I don't?"

"It's too dangerous," Eric says. "Stay back here where it's safe."

Paige shakes her head. "Screw you and your gender-normative bullshit. This is my fault, too. I'm going."

From the look in her eyes, Eric knows he's not changing her mind. So he turns to Liam instead.

"Find Jordan's car," he says. "It's a Tesla, probably hidden somewhere nearby. Disable it, if you can. And if he tries to escape—"

"He's not going anywhere," Liam tells Eric. "I'll make sure of it."

333.

"Two bombs," Eric tells Paige, as they scan the tent—

(There's a stage for the speeches, close to where they're standing. A dance floor and that goddamn string quartet. Banquet seating, and a—

crowded

—bar table.)

"Probably situated in a way to cause the most damage."

"I'll take the far side. You take the near side," Paige says. "What do we do when we find the bombs?"

"I'll get them out of here," Eric tells her. "Get them into the forest, as far away from civilization as possible."

Paige looks skeptical. "Those are live explosives. What if Jordan blows you up?"

Eric forces a smile. "I kind of deserve it. Better me than those old people, right? Even if they are godless hypocrites."

Paige doesn't smile back.

Paige doesn't think it's funny.

"Hey," Eric says, just before they disperse. "I'm sorry I flaked out so hard junior year. I know that was rotten of me. I should have, like, told you what was going on in my life."

Paige stares at him like she doesn't understand. Then she kind of laughs. "You're doing this *now*? All the freaking time you had to apologize, and you choose *this moment*, Eric?"

"I mean," Eric says. "It just felt like an appropriate time."

"You watch too many movies. Apologize when this is over. Then maybe I'll listen."

"Fine," Eric says. "But I'm sorry anyway."

Now Paige smiles. Just a little, but it's there.

It's a bonding moment.

It lightens the mood.

Paige and Eric enjoy it for a minute.

Then they make their move for the bombs.

334.

Eric hurries through the rows of tables toward the stage, where the string quartet is just finishing up. He's bumping people as he passes them. They're complaining. He's causing a scene.

Eric doesn't have time to care right now.

(His phone buzzes.)

A text message from Liam.

Found J's car. This in the center console.

There's an image attached. A picture of a piece of paper. Blank, except for three lines, written in Jordan's neat, steady hand.

Three lines.

Three phone numbers, all nearly sequential.

(Eric gets it.)

These are the numbers to Jordan's burner phones.

These are the phone numbers that will set off Jordan's bombs.

(Eric enters them into his contacts.)

335.

Eric's phone buzzes again.
He checks the screen, thinking it's Liam.
It's not.

KIK -- CAPILANO HIGH PRIVATE MESSAGE GROUP
— 08/27/16 — 06:15 PM

USERNAME: Anonymous-9
MESSAGE: Confession time: One member of the
    SUICIDE PACK couldn't be here tonight.
    She had a tragic boating accident, and
    now she's dead.

KIK -- CAPILANO HIGH PRIVATE MESSAGE GROUP
— 08/27/16 — 06:16 PM

USERNAME: Anonymous-9
MESSAGE: [A picture of HALEY KEEFER
     on Jordan's boat. She's smoking a
     cigarette and shooting the camera the
     finger.]

336.

Around the tent, hundreds of smartphones light up.
(Audible gasps from the audience.)

KIK -- CAPILANO HIGH PRIVATE MESSAGE GROUP
— 08/27/16 — 06:17 PM

USERNAME: Anonymous-9
MESSAGE: Two other PACK members should be
    here shortly. You'll recognize them.
    He's Cap High's nerdy but lovable
    STUDENT OF THE YEAR and she was in
    ITALIAN VOGUE.

337.

A murmur from the crowd. Around Eric, heads start to turn. Eric can feel people looking at him.

There's no time for this game.

He scans the room, looking for a logical place to plant a bomb. Looking for Jordan's duffel bag.

Then he spots it.

The bag is sitting under a table by the cocktail bar. It's mostly hidden by an ornate tablecloth. Above it, the table is piled high with an elaborate pyramid of crystal champagne flutes.

Eric can see immediately why Jordan chose this spot.

(Shrapnel.)

(Plus the bar is swarming with people.)

His phone's buzzing again. Eric doesn't bother to check it. He sticks to the edge of the tent. Tries to stay inconspicuous. Hurries as fast as he dares toward the champagne table, his eyes scanning the crowd, expecting any second to see Jordan.

Expecting any second to,

well,

(you know)

kablamo.

338.

People close to Eric are openly staring at him by now. They're pointing and nudging each other and whispering his name.

(And Eric's pretty sure it's not because he showed up in a hoodie.)

Eric ignores them. Reaches the back of the champagne table and ducks underneath. Stretches for the duffel bag, hooks the strap with his fingers. Drags it toward him—

(gently, gently)

—then picks it up and walks, like, *fast* for the nearest exit.

KIK -- CAPILANO HIGH PRIVATE MESSAGE GROUP
— 08/27/16 — 06:20 PM

USERNAME: Anonymous-9
MESSAGE: Haley Keefer. Paige Hammond. Eric
    Connelly. Three of the four members of
    the SUICIDE PACK, though in truth none
    of them have the balls to LEAD the
    Pack. So who's calling the shots, you
    ask?

KIK -- CAPILANO HIGH PRIVATE MESSAGE GROUP
— 08/27/16 — 06:21 PM

USERNAME: Anonymous-9
MESSAGE: Well, me.

339.

More gasps behind Eric as he bursts out of the tent. Hundreds of people talking at once, scanning the crowd, looking for the ringleader. Some of them are smiling. They still think this is a joke.

(They don't know how wrong they are.)

Eric's beyond all that now. He has the bag. He needs to get the bag out of here. He's hoping all to hell that the bag has both bombs.

And if it doesn't?

He's running back inside to help Paige find the other.

340.

Eric shoves an old dude aside as he runs for the exit. The red carpet lineup. The parking lot.

He's almost outside when someone blocks his way. A Cap student. Someone big.

It's Callum Fulchrest.

"You *asshole*," Callum tells Eric. "You and your fucking friends *ruined* me."

He has his hands raised, fists clenched, like he's ready for a fight. But Eric isn't in the mood.

"You ruined yourself," he says as he dodges past Callum—

(feeling the contents of the duffel bag jostle within).

"Next time lay off with the fucking roofies."

Callum reaches for Eric. Misses.

Eric keeps running.

"That Basquiat was a fake, anyway," he calls back.

Then he's in the parking lot, and Callum's far behind him.

341.

Eric's thinking about how he could be on a Greyhound bus right now. He could be far away from this fiasco.

He could be anywhere.

Instead he's still in Capilano, probably a wanted fugitive already, carrying a homemade IED through a parking lot full of luxury cars.

(*Live in the moment.*)

(*Just don't die.*)

342.

Eric carries the duffel bag through the parking lot. Scans the darkness for any sign of Jordan. Can't see him.

(Of course, that doesn't mean he isn't out there.)

Callum's still standing at the entrance to the tent. He's calling for security. Eric ignores this. Sooner or later, though, the rent-a-cops are going to intervene. Eric wants to have these bombs defused before that happens.

(Then he can start worrying about escaping.)

He ducks down a row of cars, kneels between a Range Rover and a Porsche Cayenne. Sets the bag to the ground and unzips it and peers in at the contents.

It's a bomb, all right. It looks just like the first one, Jordan's failed attempt. The bomb Eric resuscitated in his basement bedroom. This is both good and bad. It's good, because Jordan hasn't graduated to advanced bomb-making yet. The bomb should be easy to disable.

Where it starts to go bad, though, is the fact that there's only one bomb. And that means there's another one out there.

Eric pulls the lid off the pressure cooker. Looks in at the phone and the blasting cap and the tangle of wires, the gunpowder. Is about to reach in and dismantle the apparatus when he hears—

(no, *feels*)

—someone behind him.

He looks back.

It's Jordan,

dressed in freaking *Armani*,

smiling that mischievous smile.

Before Eric can react, Jordan PUNCHES him, hard,
sends him sprawling into the side of the Range Rover.
Jordan picks up the bag. Zips it closed again.

"Tsk, tsk," he tells Eric. "I had this whole Fix planned out, and you
freaking *ruined* it."

Eric just stares up at him. Eric thinks:

Damn.

343.

"I'm not going to lie, E, I'm a little disappointed," Jordan says. "What happened to *together to the end*, huh?"

Eric pulls himself to his knees. Rubs his cheek where Jordan punched him. It hurts.

"But then again, I'm kind of impressed, too," Jordan says. "Who knew you had all this hero stuff in you, am I right? I'm telling you, the Eric Connelly I met at the start of the summer didn't have *half* your backbone." He smiles. "You might be my favorite Fix of all, E. Excluding the grand finale, of course."

Eric stares at him.

(Tries to figure out a way to divest Jordan of that bomb.)

"You're not doing this to fix anything," he says. "It was never about that. This is just one big ego boost for you, isn't it?"

"On the contrary." Jordan shakes his head. "This town is a shithole, E. I'm doing the world a favor. And if I happen to get really, really freaking famous in the process?" He shrugs. "Well, shit. I guess that's just a perk of the job."

"You're a hypocrite. You know that, right? You're just as bad as any of these assholes."

Jordan's smile doesn't waver. "Think about how far you've come since the first day of summer. Think about all the fun we've had. It's been amazing, right?"

Eric starts to reply. Jordan holds up his hand. "Just answer me. Did you have fun?"

"We freaking *killed* people," Eric says. "That's supposed to be fun?"

"Psh," Jordan says. "Listen, E, I'm just saying, I've never steered you wrong before. Just trust me, and this will all work out fine."

(Just trust me.)

(Just *trust* me.)

(Let me *do* this and then we'll be together forever.)

(You'll thank me when this is over; just *trust me*.)

344.

But Eric's through with that bullshit.

He's friends-off with Jordan.

(Enough of that *trust me* crap.)

He looks up at Jordan. "Where's the second one?"

Jordan laughs. "Oh, is this the part where the evil bad guy is supposed to reveal his evil plan to the helpless hero?"

Eric shrugs. "I mean, whatever."

"Fine," Jordan says. "You want to know where the second bomb is, E? I'll show you."

Jordan pulls his phone from his pocket and types in a number. Presses send. "Here you go," he tells Eric.

And halfway across the lot,

a GMC Yukon blows the fuck up.

345.

Between the fireball and the chaos and the hundred car alarms, Eric's thinking—

I recognize that truck.

It's Donovan Connelly's personal Yukon. It's Eric's dad's ride.

"I meant to save that one for your dad," Jordan says. "You know, while he was in it. Just one final 'Fuck you' to the senator for all the ways he screwed up your life. But I guess I can't resist showing off for you, E. And he'll get his in the end, anyway, don't worry."

The lot is insanity now. The Yukon burns bright. What cops remain in the park are pouring in from the perimeter as rich people in tuxedos and gowns spill out of the gala. Everywhere is car alarms, sirens, and screaming. Eric can see Paige at the exit, searching the crowd. He sees Liam, too, coming out of the forest.

"You're totally crazy," Eric says. "You should be in, like, a mental institution, for real."

"Poor people are crazy, E," Jordan says, shouldering the bag. "Rich people are eccentric. That's just facts."

He turns away from Eric, walks out from between the Porsche and the Range Rover. Starts to walk toward the crowd milling around in front of the gala. And that's about when Eric pushes himself to his feet and launches his body at Jordan's.

346.

You can picture what happens next.

(Cue the ACTION-MOVIE FIGHT SCENE.)

Except we've already established that Eric's not much of a fighter. He's tall, but Jordan's taller. He's strong(ish); Jordan's *built*. Plus, his head is kind of pounding from where Jordan punched him, and oh, also, the bomb. He's hardly in the best fighting shape.

He *does* have the element of surprise, though, and that counts for something. Specifically, it counts for enough to knock Jordan stumbling down to the pavement, where he lands on all fours.

Eric lands on top of him. Police are running past, and security guards, and old rich people in five-figure formal wear. And Eric and Jordan are fighting.

It's not a fair fight. (See above.)

Jordan lets the bomb go and proceeds to kick Eric's ass. Again. Like, Eric gets a few shots in, but mostly it's Jordan with the fists and the kicking and the elbows and the knees. And eventually Jordan gets Eric pinned, and he's straddling Eric's body and raining punches, no mercy, until he's sure Eric's ass has been satisfactorily kicked.

(And Eric, for his part, can just lie there and take the punches and, like, *bleed*.)

And then Jordan lets up. Stands and picks up the Herschel

bag. Looks down at Eric—

(who's lying there, dazed, thinking he might never get up).

"I'm sorry, E," Jordan says, and he looks like he truly means it.

"I really thought we'd be famous together."

347.

It's Eric, Eric wants to tell Jordan. *My name's freaking Eric.*
But that argument seems inconsequential now,
given the circumstances.

348.

So, Eric lies there.

(Surrounded by chaos.)

Watches Jordan pick up the bag with the bomb inside and start down the rows of cars toward the gala doors.

Looks past Jordan to the crowd at those doors, and if he looks close, can see his dad in the crowd, standing with his driver, looking upset but not at all blown up.

But Paige and Liam are over there too, struggling to hold back the crowd, all those terrified gala-goers who are going to go down as collateral damage, and none of them *really* deserve it.

They're rich, and shallow, and really kind of awful, but that doesn't mean they deserve to die.

Especially not so that Jordan Grant can become the infamous Suicide Pack Killer.

So, you know what's coming.

Redemption.

(Kind of.)

349.

Jordan's cutting between a big Range Rover and a Lexus. Once he gets through, it's a clear path to the gala entrance. Nothing stands in his way.

(The time to act is NOW.)

(This is *the Moment*.)

Eric rolls over. Pulls his phone from his pocket. Scrolls through his contacts to Jordan's first burner phone. Points it at Jordan, like a remote.

(*You don't have to point it like that.*)

Presses send.

350.

Nothing.

351.

Eric scrolls down to the second burner's number. Presses send again.

(And if you're at all acquainted with the rule of three, you can figure out what happens.)

352.

Jordan keeps walking. The bomb still doesn't go off.

(Wrong number again.)

Eric scrolls to the third burner phone in his contacts. Lifts his head and finds Jordan. He's still between two cars.

"Jordan," Eric calls out. "*Drop the bomb.*"

Somehow, Jordan hears him. He looks back at Eric. He just smiles, and it kind of looks like he knows what's about to happen.

(*They'll remember my name.*)

But he doesn't stop walking. He keeps going, daring Eric to do it.

And Eric's running out of time.

So he does it.

353.

BOOM.

KIK -- CAPILANO HIGH PRIVATE MESSAGE GROUP
— 08/27/16 — 06:26 PM

USERNAME: SuIcIdEpAcK
MESSAGE: So long, Capilano. You're too
    broken to fix.

354.

(I would like to tell you that Eric saves the day, and nobody dies, and he gets away clean, and even Jordan survives.

I would like to tell you there are no consequences for the things that Eric did. But that would be a cop-out. You wouldn't feel satisfied.

Real life has consequences.)

355.

Eric wakes up in a hospital bed. He spends a few days there, and then he goes to jail—

(more accurately, a *juvenile detention facility*).

Detectives Dawson and Richards come to see him. They take him to an interview room, and they tell him that Jordan's dead. They tell Eric that with Haley and Jordan dead, and Paige already confessing, he's the only target they have left. They tell Eric he's an easy target, and they're going to take him down.

They tell him the prosecution is going to try him as an adult.

And they tell him his father ain't chipping in a dime for legal representation.

(*If you cannot afford an attorney, one will be appointed for you.*)

Basically, they tell Eric . . .
he's fucked.

356.

. . . and that's when Haley comes back.

(Okay, so there's *one* cop-out.)

It turns out Haley doesn't drown when Jordan knocks her off the Sundancer. She splashes around for a while, and she inhales a lot of seawater. She pretty well *thinks* she's going to drown.

But she doesn't.

She washes up on one of those western islands, clutching a piece of driftwood like the girl in *Titanic*. A couple kayakers find her a day or two later, soaking wet and shivering and clinging to life.

(But still alive.)

The kayakers call the coast guard, and the coast guard brings her back to the city, where they throw her in a hospital bed and nurse her back to life.

It takes a while.

And then when Haley's feeling better, she turns on the TV in her hospital room, and there's Eric's face on the news, and Haley hears the whole story.

And she decides she can't let Eric take *all* the blame.

357.

Haley's reemergence does a wonderful job of *un-fucking* Eric.

For one thing, Haley is alive, so that's one less murder charge on Eric's rap sheet. And Haley is more than willing to tell Dawson and Richards that it was Jordan who knocked her overboard, Jordan who tried to kill her. She tells the detectives that Eric was just as surprised as she was.

Further, Haley gets Eric off the hook for Mike McDougall's murder, too—

Haley tells Dawson and Richards about the conversation in the Sundancer, how Jordan bragged about killing the special effects guy. She tells Dawson and Richards how she and Eric and Paige were all together at Jordan's house while Jordan was killing McDougall, how Jordan did it all on his own.

And Dawson and Richards grudgingly accept this, especially after someone at Cap Marina tells them he remembers Jordan coming back on the Sundancer by himself that morning, no sign of pretty girls or, like, Eric.

So, boom, that's Haley and Mike wiped from Eric's list of charges. That just leaves, let me see, ▮▮▮▮▮▮▮, plus the Côte d'Azur bomb, plus, well, the Room spree, and maybe even that trashy magazine office Haley broke into way back on page 101.

That's a long list of charges.

That's a lot to answer for.

(I hate to say it, but Eric's still fucked.)

358.

Liam knows a lawyer, a Legal Aid guy named Rob. He agrees to take Eric's case as a favor.

Lawyer Rob manages to get Eric charged as a minor. He gets the ███████████ murder charges downgraded to aiding and abetting, on account of how Eric was in the lobby of the St. Regis when it actually happened.

The bombing, though, is pretty tough to dispute. Ditto the Room spree. Lawyer Rob can't do much but ask for a plea deal. The prosecution obliges, but they still come back with jail time.

"You'll be in a juvenile detention facility until you turn eighteen," Lawyer Rob tells Eric. "After that, they'll move you to an adult prison, minimum security. Give them three years with good behavior and you're out."

Three years.

Adult prison.

(So much for law school.)

359.

(On the plus side, the Connelly name is really, *really* tarnished. And you can imagine how Eric's dad feels about that.)

360.

"So, I guess I'll never be president," Eric tells Liam.

They're sitting in the visiting room at the juvenile detention facility. The dramatic stuff is over. Haley caught a three-year sentence (she'll make parole in twelve months) and Paige is under house arrest (twelve months, three years' probation, five hundred hours of community service).

(I told you rich kids get off easy.)

Right now, Eric's trying to get used to prison life. Trying to toughen up in junior jail before the big move to the big house.

(I mean, it's minimum security, but still.)

His dad hasn't visited. His mom has come, twice—

(she had to sneak out on Eric's dad to do it).

(She cried both times.)

(Eric didn't tell her about Maggie Swenson.
Or Roger Dodger.)

(He figures his mom doesn't need to hear it right now.)

But Liam keeps coming back. He's come four or five times now. And Eric doesn't ask why, because he's afraid Liam will stop, and Liam's visits, really, are the only thing that keep him sane.

"Who wants to be president, anyway?" Liam says. "Did you see what it did to Obama? Dude aged, like, thirty years by the end of his second term."

Eric laughs, despite himself.

"I just don't know what I'm going to do instead," he says. "I spent my whole life thinking I would just follow in my dad's footsteps. Now I'm, like, a convict."

"Not for long," Liam says. "You'll still be young when you get out."

"Yeah, and then what? All I ever planned for was law school and political office. I never considered other options. I don't even know where to start."

"You could come back to the health center. We could always use more help."

Eric makes a face. "What, giving needles to junkies?" He catches himself. "Sorry."

Liam laughs. "Think it over. It might not be so bad." He shrugs. "It would be nice to see you again, anyway. When you're, you know, outside."

Eric looks around the visiting room. Looks at Liam.

(Eric can see how Jordan would have liked him.)

"I mean, yeah," he says. "I mean, I would really like that."

361.

So, that's that. Eric settles into life as a convict, and it's harder and easier than he ever imagined. He reads a lot, and he lifts weights and he attends classes and tries to figure out what he'll do when he's out.

The days pass, and it's lonely and scary and rough, but Liam keeps coming, even after Eric moves to, you know, *real* prison.

And then a year passes, and it's not Liam waiting for Eric in the visitors' booth, and it's not his mom, either.

It's Paige.

She looks different. She's cut her long hair short, and dyed the blond dark. And Eric can tell by her expression that he looks pretty different too.

"So, here we are," she says when the (inevitably awkward) first moments are over. "A couple of regular criminals, huh?"

Eric nods. Regular criminals.

"Of course, we did save the whole town from a terrorist attack," Paige says, smiling wryly. "So maybe we're kind of heroes, too, just a little?"

"I killed Jordan," Eric says. "Does that make me a hero?"

Paige shrugs. "It was him or the whole town. Him or *me*. And I know . . ." She pauses. "I know it couldn't have been easy, but you did it anyway."

"Yeah," Eric says. "I thought I loved him."

Paige doesn't say anything to this, not for a while. She just looks down at her free hand for a long time, on the other side of the glass.

"He was a psychopath," she says softly. "You know that, right?"

"Yeah, but that doesn't make me feel any better."

Paige straightens. "Anyway, I didn't come here to talk about Jordan."

"No?"

"No," Paige says, and she's kind of smiling again. "You promised me a real apology that night, and you never came through.

"I'm here to collect," she says.

Eric blinks. He can feel Paige watching him, and the guards, and he knows their time is almost up. And he *is* sorry. For a lot. He just can't figure out where to start.

"I'm sorry I was such a shitty friend," he tells Paige. "I'm sorry I bailed on you junior year and never told you why I broke up with you."

Paige raises an eyebrow.

"I'm sorry I never actually broke up with you at all," Eric says. "I'm sorry I couldn't just talk to you. I'm sorry it took the freaking *Suicide Pack* to make us actually talk to each other again.

"I'm sorry about the Suicide Pack," Eric says. "I'm sorry I encouraged you to run a Fix on ▮▮▮▮▮▮▮▮, and I'm sorry I didn't have your back when you wanted to do the right thing when he died.

"I'm sorry I took Jordan's side over yours.

"I'm sorry," Eric says.

And he is.

About everything.

362.

Well, practically everything.

363.

"I'm not sorry I met Jordan," Eric says.

Paige's face darkens a little bit. She starts to say something. But Eric continues anyway.

"I'm not sorry I met Jordan, and I'm not sorry I joined the Pack," he says. "I'm not sorry about the Fix we ran on The Room, because you were right, fuck those guys for putting spikes down where homeless people try to sleep."

Now Paige smiles again, a little.

"I'm not sorry I let Jordan drag me out of my stupid internship that day, and I'm not sorry we burned down his car. I'm sorry I didn't make a confession that night, but I'm *not* sorry I was there to hear yours. I'm sorry I didn't do more to help."

Eric takes a breath.

"Basically," he says, "I'm sorry for everything shitty that I did, up to and including the crimes I've been convicted for. I'm not sorry about the Jordan and the Pack stuff because—" (Cue the sappy stuff.) "This is going to sound cheesy, but I don't think we'd be talking right now, and, like, I want to be friends again and I hope you come back."

He exhales.

(Requisite monologue complete.)

364.

Paige is quiet for a while.

She doesn't say anything, and Eric wonders what she's thinking.

Finally, she smiles, and just as the guard's coming over to tell them their time is up, Paige stands and puts her hand on the glass.

"Apology accepted," she says. "See you next week."

365.

And that's pretty much the end of the Suicide Pack.

ACKNOWLEDGMENTS

First and foremost, I'm indebted to my agent, Stacia Decker, for her wise and patient counsel. This book was a bear at times, and I would have gone nuts without a sounding board, advocate, confidante, and friend. I'm a lucky guy to have a superagent who fills all those roles and then some.

Kristen Pettit's editorial input played a vital role in shepherding this book from its nebulous beginnings to the finished product you hold in your hand. And I'm grateful to (the indispensable) Elizabeth Lynch and Jennifer Klonsky at HarperCollins, and to Catherine Knowles at HarperCollins Canada for her publicity efforts north of the border.

I'm particularly grateful to the copyeditors who worked slavishly over this manuscript and who saved me from ruin on countless occasions. If you ever happen to meet a copyeditor, hug them.

To my partner, Shannon Kyla, I'm sorry for what I said when I was hangry. Thank you for your faith in me, for inspiring me, and for sticking with me through the darkest hours. I love you.

Thanks, finally and always, to my family. Dad, Mom, Terry and Andrew, Laura and Phil: I don't want to get sappy, but you guys are the best. I couldn't have done this—any of it—without you.

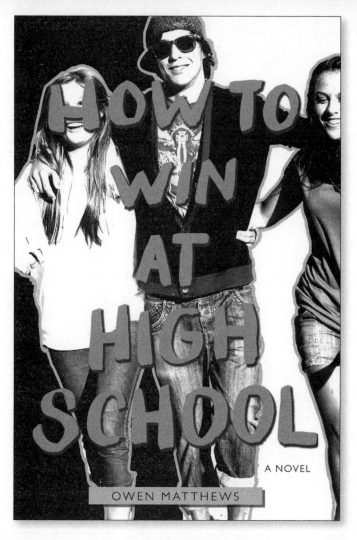

Find out how far he will go in his quest for popularity!

An Imprint of HarperCollinsPublishers

www.epicreads.com